CW01667302

# Teacher's resource

# 150 Daily Maths Lessons

YEAR 5

## Contents

| Contents | Page |
|---|---|

First published 2002
exclusively for WHSmith by

Hodder & Stoughton Educational,
a division of Hodder Headline Ltd.
338 Euston Road
London NW1 3BH



A CIP record for this book is available from the British Library.

Author: Howard Byers
Series editor: Paul Broadbent

ISBN 0340 79007 5

Typeset by Techset Ltd.
Printed and bound in Spain by Graphycems

| | Theme | Topics | Objectives – children will be taught to: |
|---|---|---|---|
| **Autumn Term** | | | |
| 1 | Multiplication and division | Understanding × and ÷<br>Mental calculation strategies (× ÷)<br>Pencil and paper procedures (× and ÷) | Understand the effect of and relationships between the four operations and the principles of arithmetic laws as they apply to multiplication.<br>Use doubling/halving: double any two digit number;<br>Halve an even number, double the other; multiply by 25, by × 100 then ÷ 4;<br>Multiply by 16, by × 8, then double; find a $\frac{1}{6}$ by halving a $\frac{1}{3}$.<br>Approximate first.<br>Use informal pencil and paper methods to support, record or explain × and ÷.<br>Extend written methods to HTU × U or U.t × U. |
| 2 | Problem-solving | Money and 'real life' problems<br>Making decisions and checking results, including using a calculator | Use all four operations to solve money or 'real life' word problems.<br>Choose appropriate operations/calculation methods.<br>Explain working. Check by estimating. Use inverse operation. |
| 3 | Fractions and decimals | Fractions and decimals | Use fraction notation, including mixed numbers, and vocabulary *numerator* and *denominator*. Change an improper fraction to a mixed number.<br>Recognise simple equivalent fractions, including tenths and hundredths.<br>Use decimal notation for tenths and hundredths, know what each digit represents in numbers with up to two decimal places. |
| 4 | Percentages and ratio | Percentages, ratio and proportion | Begin to understand percentage as the number of parts in every 100.<br>Solve simple problems involving ratio (*one for every*). |
| 5 | Handling data | Handling data<br>Using a calculator | Discuss chance or likelihood.<br>Present and interpret data on a bar chart and bar line graph: axis in 2s, 5s, 10s, 20s, 100s.<br>Recognise when intermediate points have no meaning.<br>Make a simple database on paper. Identify the mode. |
| 6 | Shapes | Shape and space<br>Reasoning about shapes | Identify and recognise properties of rectangles.<br>Classify triangles: isosceles, equilateral, scalene, lines of symmetry.<br>Recognise positions, read and plot co-ordinates in the first quadrant.<br>Solve shape puzzles. Explain methods and reasoning orally and in writing. |
| 7 | Measuring length | Measures, including problems | Understand, measure and calculate perimeter of rectangles, regular polygons.<br>Measure and draw lines to the nearest millimetre.<br>Use, read and write standard metric units of length, abbreviations and relationships. Convert larger to smaller units of length. Know mile.<br>Suggest suitable units/equipment to estimate or measure length.<br>Record estimates/measurements from scales to suitable degree of accuracy. |
| 8 | Measures problems | Measures, including problems | Read the time on 24-hour digital clock, e.g. 19:53.<br>Use all four operations to solve measurement word problems, including time. Choose appropriate operations/calculation methods. Explain working. |
| 9 | Addition and subtraction | Mental calculation strategies (+ and −)<br>Pencil and paper procedures (+ and −)<br>Money and 'real life' problems<br>Making decisions, checking results, including using a calculator | Find difference by counting up through next multiple of 10, 100, 1000.<br>Partition into HTU and add most significant digits first.<br>Use informal pencil and paper methods.<br>Extend written methods +/− of two integers less than 10 000.<br>Use all four operations to solve money and 'real life' word problems.<br>Choose appropriate operations/calculation methods. Explain working.<br>Check calculations using inverse operation, including with calculator. |
| 10 | Number sequences | Properties of numbers<br>Reasoning about numbers | Recognise and extend number sequences formed by counting from any number in steps of a constant size, extend beyond zero when counting back.<br>Know squares to at least 10 × 10. Identify factors of 2-digit numbers.<br>Solve mathematical problems or puzzles. Recognise patterns, generalise. |

# Summary of objectives

| | Theme | Topics | Objectives – children will be taught to: |
|---|---|---|---|
| **Spring Term** | | | |
| 1 | Comparing and ordering numbers | Place value, ordering, rounding<br><br>Using a calculator | Use symbols $<$, $=$, $>$, $\geqslant$, £.<br>Order a set of whole numbers less than 1 million.<br>Order positive and negative integers (number line, temperature).<br>Develop calculator skills and use a calculator effectively. |
| 2 | Multiplication and division | Understanding $\times$ and $\div$<br>Mental calculation strategies ($\times$ and $\div$)<br>Pencil and paper procedures (x and $\div$) | Begin to use brackets.<br>Use factors.<br>Use closely related facts (derive $\times 19$ from $\times 20$, $\times 12$ from $\times 10$ add $\times 2$)<br>Partition e.g. $47 \times 6$<br>Extend written methods to HTU $\div$ U (whole number remainder) |
| 3 | Problem-solving | Money and 'real life' problems<br>Making decisions and checking results including using a calculator | Use all four operations to solve money or 'real life' word problems.<br>Choose appropriate operations/calculation methods. Explain working.<br>Check with inverse operation or equivalent calculation. |
| 4 | Fractions and decimals | Fractions, decimals and percentages<br><br>Using a calculator | Order a set of fractions including mixed numbers, position on a number line.<br>Relate fractions to division and find simple fractions, including $\frac{1}{10}$ and $\frac{1}{100}$, of numbers and quantities.<br>Order a set of numbers or measurements with the same number of decimal places.<br>Round a number with one or two decimal places to the nearest integer.<br>Use a calculator effectively e.g. to convert fractions to decimals, to find fractions of numbers. |
| 5 | Shapes, lines and angles | Shape and space<br><br>Reasoning about shapes | Visualise 3-D shapes from 2-D drawings and identify nets of open cube.<br>Recognise directions, and perpendicular and parallel lines.<br>Understand and use degrees.<br>Identify, estimate and order acute and obtuse angles.<br>Use protractor to measure and draw acute and obtuse angles to 5°.<br>Make patterns from rotating shapes.<br>Calculate angles in a straight line.<br>Recognise and explain patterns and relationships, generalise and predict. |
| 6 | Area | Measures including problems | Understand area measured in square centimetres.<br>Use formula in words for area of rectangle. |
| 7 | Measuring mass | Measures including problems<br><br>Handling data | Use, read and write standard metric units of mass, abbreviations. Know relationships between them. Convert larger to smaller units of mass.<br>Suggest suitable units and equipment to estimate or measure mass.<br>Read measurements from scales.<br>Use all four operations to solve measurement word problems.<br>Choose appropriate operations/calculation methods. Explain working.<br>Represent and interpret data in a line graph (e.g. weight of a baby at monthly intervals from birth to one year).<br>Recognise when points can be joined to show trends. |
| 8 | Addition and subtraction | Mental calculation strategies (+ and −)<br><br>Pencil and paper procedures (+ and −) | Identify near doubles e.g. 1.5 + 1.6.<br>Add/subtract multiple of 10 or 100 and adjust.<br>Use relationship between addition and subtraction.<br>Extend written methods to addition of more than 2 integers less than 10 000, and + and − of pair of decimals both with 1 or 2 decimal places. |
| 9 | Money problems | Money and 'real life' problems<br>Making decisions, checking results, including using a calculator | Use all four operations to solve money or 'real life' word problems.<br>Choose appropriate operations and calculation methods.<br>Check by adding in reverse order, including with calculator. |
| 10 | Properties of numbers | Properties of numbers<br><br>Reasoning about numbers | Recognise multiples of 6, 7, 8, 9 up to the 10th multiple.<br>Recognise and extend sequences formed by adding 6, 7, 8, 9…, starting from any number.<br>Know and apply tests of divisibility of 2, 4 , 5, 10 or 100.<br>Make and investigate a general statement about numbers, by finding examples that satisfy it. Suggest extensions. |

| | Theme | Topics | Objectives – children will be taught to: |
|---|---|---|---|
| **Summer Term** | | | |
| 1 | Multiplication and division | Understanding × and ÷<br><br>Mental calculation strategies (× and ÷)<br>Pencil and paper procedures (× and ÷) | Express a quotient as a fraction, or as a decimal when dividing a whole number by 2, 4, 5, 10 or when dividing £ and pence.<br>Round up or down depending on the context.<br>Use relationship between × and ÷.<br>Use known facts and place value to multiply and divide mentally.<br>Extend written methods to TU × TU (long multiplication). |
| 2 | Money problems | Money and 'real life' problems<br>Making decisions and checking results including using a calculator | Use all four operations to solve money or 'real life' problems, including percentages.<br>Choose appropriate operations/calculation methods. Explain working.<br>Check results. |
| 3 | Fractions, decimals and percentages | Fractions, decimals and percentages | Relate fractions to decimal forms (including tenths, hundredths), and to percentages.<br>Find fractions and simple percentages of whole number quantities. |
| 4 | Ratio and proportion | Ratio and proportion | Solve problems involving ratio (*1 for every*) and proportion (*1 in every*). |
| 5 | Handling data | Handling data<br><br><br>Using a calculator | Solve a problem by representing and interpreting data in bar line charts: axis in 2s, 5s, 10s, 20s, 100s. Discuss cases where intermediate points have no meaning and cases where points may be joined to show trend.<br>Find the mode and calculate the range of a set of data.<br>Use a computer to compare different presentations of the same data. |
| 6 | Reflections and symmetry | Shape and space<br><br><br>Reasoning about shapes | Recognise reflective symmetry in regular polygons.<br>Complete symmetrical patterns with two lines of symmetry at right angles. Reflect shapes in mirror parallel to one side.<br>Recognise where shape will be after translation.<br>Make and investigate a general statement about shapes. |
| 7 | Time | Measures including problems | Use timetables. Know and use relationship between units of time.<br>Use all four operations to solve measurement word problems, |
| 8 | Capacity | Measures including problems | Use, read and write standard metric units of capacity, including abbreviations and pint, gallon.<br>Know and use relationships between them.<br>Convert larger to smaller units of capacity, including gallons to pints.<br>Suggest suitable units and equipment to estimate or measure capacity.<br>Read measurements from scales.<br>Choose appropriate operations/calculation methods. Explain working. |
| 9 | Addition and subtraction | Mental calculation strategies (+ and −)<br><br>Pencil and paper procedures (+ and −)<br><br>Money and 'real life' problems<br><br>Making decisions, checking results, including using a calculator | Add several numbers.<br>Use known facts and place value for mental addition and subtraction.<br>Extend written methods; addition and subtraction of integers less than 10000, and decimals with up to two decimal places.<br>Use all four operations to solve money or 'real life' word problems, including percentages.<br>Choose appropriate operations/calculation methods. Explain working.<br>Check using sums/differences of odd or even numbers. |
| 10 | Properties of numbers | Properties of numbers<br><br>Reasoning about numbers | Find all the pairs of factors of any number up to 100.<br>Make general statements about odd and even numbers, including sums and differences.<br>Explain a generalised relationship in words. |

# Year 5

## Mental maths starters

1 Multiplication facts – hold up numeral cards to answer multiplication questions. Estimate answers to TU × U. Division Facts – children respond to quick questions using numeral cards.

2 'Word Problems Bingo' – write down five numbers between 1 and 10, then cross them off as they answer questions such as 'I buy five CD's all the same price for a total of £40. How much was each CD?'

Children also derive quickly division facts corresponding to tables up to 10 × 10.

3 'Fractions Bingo' – write five different numbers between 1 and 10 on paper. Ask fraction questions, *e.g. 'What is a third of 12?'*. Children cross out correct answers. First child with all numbers crossed out wins. Also use division to find simple fractions of numbers.

4 'Ratio Race' – roll two dice to generate ratios (*e.g. 1 : 5*). Groups hold up a tower with the correct ratio of colours. Continue to derive division facts corresponding to tables.

5 Derive quickly doubles of all whole numbers 1 to 100. 'How did I get that?'. Put a given number in a calculator and decide how you can reach that answer. What operations would you use?

6 Describe and visualise 2-D shapes. 'What is the question?'. Write a 'blank' division question on the board: □ divided □ = 3. How many different questions can you make with the answer 3?

7 'Class conversion' – give the children a measurement in metres (*e.g. 2 m*). Ask them how many centimetres that is. Repeat with 1.75 m and other examples. Repeat for millilitres and kilometres.

8 Derive quickly all pairs that total 100 (*e.g. 43 + 57*). 'Approximate Answers' – show a 3-digit number on the board then cover it up and ask the children to approximate it to the nearest 10 or 100.

9 'Multiply and Divide by 10'. After a number of examples ask the children what they notice. Round 5-digit numbers to the nearest 10,000, 1000, 100 and 10.

10 'Mystery Number'. Tell the children you are thinking of a 1-place decimal number between 1 and 20. They must ask questions to find out what the number is. The answers can only be yes or no. Derive quickly or continue to derive quickly all two-digit pairs that total 100.

11 Children hold up numeral cards in response to quick-fire multiplication questions. Work out various angles in triangles using 180 degrees.

12 Ask for areas of simple shapes given limited dimensions (a square that measures 4 cm). Derive quickly the corresponding halves of all doubles of whole numbers 1 to 100.

13 Convert grams to kilograms and vice-versa at speed. 'Pairs to make 1000' – give the children a multiple of 50 and ask how many more to make 1000.

14 'Subtraction from 10 s' – ask the children to work with a partner, writing down as many subtractions from a 2-digit multiple of 10 that have an answer of 19 or 21 (*e.g. 90 – 71*). Derive quickly or continue to derive quickly decimals that total ten.

15 Derive quickly division facts corresponding to tables up to 10 × 10. Use known facts and place value to multiply and divide mentally.

16 Change £s and pence into just pence and vice-versa. Round any integer less than 10,000 to the nearest 10, 100 or 1000.

17 Relate fractions to division and use division to find simple fractions of numbers and quantities. Derive quickly all two-digit pairs that total 100.

18 Count up and back in steps of 5, 10 and 20. Ask questions relating to 5×, 10× and 20× tables. Class can respond in groups.

19 'Think of a Number' – ask questions based on known facts *e.g. 'Think of a number between 20 and 30, it's an even number and a multiple of 3 and 4'*. Repeat.

20 'Invent a Loop' – give out 2-digit number cards. The children must say what calculation they would do to their number to get to the number of the child sitting next to them. Go round the class.

21 'How many minutes in 4 hours = 4 × 60 = 4 × 6 + 0 = 240 etc'. Extend to minutes and seconds as well. Know by heart all multiplication facts to 10 × 10.

22 Convert millilitres into litres and vice-versa. Using numeral cards answer quick fire multiplication and division questions.

23 Count on in steps of 0.1 and 0.5. Time the children individually at how fast they can say their tables. Can they beat their time?

# Theme 1 Multiplication and division

## Objectives

- To understand the principles of arithmetic laws as they apply to multiplication
- To perform pencil and paper multiplication
- To use pencil and paper methods to support calculations
- To use pencil and paper methods to multiply two-digit whole numbers by single digit decimals
- To halve and double
- To review multiplication methods

## Vocabulary

multiple, product, multiplied by, double, row, column, brackets, product, ... lots of ..., halving, doubling

## Resources

Copymasters 1 and 2. Homework Copymaster 1.

## Assessment

*At the end of this theme is the pupil able to:*

- Understand the effect of and relationship between the four operations and the principles of arithmetic laws as they apply to multiplication;
- Use doubling and halving;
- Double any two-digit number;
- Approximate first;
- Use informal pencil and paper methods to support, record or explain $\times$ and $\div$;
- Extend written methods to HTU $\times$ U or UT $\times$ U?

## Mental maths starter 1

## Lesson 1

### Introduction

Quick-fire questions. Pupils answer on white boards e.g. *What is double 32? 6 times 8? 12 multiplied by zero? What is the product of 15 and 2? What is the product of 2, 3 and 4? Is 45 a multiple of 9? Add three to the product of 4 and 4.* Provide help/remediation as the need becomes apparent. This activity is more in the nature of consolidation.

Depending on the needs of the group review/introduce informally the use of brackets: give out or draw a square of 5 dots by 6 dots. Initiate discussion along the lines: *What calculation will give the total number of spots in this pattern?* Guide the responses towards (starting at the top) $5 \times 6$ (or $6 \times 5$) but accept initially $5 + 5 + 5 + 5 + 5 + 5$ or $6 + 6 + 6 + 6 + 6$, $4 \times 3$ (or $3 \times 4$), $4 \times 12$ (or $12 \times 4$), $6 \times 12$ (or $12 \times 6$). When the multiplication solution is recognised by all, illustrate how, for example, $5 \times 6$ can be split up into $5 \times 2$ and $5 \times 4$ – these may be marked on the OHT. Touch lightly on the fact that brackets may be used to show this splitting up e.g. $4 \times 12 = (4 \times 10) + (4 \times 2) = 40 + 8 = 48$. Illustrate with a few more examples, involving pupils whenever possible. (Dot patterns make an ideal visual aid.)

### Activities

Working in pairs, children complete the first half of Copymaster 1. *Ask pupils to check each other's table squares.*
*What patterns have you noticed? Can you use these to check the multiplications? What do you notice about the numbers following down a column or going across a row?* Allow free-ranging discussion, but encourage correct mathematical language, e.g. *multiples are in rows or columns; ... is added each time.*
Working in pairs, children complete the first 7 of the second half of Copymaster 1. Remediate in individual pairs – guiding towards an understanding that multiplication is repetitive addition and a 'feel' for partition.

### Differentiation

*Low Attainers* – Complete Copymaster 1 with adult support.
*High Attainers* – Complete Copymaster 1 with the added challenge to use brackets to show how to split up multiplications such as $17 \times 9$. If possible allow them to 'discover' and justify $17 \times 9 = 17 \times 10 - 17$.

### Plenary

Computers and calculators usually do multiplications by addition. What does this mean? Allow pupils to reiterate that multiplication is repetitive addition. Focus on the correct use of vocabulary. Write down on the board $47 \times 5$. What does this mean? Guide to '47 lots of 5', '47 added 5 times' etc. Add '= 535' What is the answer to '5 times 47'? How do you know? Ensure that the class appreciates that order does not matter in multiplication. (Use dot patterns if needed.) *Does order matter in addition, subtraction, division? Give some examples.* Accept fairly informal answers – but insist on concrete examples. *Several hundred years ago people used multiplication tables a lot more than now, but most of them were in the shape of triangles, not squares like the one you completed. Why do you think this was?* Allow free-ranging discussion. *What is the minimum number of table facts you need to know to recall up to 10 × 10?*

## Lesson 2

### Introduction

Mental activity. On the board, reveal/write one at a time calculations such as $2 \times 10$, $2 \times 100$, $2 \times 1000$ and $2 \times 2$, $2 \times 20$, $2 \times 200$ and $20 \times 2$, $200 \times 2$ and so on, (note the pattern in questions).
Encourage pupils to give their answers orally as a group. In the last couple of minutes ask if they can see any patterns and encourage them to make conjectures.
For example, to calculate $20 \times 400$ it may help to verbalise this as 20 lots of 400, giving 80 lots of 100 or 8000.

### Activities

Read out about ten multiplication problems of the type $3 \times 40$, $50 \times 6$, $7 \times 60$, $500 \times 3$ and so on. *What are ... lots of ...?* (This may help the lower attainers – *e.g. three lots of four hundred.*) *What is ... multiplied by ...? What is the product of ... and ...? What is double ...? What is ... times ...?* Ask pupils to write down the actual multiplication, then to work it out. Allow pupils to check their own answers with a calculator.
To reinforce, allow a few minutes for pupils to make up and do and check some calculations of a similar type for themselves
Write on the board $43 \times 7$. *How could we work this out?* (With the emphasis on HOW.) If little response then remind the group of the previous lesson's work on splitting up multiplications. Allow the discussion to run its course and then recap: give a purely verbal version; encourage pupils perhaps to close their eyes in order to 'see' what is happening.
*Forty-three is forty plus three. Forty times seven is two hundred and eighty. Three times seven is twenty-one. Twenty-one add two hundred and eighty is three hundred and one. So forty-three times seven is three hundred and one.*
If necessary repeat with $28 \times 8$ etc.
*On your own try to answer these. Jot down all the steps in your calculation.* Write on the the board: $12 \times 9$, $6 \times 18$, $29 \times 9$, $5 \times 27$, $52 \times 6$, $6 \times 21$ etc. Remediate whilst pupils are working: their jottings will provide useful clues as to the efficiency or otherwise of their methods. Depending on circumstances pupils could be encouraged to work though their solutions aloud. Working in pairs test each other on some similar multiplications. *Keep a record of any which either of you found difficult.*

### Differentiation

*Low Attainers* – Give these pupils more practice in recognising the pattern in the calculations, and the answers, of the form $3 \times 2$, $3 \times 20$, $3 \times 200$ etc.
*High Attainers* – Find as many multiplications as possible which have an answer of 4800. Try multiplications of the type $160 \times 21$ or $240 \times 71$, checking their own answers with a calculator.

### Plenary

*Which multiplications did you find most difficult? Give me some examples.* Collect these on the board with short discussion as to why.
*As a final challenge try, in pairs, to calculate 163 × 4. You have about a minute.* Collect answers on the board. Ask one 'correct' pair to talk the class through their solution.

## Lesson 3

### Introduction

*Jot down the answers to these multiplications.*
*Remember it usually helps to split a number up into smaller parts.*
Write some questions on the board e.g. *201 × 4, 402 × 3, 903 × 3, 211 × 5.* Pupils show the answer after each question. As a quick recap, write on the board e.g. *201 × 4 = (200 + 1) × 4 = 801.* Depending on the group, work through another example orally.

### Activities

*Working in pairs, complete a selection of multiplications.*
Remediate as needed. Depending on the group, allow self-marking.
*It sometimes helps to lay out your multiplications in a certain order. Here is one way.*
On the board, line by line, work through 4 × 312 or similar (stress that this is the same as 312 × 4). Involve pupils in this calculation.

```
              3 1 2
              × 4
3 0 0 × 4 = 1 2 0 0
  1 0 × 4 =     4 0
    2 × 4 =       8
            1 2 4 8
```

When appropriate show pupils the short cut:

```
 3 1 2
 ×   4
 1 2 4 8
```

(allow 'carries' to arise naturally)

If necessary work through another example, involving the pupils as much as possible. Solve difficulties as they arise.

### Differentiation

By outcome.

### Plenary

Recap progress made over the lesson, then pose the question:
*How can we check the answer to a multiplication?*
Allow and record on the board all reasonable suggestions in the time available.
This is only the first visit so allow informal methods and involve as many of the class as possible.

## Lesson 4

### Introduction

As appropriate divide the class into two groups and play the multiplication and division 'circle' game on Copymaster 2. Record the time taken to complete the game – to be compared with the corresponding time at the end of the lesson.

### Activities

(Some pupils may not be as secure with decimals generally, therefore it may be useful to have a scale with graduations marked in 0.1 divisions as a supporting resource.) Write the calculation 3 × 0.2 on the board. *How could you work this out?* Involve as many of the class as possible. Ensure that 0.2 + 0.2 + 0.2 is considered – justify this by reminding the class that multiplication is repeated addition and that the order of multiplication does not matter so 0.2 × 3 gives the same answer. When appropriate remind pupils that 3 and 3.0 are 'worth' the same.
Repeat as necessary for 4 × 0.2 and 2 × 0.3. Do not, at this stage, use the calculator as an 'arbiter' but use the opportunity to reinforce correct mathematical language with decimals such as 'zero point three' etc. Write this on the board, saying aloud each line:
*Here is part of the 0.3 times table.*

1 × 0.3 = 0.3
2 × 0.3 = 0.6
3 × 0.3 = 0.9

Invite pupils to come to the board to continue the '0.3 times table' and establish that 4 × 0.3 = 1.2. Challenge pupils: *How can you tell that 6 × 0.3 cannot be 0.18?* Guide the class into realising that '6 lots of 0.3 must be greater than 0.18'. Use further examples to ensure that all pupils are able confidently to recall the answer to the product of a single-digit whole number and a single-digit decimal.
Write this calculation on the board: 7 × 2.3 *There is a method to work this out.*
Work through the method ensuring as much pupil participation as possible.

| × | 2 | 0.3 | |
|---|---|---|---|
| 7 | 14 | 2.1 | = 16.1 |

Stress to pupils that approximation can be useful as a check: for this example 7 × 2 = 14,which suggests that 16.1 is reasonable.
Work through as many examples as the class needs.

### Differentiation

Differentiation by outcome but all pupils should experience success with at least one question from each of the three sections.

### Plenary

Repeat the multiplication and division 'circle' game on Copymaster 2. Compare the completion time with that of the start of the lesson.

## Lesson 5

### Introduction

A quick question and answer session with pupils answering on number fans or wipe boards.
Encourage pupils to volunteer **HOW** they arrived at their answers.
Ask questions on doubling whole numbers and halving even numbers, e.g. *Double 26. Twice 35. Write down a number twice as big as 51. What is half of 26? Divide 60 by 2. I'm thinking of a number. I double it and add 2. The answer is 52. What was my number?*

### Activities

In pairs, pupils continue the Q + A game described above.
Invite pupils to give examples of what they consider to be 'hard' 3-digit by 1-digit multiplications. Encourage discussion as to why this is so – this will reveal any major misconceptions or tables which could be better learned. Depending on the situation, the class could be grouped by attainment in order to make more efficient use of time.

### Differentiation

Essentially by outcome, but ensure that all pupils attempt some questions from each section of Homework Copymaster 1.

### Plenary

Recap the basic rules of multiplication, including (informally) commutivity and multiplication as repetitive addition.

# Theme 2 Problem-solving

## Objectives
- To use all four operations to solve word problems involving numbers in 'real-life'
- To check calculations by estimating and doing the inverse operation
- To choose and use appropriate arithmetic and calculation methods
- To explain working and calculation methods

## Vocabulary
undo, inverse, trial and improvement

## Resources
Copymasters 3 and 4, Homework Copymaster 2. A collection of shopping items labelled with costs. Number cards.

## Assessment
*At the end of this theme is the pupil able to:*
- Use all four operations to solve money or 'real life' word problems;
- Choose appropriate operations/calculation methods;
- Explain working;
- Check by estimating;
- Use inverse operation?

## Mental maths starter 2

---

# Lesson 1

## Introduction
Divide the class into pairs, as some of the questions are quite challenging, and play a 'circle' game using problem solving questions such as: *Amy has 65 picture cards. She buys 35 more. How many does she have in total?* Record the time taken to complete the circle – to be compared with the corresponding time at the end of the lesson. Stress that, rather than answers, the calculation is required. Observation will highlight serious weaknesses and allow remediation. As a quick activity invite pupils to make up word problems (orally – not written down) to fit calculations (written on the board) such as $12 \times 3$, $12 \times 4$, $12 - 4$. Invite contributions from all pupils.

## Activities
Give out or use an OHT of Copymaster 3. Ask pupils to look at the first problem, but not to state the answer or working required – yet. *What is the problem asking? What information do we know? What else do we need to find out or calculate? What calculation is needed: addition, subtraction, multiplication or division?* Set the pupils to work through Copymaster 3 in pairs, but insist that they show their working so that someone else reading it is able to understand exactly how they went about solving the problem. When needed, pupils should be allowed access to calculators.

## Differentiation
*Lower attainers* – Invite them to think aloud how they would tackle the problems in Section A.
*Higher attainers* – Begin with Section B – these are multi-step problems. Depending on the time available invite these pupils to make up similar problems for themselves, trying them out on each other. These might form a useful collection of such problems as a resource for later on.

## Plenary
Recap on the questions asking pairs to say which problems they found the most difficult. Emphasise that the 'trick' is to 'see' the calculation hidden in the words. Point out the importance of checking answers against the original problem.
Replay the 'circle' game and compare the time with that taken at the start of the lesson.

---

# Lesson 2

## Introduction
Divide the class into groups of 2 or 3 pupils. Each group picks 6 number cards and puts them face up on the table. Ask a series of multiplication and division facts: if a group has the answer on one of their cards it can be turned over. The cards count as digits, so an answer of 24 would use up '2' and '4'. The first group to turn over all their cards wins.
Try mental activity based on money – questions of the type: *How many pence is £1.57/£10/£4.07/£5.50? Jot these down in pounds: 150p/50p/650p/700p. A CD costs £6. How long would it take to save up for at 50p a week? Which four coins make 10p/33p/90p? Which three coins make 20p? How many 5p coins make £1? How many 20p coins make £6? What is the least number of coins needed to make 39p? What is the change from £1 for 8 felt tip pens at 5p each? I spent £5.45. What was my change from £10? Mercury bars cost 35p each. How many can be bought for £1?*

## Activities
Give pairs of pupils a selection of shopping items and ask them to add various prices together. How much change will they get from £1? From £5? Lower attainers may need to have access to a calculator to check their answers.

## Differentiation
*Low Attainers* – Tackle the price exercise with a calculator to hand.
Ask children to
- Find the sum of … and …;
- What is the difference between … and …;
- What is the product of … and …;
- What is … shared by …;

*High Attainers* – Complete the exercise without using a calculator..

## Plenary
Ask each pair to summarise their calculations.

## Lesson 3

### Introduction

Read out (or show on the OHP) some simple numerical problems such as those shown below. Pupils are to jot down the calculation required – but not the actual answer. When completed discuss with pupils why they chose their particular calculations. Depending on circumstances pupils may be invited to work out the actual answers on the board – a useful vehicle for revision. *24 people go on a picnic by car. Each car holds 4 people. How many cars are needed? In a class of 32 children, the children sit in groups of 4. How many groups are there? In a class of 32 children, half of them are away with flu. How many are away? James saves £12. He spends £7 on a CD. How much has he left? There are 8 people in a lift. Five people get out and two get in. How many are now in the lift? Felt tips are sold in packs of 12. How many felt tips are there in 3 packs? In a school there are 6 classes. Each class has 40 pupils in it. How many pupils are in the school? Aijaz has 25 CDs? His brother Franklin has 6 fewer. How many CDs does Franklin have?*

### Activities

Here are three numbers: 7, 8 and 15. Use these to make as many different additions and subtractions and their answers as you can, *e.g.* $7 + 8 = 15$. Quickly establish that there are just four different calculations possible ($7 + 8 = 15$, $8 + 7 = 15$, $15 - 7 = 8$ and $15 - 8 = 7$). Repeat for some other numbers, *32, 64, 96 and 23, 54 and 77.*

We can use this to check subtractions. *83 − 21 = 62 is correct because 62 + 21 is equal to 83.* Repeat with some other examples until the class is secure.

Write 24 then $24 - 3 = 21$. *How can we get back to 24 starting from 21?* Quickly establish that $+3$ will 'undo' the $-3$. Repeat with some other subtractions making certain that pupils understand the general principal that 'addition' will undo 'subtraction'. Carefully introduce the term 'addition is the inverse of subtraction'. *What do you think the inverse of addition is?* Challenge pupils to provide examples.

Invite the class to check these subtractions by adding and to find which of them have wrong answers.

| | | | |
|---|---|---|---|
| $29 - 14 = 14$ | $87 - 25 = 61$ | $41 - 34 = 9$ | $54 - 38 = 16$ |
| $57 - 32 = 35$ | $81 - 33 = 48$ | $63 - 28 = 35$ | $45 - 13 = 32$ |

(For children grouped by attainment level a page of such calculations against the clock with $-1$ for each incorrect 'right' or 'wrong' would make a useful activity to 'sharpen up' number bonds.)

*How can we use inverses to check subtractions and additions?* Encourage pupil participation. Show, for example that if $34 - 2 = 32$ then $32 + 2$ should be 34, similarly for $56 + 4 = 60$ etc. Point out that checking additions by subtraction may be harder than the original calculation. *Are there any other methods of checking additions and subtractions?* Encourage all pupils to be involved, but consider at least these: make a rough estimate (not always useful with addition and subtraction); redo the calculation – perhaps in a different order for addition.

### Differentiation

*Low Attainers* – May need to perform the checking calculation using a calculator.

*High Attainers* – May need more challenging examples and less time to check, with greater emphasis on checking

### Plenary

Write a series of additions and subtractions on the board and invite pupils to think aloud how they would check them. Accept various strategies.

## Lesson 4

### Introduction

Write 25 2-digit numbers on the board and ask pupils to collect numbers that sum to 100. The object is to form as many of these as possible in the time allowed. Finish this activity with a short discussion as to what strategies pupils employed. Lower attainers may need to have a calculator to hand. Higher attaining pupils could make up and test a similar puzzle for themselves.

### Activities

The object of this activity is to give pupils practice in using calculators in a puzzle context. Where possible, and depending on the levels of attainment, pupils should be encouraged to use 'number sense' rather than trial and improvement – the former should be discussed after the activity. Give pupils a copy (or use an OHT) of Copymaster 4 (section A). Lower-attaining pupils should not be expected to complete the whole of Section A. Some classes may need to be shown what is expected. The object of these questions is to develop number sense rather than trial and improvement: for example a suitable strategy for question 1 is *27 is about 30 and 13 is about 10, so a rough answer would be about 30 × 10 or 300, so the missing digit will be 3 – a calculator check shows this to be the case.* After 10–15 minutes instigate a short discussion on the pupils' strategies. Allow pupils several minutes to complete Section B, then quickly go through and discuss any difficulties experienced. Allow sufficient time for the vast majority of pupils to complete the six problems.

### Differentiation

*Low Attainers* – Should be encouraged to complete the first 4 or so in each section.

*High Attainers* – Should complete Copymaster 4 – including Section C.

### Plenary

Lead a discussion as to which calculations pupils would use 'mental', 'pencil and paper' or 'calculator' for. Highlight the fact that many people would do most of Section C in their head, but lower attainers obviously need sympathetic consideration. This might be a useful point at which to stress the usefulness of knowing tables and other number bonds by heart. If there is sufficient time, round off the lesson with a quick-fire tables test using questions similar to that in Section C on Copymaster 4.

## Lesson 5

### Introduction

Write these calculations and answers on the board and invite groups of 3 or 4 to jot down a sentence or so (a number story) to describe a situation where the calculations might arise.

| | | |
|---|---|---|
| $124 + 302 = 426$ | $7 \times 24 = 168$ | $367 - 33 = 334$ |
| $168 \times 12 = 14$ | $34 + 35 + 31 = 100$ | $52 \times 45 = 2340$ |

Invite the groups to share their stories with the rest of the class, asking appropriately attaining groups to explain how they would actually carry out the calculation itself.

### Activities

In the same groups ask pupils to complete more calculations similar to those above but stress the importance of clear working and the understanding that groups may have to explain their methods and working to the rest of the class – in other words the maths behind the 'story'.

### Differentiation

*Low Attainers* – Work with adult supervision.

*High Attainers* – Use more challenging calculations.

### Plenary

Invite groups to explain their methods and how they worked out the answers to the rest of the class.

# Theme 3 Fractions and decimals

### Objectives
- To use fraction notation and recognise the equivalence between fractions
- To use decimal notation and know what each digit in a decimal fraction represents

### Vocabulary
Proper/improper fraction, mixed number, numerator, denominator, equivalent, reduced to, cancel.

### Resources
Decimal number lines, fraction cards, share price lists.
Copymasters 5 and 6, Homework Copymaster 3.

### Assessment
*At the end of this theme is the pupil able to:*
- Use fraction notation, including mixed numbers;
- Recognise the equivalence between an improper fraction and a mixed number;
- Recognise simple equivalent fractions including tenths and hundredths;
- Use decimal notation for tenths and hundredths;
- Identify what each digit in a decimal fraction represents;
- Compare pairs of decimal fractions?

### Mental maths starter 3

## Lesson 1

### Introduction
On the board draw a variety of shapes with various fractions shaded. Ask the children *What fraction is shaded.* Revise fraction language and notation at this point. Give the children a sheet of examples where they have either to write down a fraction from a set of shaded diagrams or they have to produce a shaded diagram given a fraction.

### Activities
Ask the children to say these fractions as you write them on the board: $\frac{1}{2}$, $\frac{2}{3}$, $\frac{2}{5}$, $\frac{18}{100}$, $\frac{8}{10}$, $\frac{54}{100}$.

Tell the children that the top number in a fraction is called the numerator and the bottom number is called the denominator. Write the words on the board. Point to different fractions in turn and ask – *What is this fraction? What is its numerator? What is its denominator?*

Tell the class that a mixed number is a mixture of whole numbers and fractions. Illustrate this fact by drawing $2\frac{1}{2}$ whole cakes and 5 half cakes on the board. Write $2\frac{1}{2}$ and $\frac{5}{2}$ underneath. Explain that these have the same value although they are written in different ways.
Point out that an improper fraction is not a proper fraction because the numerator is greater than the denominator (it is more than one whole)
Write on the board $2\frac{1}{2} = \frac{5}{2}$

*Working in pairs* – Use Copymaster 5 and ask one child to point to a plate and say the mixed number for how much cake there is and the other child say the improper fraction. They can record each equivalence in their books.

### Differentiation
*Low Attainers* – They could use shapes divided into segments to visualise the fractions.
*High Attainers* – They could draw number lines for fifths, sixths, eighths and tenths.

### Plenary
Draw this number line on the board-

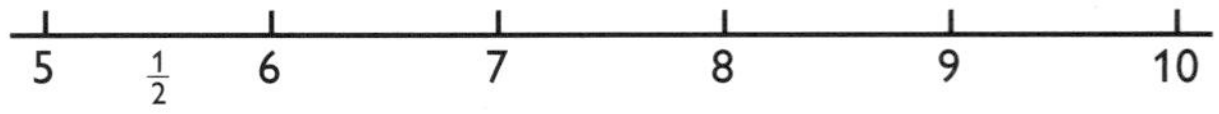


Ask the children to copy the number line and fill in the numbers $6\frac{1}{2}$, $7\frac{1}{2}$, $8\frac{1}{2}$. Write $\frac{10}{2}$, $\frac{11}{2}$, $\frac{12}{2}$ etc above the number line, in the appropriate positions. Ask the children, *Where would the improper fraction $\frac{17}{2}$ go?*
Give the children improper fractions to change to mixed numbers and vice versa, selecting numbers appropriate to each child. Write the equivalencies on the board.

## Lesson 2

### Introduction
The children count in quarters up to twelve quarters;
'One quarter, two quarters, three quarters,' etc.
Then they count up to 4 saying the fractions in their lowest terms;
'One quarter, one half, three quarters, one whole, one and one quarter,' etc.
Repeat, counting sixths up to twenty-four sixths. Record on the board
$\frac{1}{6}$, $\frac{2}{6}$, $\frac{3}{6}$, $\frac{4}{6}$, $\frac{5}{6}$ etc.
$\frac{1}{6}$, $\frac{1}{3}$, $\frac{1}{2}$, $\frac{2}{3}$, etc.
*What is two sixths in thirds? What is one half in sixths?*

### Activities
One child stands with a card with 0 on it in front of the class. A little way away another child stands with a 1 card. Give another child a card with $\frac{5}{10}$ on it and ask the class where this should go between the other two. Repeat for $\frac{1}{10}$, $\frac{3}{10}$, $\frac{8}{10}$, and $\frac{9}{10}$.

Then ask five children with cards that have on them $\frac{10}{100}$, $\frac{30}{100}$, $\frac{50}{100}$, $\frac{80}{100}$ and $\frac{90}{100}$ to stand in front of those children with the tenth cards. Talk about the equivalence of tenths and hundredths and ask:
*How many hundredths is seven tenths?*
*How many tenths are equivalent to thirty hundredths?*
*Working in pairs* – Write down as many fractions that you can that are equivalent to a half. Give the children some more examples of equivalent fractions to complete by either filling in the numerator or the denominator.

### Differentiation
*Low Attainers* – Use only tenths and their equivalent hundredths.
*High Attainers* – Give them some fractions and ask them to give you an equivalent fraction.

### Plenary
Fill in 'fraction walls' for halves, tenths, fifths and other fractions familiar to the children.
Put a selection of fractions on the board and have a competition to see who can recognise the most that are equal to $\frac{1}{3}$ or $\frac{1}{2}$ or $\frac{1}{10}$ etc

## Lesson 3

### Introduction

Revise the place value of tenths and hundredths by drawing columns on the board. Refer to amounts of money. Use the children's pocket money as an example or prices from a catalogue. Emphasise the importance of the decimal point, which separates the pounds from the pence.

### Activities

On the board, draw a table with columns labelled '£.p' and 'p'. Choose amounts of pence greater than £20 to exchange into pounds and pence. Show the children how these monies are written down e.g. *7125p = £71.25*
Remind the children that we write amounts of money with trailing zeros e.g. *£27.40* and emphasise that there are always two digits after the decimal point to show pence as fractions of pounds.
*Working in pairs* – Using Share Price lists in newspapers the children can see that sometimes large amounts of money are listed as pence. Ask each pair to list the ten most expensive shares. (If time permits these share prices could be followed through the week and the list changed).

### Differentiation

*Low Attainers* – Let the children have plenty of experience of using a place value grid. Invite individual children to come to the board and write up one of their answers.
*High Attainers* – Discuss how the system can be extended to include $\frac{1}{1000}$, $\frac{1}{10000}$ etc.

### Plenary

Discuss how a very small amount of pence would be represented, for example, writing 4p as £0.04. Finish with oral questions such as; *How many pence is £3.67? How many pounds is 426pence?*
Look at the same method for writing kilometres and kilograms *e.g. 2.5 kg = 2500 g or 3400 g = 3.4 kg*

## Lesson 4

### Introduction

Practise counting in decimals.
Count up in steps of $\frac{1}{10}$ from 3 to 5, and then back in steps of 0.1.
Count up in steps of $\frac{1}{100}$ from 0 to 0.2, then back in steps of 0.01.
Ask the class: *What is one tenth more than 3.6? What is one tenth less than 1.9? What is two tenths more than 3.7? What is 0.2 more than 6.5?*

### Activities

Saying or writing 'zero point one five,' 'fifteen hundredths,' 'one tenth and five hundredths,' '0.15' and '$\frac{15}{100}$' are different ways of expressing the same value.
Place 6.34 on a demonstration place value grid. Ask the whole class the following: *How do we say this number?* (Six point three-four) *Can anyone write it for us?* (6.34) *What is the value of each digit?* (Six units, three tenths, four hundredths)
Continue with *In the number 5.3, what does the three stand for?* (Thirty hundredths or three tenths)
*Working in pairs* – Using Copymaster 6, ask the children to write the digits in the number 8.34 in the correct columns. Repeat this with the other numbers on the sheet.

### Differentiation

*Low Attainers – How do I write $\frac{30}{100}$ which is $\frac{3}{10}$ as a decimal?* (0.3). *How do I write $\frac{50}{100}$ which is $\frac{5}{10}$ or $\frac{1}{2}$ as a decimal?* (0.5) etc.
*High Attainers – In the number 23.06, what does the digit 0 stand for?* (no tenths) etc.

### Plenary

Construct a number by pointing to each row in turn, and ask the children to say and write the number, e.g. *5678.95 is five thousand six hundred and seventy eight point nine five*. Emphasise two rules: the point is used to separate whole numbers from decimal fractions. Each decimal digit is spoken without the 'tenths, hundredths, thousandths' language. Only the position of the digit tells you its value. *E.g. 0.56 is read as nought point five six and as nought point fifty-six.*

## Lesson 5

### Introduction

Use a decimal number line.
Write these numbers on the board: 0.3, 0.6, 0.67, 0.69, 0.45, 0.23 etc. Choose two of the decimals such as 0.6 and 0.45, and ask the children to say where the numbers would go on the decimal number line. Then ask the class which is the smaller and which is the larger. Repeat using other numbers.

### Activities

Write on the board $0.45 < 0.6$ and $0.6 > 0.45$ (you may need to remind the class how to position these signs properly) and ask the children to copy the two statements. Remind them to compare digits with the greatest place value first. Let each child choose three pairs of numbers from a list on the board and work out where they would go on the number line. Ask them to write two statements for each pair using the signs $<, >$. Ask children to read out their statements. Write these on the board and go through them with the class using the number line.

### Differentiation

*Low Attainers* – Could practise counting along the number line in tenths to help them work out the position of the numbers.
*High Attainers* – Could estimate the positions of numbers with three decimal places.

### Plenary

Using the decimal number line, mark positions with letters for the children to place a list of various numbers to 2+ decimal places next to each letter. Again remind the children that it would be easier to mark those numbers with the greatest place value first. Go through Homework Copymaster 3.

# Theme 4 Percentages and ratio

## Objectives
- To recognise and understand simple ratio (... for every ...)
- To solve simple ratio patterns
- To solve simple ratio problems
- To begin to understand percentage as the number of parts in every 100
- To understand percentage as the number of parts in every 100 and to recognise the simple fraction equivalents of 25%, 50% and 75%

## Vocabulary
ratio, ... part to ..., ... for every ...

## Resources
Copymasters 7 and 8, Homework Copymaster 4. A blank 100 square.

## Assessment
*At the end of this theme is the pupil able to:*
- Begin to understand percentage as the number of parts in every 100;
- Solve simple problems involving ratio (*one for every*)?

## Mental maths starter 4

---

## Lesson 1

### Introduction
Write these divisions on the board:

| | | | | | |
|---|---|---|---|---|---|
| 16 ÷ 4 | 24 ÷ 4 | 12 ÷ 4 | 8 ÷ 4 | 12 ÷ 3 | 40 ÷ 4 |
| 24 ÷ 6 | 50 ÷ 10 | 48 ÷ 8 | 6 ÷ 2 | 20 ÷ 2 | 25 ÷ 5 |

*Working in pairs, group these divisions into ones which have the same answer.* When most pairs have finished, ask them: *What do you notice?* Give as many pupils as possible the opportunity to participate. Guide the class to the realisation that doubling each 'side' of a division does not alter the result. Invite pupils to produce (and check) some examples of their own.

### Activities
*Ratio is about comparing amounts. Here are some glasses of water and some glasses of undiluted lime juice. Which set will give the strongest drink when mixed?*

(a)

(A) (B) (C)

(b)

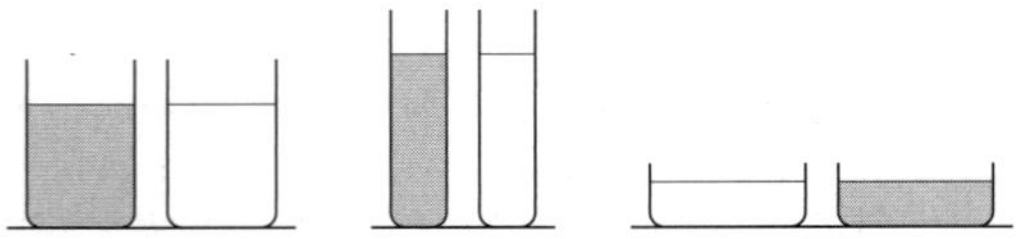

(A) (B) (C)

Establish that in (a) [A] is the strongest and that in (b) all are the same strength, and begin to use the language *1 part of water to ... parts of juice*.
Ensure that all pupils are secure in this (working through another example may be necessary).
*John says that these two mixtures have different strengths; Jean says they are the same. Who is right? Give reasons for your answer.*

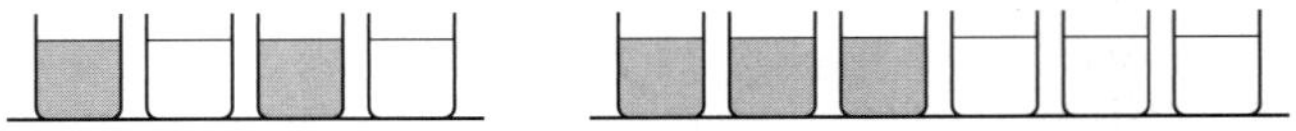

Encourage as many of the class as possible to contribute to the discussion, but insist on explanations rather than the mere answer. Make the end point of the discussion the observation that in both cases there is one glass of water for one glass of juice.

### Differentiation
By outcome.

### Plenary
Recap on the content of the lesson, perhaps inviting pupils to make up for themselves questions based on some of the diagrams.

---

## Lesson 2

### Introduction
A quick 'no frills' halving and doubling exercise, concluding with a short discussion on how pupils remembered these facts – but only if productive. *Jot down the answers to these:*

| | | | | |
|---|---|---|---|---|
| *double 23* | *two times 65* | *half 30* | *64 divided by 2* | *double 45* |
| *half of 90* | *double 53* | *86 divided by 2* | *63 add 63* | *two 83s* |

### Activities
*In this pattern 1 in every 3 squares is black.* Draw these on the board; some pupils may need a quick recap/reminder about strip patterns.

*If a strip of this pattern has a total of 12 squares, how many will be black/white? If a strip of this pattern has a total of 15 squares, how many will be black/white? Are there any other ways of describing the proportion of black and white squares?* Allow a free-ranging discussion, ensuring that at least the following are considered:
*There are twice as many white squares as black squares. There are half as many black squares as white squares. The ratio of black to white squares is 1 black square for every 2 white squares.*
Use another drawing such as this to reinforce the above two ways of regarding ratio. Insist that pupils use the correct language.

### Differentiation
By outcome.

### Plenary
Repeat the introductory exercise, noting the time taken.

## Lesson 3

### Introduction
Write this statement on the board, ensuring that all pupils can read it: 'Anita has 1 football sticker for every 2 stickers that Ben has.' *I'm going to read out some statements about this. Put a cross if they are wrong and a tick if they are correct.* Ensure that pupils do not mismatch question numbers! Write statements like: *Anita has fewer stickers than Ben. Anita has twice as many stickers as Ben. If Ben has 20 stickers, Anita has 10 stickers. Anita has half as many stickers as Ben. If you added together Anita's and Ben's stickers, half would belong to Ben. One third of all the stickers belongs to Anita. Ben has the most stickers. If Anita had 100 stickers Ben would have 50 stickers. Ben has twice as many stickers as Anita. If they have a total of 30 stickers, Ben has 20 stickers.* Extend the time slot to allow full discussion of each question.

### Activities
Give pairs of pupils a copy of Copymaster 7 to complete. Stress that mere answers are not sufficient and that they will be expected to explain their method of solution and thinking behind it.

### Differentiation
*Low Attainers* – Tailor the initial activity to suit the level of attainment. Support will be needed to complete Copymaster 7.
*High Attainers* – Extend the initial activity to '2 football stickers to every 3 stickers'.

### Plenary
Go through Copymaster 7. Insist that pupils share their methods of solution with the rest of the class.
Recap and consolidate the context covered during the lesson.

## Lesson 4

### Introduction
Write the twelve numbers *2, 3, 4, 5, 6, 7, 8, 9, 10, 35, 36* and *80* on the board. *Using all these numbers once only, make as many divisions and their answers as you can.* (In fact all the numbers can be used in 4 calculations and their answers.) Invite pupils to write their answers on the board.

### Activities
Many pupils are inclined to become confused with ratio and '1 in every ...' For example, in a class of 30 pupils if 1 in 3 pupils are boys there are 10 boys and 20 girls, but the ratio of boys to girls is 1 to 2. Care should be taken not to muddle the two concepts.

*1 in 5 of these squares are black.*

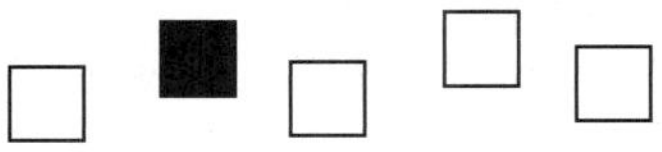

*We sometimes say 1 square in 5 is black. What could you say about these?*

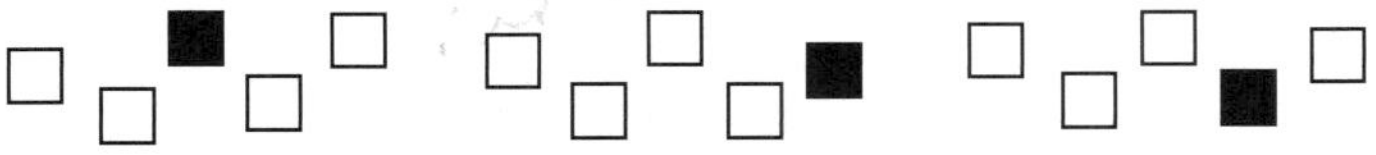

Collect in the answers. Initially allow *1 in 5, 2 in 10 and 3 in 15*, but state that these are the same. Ensure that all pupils are convinced that this is the case – invite other pupils to do the convincing.
Give each child a copy of the blank 100 square (Copymaster 8).
*How many small squares are here?* (Establish that it is 100.) Colour 1 square. *What proportion of the large square have I coloured in?* Confirm with the class that the answer is '1 part in every 100'. Use 'proportion' and '... parts ...' with other colouring in to fix in pupils' minds the equivalence of the two. When this is secure continue: *We have a special name for "parts in every 100". It is called "per cent". So rather than saying, for example, "11 in every 100" we say "11 per cent".*
Give pupils Copymaster 8 to work through on their own. Provide help as and when required. When pupils have completed the copymaster, quickly go through it with the whole class.

### Differentiation
*Low Attainers* – Extra support will be needed (see note at beginning).
*High Attainers* – Invite pupils to find what per cent of a square is shaded when $\frac{1}{2}$, $\frac{1}{4}$ or $\frac{3}{4}$ is shaded.

### Plenary
*Percentages are used in everyday life. Can you give me some examples?* Collect these on the board without comment. *Why are percentages used?* (To make comparisons easier.) Allow as wide a discussion as possible.
Recap on the lesson content i.e. "... parts in every 100" to "per cent" and show the class the % symbol, stating that it means "out of a hundred".

## Lesson 5

### Introduction
Write 3 or 4 numbers between 1 and 20 on the board. Invite pupils to make up word problems involving multiplications or divisions having one of these numbers as the answer.
If it is felt useful this activity may be repeated using additions or subtractions but with a target number in the range 50 to 100.

### Activities
Use the blank 100 square for this activity, the aim of which is to establish/revise the equivalence of "... parts in ...", "fractions of a whole" and "per cent". Shade in 1 small square. *How many parts in a 100 are shaded? What fraction of the large square is shaded? What percentage is shaded?* Quickly establish the correct answers from the pupils.
Repeat for 10 squares (establishing in the process the equivalence of $\frac{10}{100}$ and $\frac{1}{10}$). 25 squares (establishing the equivalence of $\frac{25}{100}$ and $\frac{1}{4}$), for 50 squares and 75 squares.
Recap the percentage of equivalents of $\frac{1}{4}$, $\frac{1}{2}$ and $\frac{3}{4}$.
In pairs, children should reflect this game.

### Differentiation
*Low Attainers* – Work with an adult. Do on a 1-to-1 basis.
*High Attainers* – Work together in pairs.

### Plenary
Go through the pupils' work challenging them on how they arrived at their answers.
In order to recap the lesson, pupils could be invited to shade a certain percentage of an OHT of the 100 square and produce questions based on it for themselves.

# Theme 5 Handling data

## Objectives:

- To discuss chance or likelihood and informally order probabilities
- To interpret data on a bar chart with axis in 2s and 5s
- To interpret data on a bar line chart with axis in 5s and 10s
- To present and interpret data on a bar line graph, identifying the mode
- To make a simple database on paper

## Vocabulary

fair, unfair, likely, unlikely, likelihood, certain, uncertain, probable, possible, impossible, chance, good chance, poor chance, no chance, risk, doubt, frequency, axis, bar chart, graduations in …, bar line chart, plot, mode, database, data

## Resources

Copymasters 9 and 10, Homework Copymaster 5. Sets of 0 to 9 digit cards.

## Assessment

*At the end of this theme is the pupil able to:*

- Discuss chance or likelihood;
- Present and interpret data on a bar chart and bar line graph (axis in 2s, 5s, 10s, 20s, 100s);
- Recognise when intermediate points have no meaning;
- Make a simple database on paper;
- Identify the mode?

## Mental maths starter 5

# Lesson 1

## Introduction

This game is based on a TV game. It should give pupils very informal experience in using probability. However do not attempt to force the formal aspects. Pupils play in pairs, and each pair needs a set of 0 to 9 digit cards.
Players shuffle the cards, put them in a line and turn over the first card.

The first player has to guess if the next card in the line is higher or lower. They turn the card over and if their guess is correct they win a point. The other player then tries to guess if the third card is higher or lower than the second and so on. When all the cards have been used, shuffle and start again. The first player to ten points wins. This game could be played by the whole class, suspending large digit cards on a washing line in front of the class.

## Activities

Ask pupils what statements such as these mean: *It will probably rain tomorrow. It's probable that the sun will shine next week. I don't feel well. I've probably got a cold. Someone probably has a birthday tomorrow.* Open the discussion to all, leading the class to appreciate informally the meaning of 'probability'.
Working in pairs, invite pupils to jot down two events which are impossible, two which are certain and two which are neither impossible nor certain. Collect in the events: 'certain' on one side of the board, 'impossible' on the other and 'neither' in between.

As a class, discuss the groupings, clarifying in pupils' minds what is meant by 'impossible' and 'certain'. The next activity invites pupils to order probabilities and justify the ordering.
Draw this line on the board

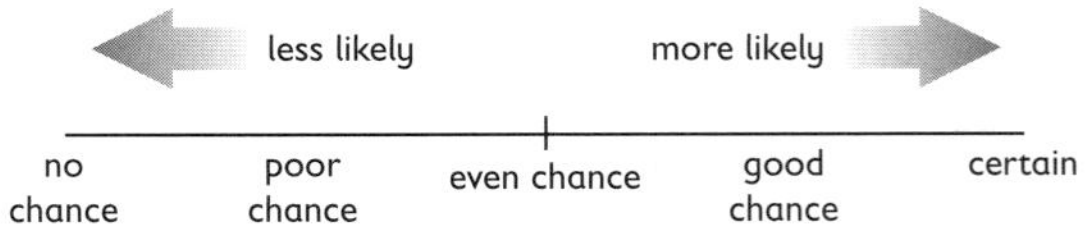


Invite pupils to put each of the events discussed on the probability line. Challenge pupils to justify their choices. Involve as many of the pupils as possible. Use the opportunity to use and draw pupils' attention to the vocabulary of probabilities.

## Differentiation

*Low Attainers* – Will need extra support in order to gain confidence.
*High Attainers* – Can be asked more challenging questions and to justify their answers.

## Plenary

Recap on the lesson using the game *higher or lower* as a vehicle: for example, how likely is it that the next card is higher (or even)? It may be useful to list the 'possible' cards on one side, like this:

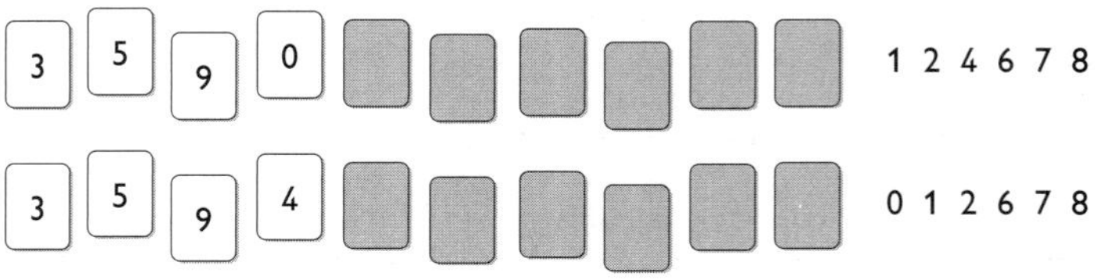


# Lesson 2

## Introduction

Some quick fire, no frills questions involving doubling and halving, with up to 2-digit numbers, such as: *half of 98, double 56, 82 divided by 2, 2 lots of 27.* Give the whole class a ten-question tables test. Quickly mark by swapping sheets. Collect in the sheets to be used again in Lesson 5.

## Activities

These whole-class question/answer/explanations are based on the bar charts shown on Copymaster 9. The copymaster may be distributed or displayed on the OHP. Some of the earlier questions are more of a quick revision and can be quickly passed over. By the end of the session all pupils should have a working understanding of frequency and be able to read from a bar chart graduated in 2s or 5s. As always, challenge pupils as to how they arrived at their answers. Depending on the time available pupils could make their own questions up and give these at the final plenary session.
**Chart A** *Is the chart clear? Can you understand it? In a couple of words what does it tell you? How many families had 4 children?* To force pupils to differentiate between 'frequency' – numbers of families and numbers of children in each family: *How many families were in the survey?*
**Chart B** The situation may have to be explained: *Could the title have been improved? What does frequency mean? What does difference mean? Which difference is most popular? Which difference is least/most likely? How many times did a difference of 5 occur?* (Ensure that pupils are confident with scale in 2s.) *Why is a difference of 6 impossible?*
***Chart C*** The situation may need to be explained: *Could the title have been improved? How many times was the smallest number 4? How did you work this out?* (Repeat as necessary.) *According to the bar chart the smallest number was never 6 – does this mean that it is impossible to get a smallest number of 6? Explain.*
***Chart D*** Similar questions to Chart C.

## Differentiation

*Low Attainers* – Match the questions to their level.
*High Attainers* – Move at a quicker rate and ask more challenging questions.

## Plenary

Invite pupils to make up their own questions based on the charts. Recap the lesson's progress including what every chart must have – title, labelled axes etc.

## Lesson 3

### Introduction

Quick mental arithmetic problems of the type: *Find three pairs of numbers between 200 and 300 that add up to 476. Pick two numbers from this list which add up to 100: 26, 35, 23, 56, 71, 44, 31, 22, 79, 87. Jen saves £4 a week of pocket money. How many weeks will it take her to save £60? Cakes cost 13p each to make and are sold for 20p each. How much profit is there in selling 100? Which is the largest of these numbers: 5, 6, 4, 7, 1, 7, 3, 9? Jot down three whole numbers that add up to 7. Subtract 8 plus 9 from 8 times 9. A coach can carry 52 people. How many of these coaches will be needed to carry 137 people? Which four coins add up to £1? Jot down three multiplications that have 36 as an answer.*

### Activities

Give pairs of pupils Copymaster 10. Provide help as and when needed.

### Differentiation

*Low Attainers* – Do Copymaster 10 Part 1 with support with the reading.
*High Attainers* – Do the whole of Copymaster 10 including the challenge. Invite pupils to report their conclusions/findings to the rest of the class during the plenary session.

### Plenary

Discuss as a class the answers to the copymaster, challenging pupils to justify their answers where appropriate. Recap the content of the lesson.

---

## Lesson 4

### Introduction

Play the game *Yes/No* – the teacher or a pupil chooses a secret whole number less than 100. The rest of the group has to find what the number is by using questions which can be answered by a yes or no e.g. *Is it less than …? Is it in the … times table? Is it a factor of …?* Play the game several times, perhaps in groups.

### Activities

*Why do you think dice are used in a lot of board games?* Lead the class to consider unpredictability and fairness at an informal level. This activity generates data (pupils' choice of 'random' numbers from 1 to 9), which can be displayed in the form of a bar and chart and used as a vehicle to revisit informal probability, including fairness. Ask pupils to jot down any number between 1 and 9. Quickly collect these on the board, with no comment or opportunity for pupils to change their minds. *If you were to plot a bar line chart of these results what sort of shaped chart would you expect?* Allow as many pupils as possible to voice an opinion, perhaps sketching their answers. Lead the class to the conclusion that a chart with more or less equal height lines might be expected. Working in pairs, ask pupils to plot a bar line chart of the numbers on the board. Provide graph paper, but give pupils a free hand and allow them to decide on their own methods. Set a target time for this – say 10–15 minutes. Initiate a full class discussion about how they went about the task. In the discussion, bring out the importance of labelling charts, using a sensible scale and, at the very start, making a tally chart. In all probability the charts will have peaks at '3' and '7'. Should this be obvious (or if any number(s) are unduly represented) make an issue of this, pointing out that humans don't make good dice!

### Differentiation

*Low Attainers* – Will need some support in the 'open ended' plotting activity.
*High Attainers* – As an extension activity, ask them if throwing two dice and adding the scores would be a fair way of choosing 'fair' numbers from 2 to 12. Invite them to investigate this practically.

### Plenary

Recap the questions based on Copymaster 9.

---

## Lesson 5

### Introduction

Give the whole class a ten-question tables test (a different one from that given in Lesson 2). Quickly mark by swapping sheets. Collect in the sheets or the marks. The compilation of the database does not necessarily require pupils to be identified so the sheets do not require a name on them.

### Activities

*We now have two collections of marks from the two tables check ups: the one you have just done and the one you did earlier in the week. When we collect together both sets of marks we shall have what is called a database – a collection of data which we can use.* Quickly write on the board or OHP in two unordered lists the two sets of test results. *We want to use this database to help check some statements such as: most of the class got 8 out of 10 right in both tests; the class did better in the second test; very few of the class got full marks in either test; all the class got over half the questions right.* Discuss with the class how the statements may be checked, including consideration of what information is needed and how it can be collected and displayed. In the course of the discussion suggest that the mode is a useful measure of 'how most of the class did' and that bar or bar line charts are a useful way of comparing sets of results. Allow pupils to pursue their 'guided choice' of method, working in groups of 2 or 3. Advise them that they may have to make a mini presentation to the whole of the class on their findings. Provide help and remediation where needed.

### Differentiation

*Low Attainers* – Will need extra support, perhaps being provided with a list of the marks on paper.
*High Attainers* – Could be invited to investigate, using the raw data, if any particular questions were found difficult. Or work out together how they might investigate which operation pupils experienced most difficulty with, pursuing this at a later date.

### Plenary

Recap the lesson content using presentations by two or three groups – encourage constructive criticism where appropriate.

# Theme 6 Shapes

## Objectives

- To recognise and use the appropriate vocabulary associated with scalene, isosceles, equilateral and right-angled triangles
- To recognise the properties of rectangles and use and understand the term 'congruent'
- To read and plot points in the first quadrant
- To use and understand the vocabulary associated with the first quadrant coordinate grid
- To solve shape puzzles, giving verbal and written explanations of solutions

## Vocabulary

parallel, perpendicular, equilateral and right-angled triangles, scalene triangle, isosceles triangle, square, pentagon, hexagon, heptagon, octagon, congruent, diagonals, bisect, coordinates, x-axis, y-axis, origin, vertices, vertex, explain, polygon, tangram, tan.
(Pupils may need reminding of some of the shape vocabulary to date.)

## Resources

Rulers, Copymasters 11 and 12, squared and triangular spotty paper, square and triangular pin boards, possibly squared paper for drawing first quadrant coordinate grid. Squared dotty paper, scissors, tracing paper, thin card (optional), a slide projector (or appropriately de-focused OHP) for casting sharply focused shadow onto the wall or screen, some prepared cardboard shapes (square, rectangle, triangles, various polygons), Homework Copymaster 6.

## Assessment

*At the end of this theme is the pupil able to:*

- Identify and recognise the properties of rectangles;
- Classify triangles – isosceles, equilateral and scalene;
- Describe lines of symmetry;
- Recognise positions;
- Read and plot coordinates in the first quadrant;
- Solve shape puzzles;
- Explain their methods and reasoning orally and in writing?

## Mental maths starter 6

## Lesson 1

### Introduction

Explain to pupils the idea behind subtraction crosses i.e. Invite pupils to solve some subtraction crosses such as these:

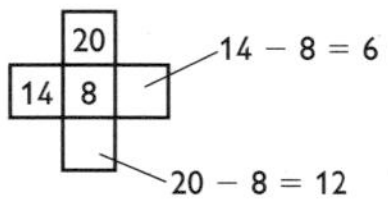


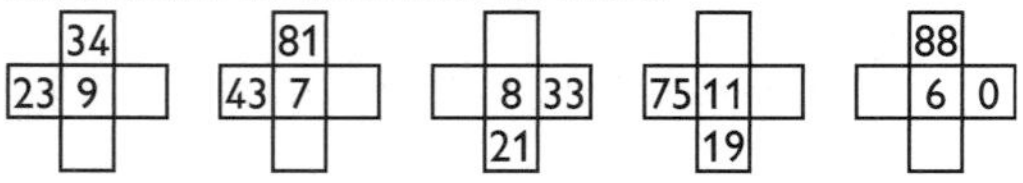


Challenge pupils, working in pairs, to find a connection between the difference between the right-hand cell and the bottom cell and the difference between the left-hand call and the top cell. Guide pupils into realising the importance of working methodically and of testing any rules they might find. Spend several minutes collecting the class' observations. Low attainers can be involved by asking them to solve more straightforward puzzles similar to the initial two and the example.

### Activities

Write the words 'parallel' and 'perpendicular' on the board. *Can anyone read these words? Can someone tell me what they mean?* Encourage pupils to supplement their explanations by drawings. Filter out the incorrect and home in on 'lines which stay the same distance apart' or equivalent and 'at right-angles to' or equivalent. Either give out or use on OHT Copymaster 11 and invite pupils using (a) and (b) to draw and label some lines which are parallel or perpendicular using the spots as ends of the lines. This activity will quickly indicate any pupils with problems.

Quickly draw some triangles on the board – include right-angled, isosceles, equilateral, and scalene – making no comment. What are these called? Very quickly establish triangles. Are there any special sorts of triangle? Depending on the group, take sufficient time to revise (writing the words on the board) equilateral, isosceles and introduce 'right-angled' and 'scalene'. Challenge pupils to find as many of these as possible on Copymaster 11, using the spots as vertices (this word may need revising) – insist on their using ruler and pencil.
At this point, depending on facilities, it would be useful to give pupils the opportunity to use a computer program such as *Tree of Knowledge* or *Branch*, perhaps in groups over the duration of this theme.

### Differentiation

*Low Attainers* – May find using pinboards and elastic bands a useful precursor to drawing on the copymaster. Ask them to make at least one of each of the three types of triangle using elastic bands and a pinboard.
*High Attainers* – May be given sheets of triangular and square dotty paper and encouraged to find some less obvious triangles, and to check the sides by measuring.

### Plenary

Invite individual pupils to draw 'different' triangles on an OHT of Copymaster 11 (no repeats allowed). Encourage constructive comments and discussion as to whether the differences are real and make an issue about the importance of measurement as the final arbiter.
Quickly recap the triangles – scalene, isosceles, equilateral and right-angled – insisting on correct mathematical language.

## Lesson 2

### Introduction

Write these words on the board: *scalene triangle, isosceles triangle, square, pentagon, hexagon, heptagon, octagon.*
Invite students to draw these shapes on Copymaster 11 with spots at the vertices. This is a quick activity to revise some of the 2D shape vocabulary. Quickly check and remediate any problems.

### Activities

Using Copymaster 11 ask pupils to draw – with vertices on spots – as many different rectangles as they can.
Force the issue of what to do with rectangles like these:
Establish by measurement that they are the 'same'.

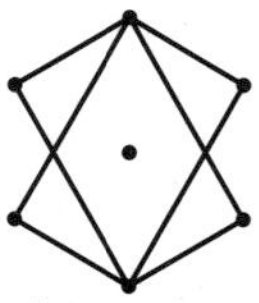

*Using 'the same' is a bit vague – all rectangles have the same number of sides but can be different sizes. When shapes are the same is every way – apart from position we say they are 'congruent'.* Reinforce this by asking pupils to point out other rectangles that are congruent to each other.
Provide help as and when needed. Give a target time, say ten minutes, then ask pupils, in pairs, to jot down anything which they notice that all rectangles have (if appropriate the word 'property' may be used).
Collect pupils' properties of rectangles on the board. Guide the group into considering these properties of rectangles: all angles are right angles; opposite sides are equal and parallel; the diagonals are equal in length; the diagonals bisect each other (the latter may not emerge and can be given to pupils as a suggestion for them to investigate quickly. It is a new piece of vocabulary so may need special attention).

### Differentiation

*Low Attainers* – May find a pinboard and elastic bands a useful aid.
*High Attainers* – As in the previous lesson, may use separate sheets of square and triangular spotty paper.

### Plenary

Recap the content covered in the lesson, drawing pupils' attention to the new vocabulary encountered, especially 'congruent', and 'bisect'.
Challenge pupils: *Is a square a rectangle? Can a rectangle be a square? What is special about an oblong? Is a square an oblong? How could you test that two shapes were congruent?* (Make a tracing.) Remember that a square is an equilateral rectangle and an oblong a rectangle with unequal pairs of sides.
A quick investigation: How many congruent rectangles measuring 3 units by 1 unit (show on OHT) can you find in this grid? (Indicate one of the square grids on Copymaster 11.) On a 3 × 3 square grid of spots a total of 76 triangles can be made, only 8 of which are non-congruent. It is impossible to make an equilateral triangle?

# Lesson 3

## Introduction

Play 'What am I called?' using shapes e.g. *I have six sides. What am I called? Hexagon!* Two teams can compete against each other or against the clock or pupils could play in pairs, high attainers assisting low attainers. Remediate any serious problems.

## Activities

Quickly revise coordinates. Refer to coordinates being 'starting from the origin then so many across followed by so many up'.
Point out the following features of the grid: origin, x-axis, y-axis (and, if appropriate, the fact that we refer to the region where both x and y coordinates are positive as being the first quadrant).
Ask the pupils to draw a grid then ask questions like these, ensuring that as many as possible of the class make an oral contribution.
Depending on circumstances teams could make up and test questions of a similar type: *Draw the shape made by joining the points (1, 1), (3, 1), (3, 3) and (1, 3). What is the name for the shape? Draw a straight line joining the points (6, 5) and (9, 8). Draw a straight line joining the points (1, 4) and (1, 8). Jot down the coordinates of the mid-point of the line. What can you say about the triangle with vertices at (5, 6), (3, 8) and (3, 6)? These points are the coordinates of the vertices of a shape: (5, 3), (9, 3), (9, 4), (5, 4). What is the name of the shape?*

## Differentiation

*Low Attainers* – May need some support during this activity.
*High Attainers* – Can investigate the connection between the coordinates of the end points of a straight line and the coordinates of its mid-point.

## Plenary

Explain to the class the more general definition of diagonal: *a line joining two vertices* (if appropriate qualify this by vertices which are not next – adjacent – to each other.) Reinforce 'diagonal' by showing some of the 5 diagonals in a pentagon, for example:

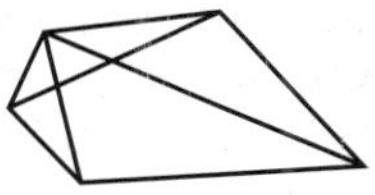

This will give the opportunity to recap on regular/irregular polygons.
Ask pupils to find the total number of diagonals.
Depending on level of attainment, quadrilaterals and hexagons could also be investigated. The very able should be encouraged to find a number linking the number of diagonals with the number of sides of a polygon.

# Lesson 4

## Introduction

A no-frills multiplication tables test. Take the opportunity to probe which tables might need a little more work.

## Activities

Give each pupil a copy of Copymaster 12. Use the opportunity to encourage reading aloud – pupils read through each task. Invite any queries. Then either allow a free or guided choice, working in pairs or individually. Set a target time and state that after this time some of the class will be expected to tell the class what they found. Most of the activities lend themselves to use of the OHP (with question 4 for example, thin cardboard shapes will project well as shadows). Provide support where necessary.

## Differentiation

Differentiation is by outcome.
*Low Attainers* – May need extra support to start them off.

## Plenary

Ask selected pairs or individuals to report back to the group – encourage the whole class to participate constructively. Make an issue of using correct mathematical language – this is a useful time to recap on the new vocabulary encountered during the theme.
Depending on the outcome from the start of the lesson have another quick tables test or play the 'What am I called?' game again to see if groups can improve on their performance from the previous lesson.

# Lesson 5

## Introduction

Show the class how shadows are cast, then ask them *Can you use a square to make a triangular shadow?* Collect answers then invite a pupil to try for him/herself. The important part of this activity is the use of language and the visualisation. Challenge the class with other questions such as: *Can you make a square shadow from a rectangle/triangle/hexagon? Can you make a triangle shadow from a rectangle/hexagon? Can you make a right-angled triangle shadow from this scalene/isosceles triangle?* Invite pupils to suggest similar questions of their own.

## Activities

All the activities are based on tangrams. Whilst making a tangram is a useful exercise in drawing and measuring, some low attaining pupils may find a set of pre-prepared tangrams useful. These may be made more permanent by using the thick acetate sheets used to make folders. This material is easy to cut and is available in different colours.
Repeat the activity from the previous lesson using Part 2 of Copymaster 12, but with the understanding that they have to 'tell the story' of their investigation. It may be necessary to explain what a tangram is to the whole class (and that a single piece is called a tan).
Stress that you are not expecting a fully polished account: just a few sentences and diagrams so that someone else can understand.

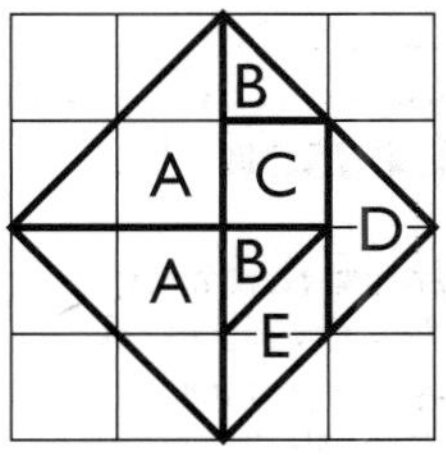


Depending on the attainment level of the group, pairs' work could be circulated to see if the writing/diagrams do their job. Set a time limit based on your knowledge of the group. Some groups may find it useful to begin with a whole class activity using a 'standard' tangram made from card and projected with an OHP.

## Differentiation

Differentiation is by outcome.
*Low Attainers* – Will need extra support with their writing. In some cases diagrams or sketches may be a sufficiently realistic challenge.

## Plenary

Groups feed back their findings, perhaps reading them aloud and showing diagrams with the aid of the OHP. Encourage as many pupils as possible to contribute and pay attention to the use of correct mathematical language.

# Theme 7 Measuring length

## Objectives

- To use, read and write standard units of length and their abbreviations; convert between these units of length make; estimates of lengths
- To understand, measure and calculate the perimeter of rectangles and regular polygons
- To estimate lengths and to measure and draw lines to the nearest millimetre
- To recognise simple fractions of a metre expressed in centimetres and simple fractions of a kilometre expressed in metres
- To recognise and use the approximation that a mile is a little bit more than one and a half kilometres and to suggest suitable estimates/equipment to measure length

## Vocabulary

millimetre, centimetre, metre, total, sum, estimate, perimeter, rectangle, pentagon, hexagon, heptagon, polygon, approximate, difference, total, one tenth, one hundredth, mile

## Resources

Sufficient 30 cm and metre rules and 10 m measuring tapes for the whole class (possibly trundle wheels if available), a collection of objects to be measured such as pieces of string, cotton-wool balls (to be 'thrown' and distance thrown measured), some thick and thin paperbacks, squared paper. Copymasters 13 and 14. Homework Copymaster 7.

## Assessment

*At the end of this theme is the pupil able to:*

- Understand, measure and calculate the perimeter of rectangles and regular polygons;
- Measure and draw lines to the nearest mm;
- Use, read and write standard metric units of length, abbreviations and relationships;
- Convert larger units of length to smaller units;
- Suggest suitable units of length and equipment to measure length;
- Record estimates/measurements from scales to a suitable degree of accuracy?

## Mental maths starter 7

# Lesson 1

## Introduction

Ask pupils to jot down as many different calculations as they can in five minutes that fit these:

| | | | |
|---|---|---|---|
| *… ÷ … = 5* | *… ÷ … = 10* | *… × … = 12* | *… × … = 24* |
| *… ÷ … = 3* | *… × … = 32* | *… × … = 32* | *… ÷ … = 7* |

## Activities

In a quick question and answer session revise the standard metric units of length (mm, cm and m) and the relationship between them. Also make a point of revising their abbreviations. Some lower attaining pupils may find copying down a short list of the units and their relationships useful. Illustrate centimetres and metres by making use of the 30 cm and metre rules.

If necessary illustrate on the OHP using a transparency and transparent ruler the more common errors which are made in using a ruler. Challenge pupils to state what is wrong – don't merely tell them. The common errors are (for completeness): measuring from '1' rather than zero, using the ruler at an angle to the subject line, using the scale upside down.

Working in pairs, set the class out on a length measuring circus, involving about 10 diverse length measurements. Ask pupils to measure the lengths as accurately as they can, but provide no other hints, allowing them to make decisions for themselves. Possible activities are:

- *Thickness of paperbacks (one thick, one thin)*
- *How far can you throw a cotton-wool ball?*
- *How long is your middle finger?*
- *How wide is your thumb nail?*
- *How high/wide is the doorway?*
- *How tall are you?*
- *How high is the desk top from the floor?*
- *How thick is a pencil?*

Remediate where pupils are obviously having problems, but wherever possible allow pupils to make their own decisions.

## Differentiation

*Low Attainers* – May need some initial support in the measuring activity.
*High Attainers* – Could be given more challenging measurements, perhaps involving inaccessible dimensions and requiring two or more steps.

## Plenary

Go through pupils' measurements, taking the opportunity to make an issue of giving units. Finish the lesson with a simple quick fire activity asking questions such as: *What object in the room measures about five metres/millimetres/centimetres?* Take the opportunity to encourage pupils to give their rationale.

# Lesson 2

## Introduction

This activity is designed to give pupils practice with mental addition and in remembering numbers – no writing down is allowed. The object of the activity is to begin on the central square and to imagine a path to one of the sides. The path must not go through any square more than once. It must not go diagonally, only up down or across.

The squares may be shown on the OHP.

| | | | | |
|---|---|---|---|---|
| 2 | 3 | 4 | 6 | 1 |
| 3 | 10 | 6 | 9 | 6 |
| 3 | 2 | 2 | 3 | 2 |
| 7 | 7 | | 5 | 3 |
| 6 | 8 | 4 | 7 | 2 |
| 5 | 2 | 7 | 1 | 8 |
| 4 | 1 | 3 | 2 | 4 |

| | | | | |
|---|---|---|---|---|
| 9 | 1 | 4 | 2 | 1 |
| 3 | 7 | 2 | 7 | 10 |
| 3 | 7 | 8 | 6 | 2 |
| 7 | 8 | | 7 | 9 |
| 3 | 4 | 6 | 1 | 8 |
| 6 | 10 | 7 | 3 | 4 |
| 7 | 2 | 2 | 6 | 1 |

| | | | | |
|---|---|---|---|---|
| 23 | 15 | 48 | 13 | 29 |
| 66 | 7 | 12 | 8 | 4 |
| 3 | 44 | 10 | 6 | 88 |
| 77 | 27 | | 14 | 71 |
| 23 | 33 | 6 | 26 | 88 |
| 86 | 72 | 11 | 34 | 24 |
| 43 | 12 | 19 | 6 | 15 |

Depending on attainment level, questions can be: *Which side gives the smallest/greatest total? Your score is the total of the numbers from the centre to this side (indicate) in five squares. What is the smallest/greatest score?*

If appropriate invite pupils to share their strategies for remembering numbers.

## Activities

Recap on the conversion between different metric units of measurement by asking questions, for example: *The average doorway is two metres tall. How many centimetres is this? Which is longer: a string half a metre long or one 40 centimetres long? Explain your answer. About how tall are you in centimetres?* Take the opportunity to reinforce and internalise everyday lengths and establish a 'feel' for them.

Give out Copymaster 13 for pupils to do individually.

## Differentiation

*Low Attainers* – May only achieve success on the simpler number squares and should not be expected to find all the solutions on Copymaster 13. These pupils need to begin on 1(a).
*High Attainers* – Will need the challenge of the 'harder' number squares in the initial activity and could profitably design and test their own versions of the activities on Copymaster 13. They could omit 1(a).

## Plenary

Go through Copymaster 13 using the OHP, remediating and involving pupils as much as possible.

Finish with some questions of the form *Estimate the distance from here to here.* Make an issue over using the correct units, and, if appropriate, invite pupils to share their estimation strategies with the rest of the class.

## Lesson 3

### Introduction
Revise the definitions of the common polygons. Depending on the attainment level of the group it may be useful to draw the distinction between 'regular' and 'irregular' polygons.

### Activities
Quickly recap on the meaning of perimeter, beginning perhaps with *Can anyone tell me what a perimeter fence is?* Invite pupils to draw some rectangles on squared paper, using the lines so that all the sides are whole number lengths. Then ask them to find the perimeters of their rectangles. Take this opportunity to give support to any low attainers who might be struggling. Collect the results in a table on the board. In order to avoid confusion it may be useful to tell pupils that 'length' is the longer side and 'breadth' the shorter side.

| LENGTH | BREADTH | PERIMETER |
|---|---|---|
| 4 cm | 1 cm | 10 cm |

Invite pupils to find a connection between the length and breadth and the perimeters of their rectangles.
Discuss responses and ask how they might be written as a formula in words.
Guide the class into considering 'perimeter = 2 × (length + breadth)'.
Challenge the class: *What formula could you use to find the perimeter of a square?*

### Differentiation
*Low Attainers* – Will need support with the word equations and might reasonably be expected only to gain complete understanding with the case of the square.
*High Attainers* – Should be asked to give proper algebraic formulae for the perimeters of regular polygons.

### Plenary
Review the lesson's content and finish with some recap questions of the type: *A square has a perimeter of 20 cm. What is the length of one of its sides? A (regular) hexagon has sides each of length 5 cm. What is its perimeter? One side of a rectangle is 4 cm. Its perimeter is 10 cm. What is the length of each of the shorter sides?* And for challenge: *Two squares each have a perimeter of 24 cm. They join together to make a rectangle. What is the perimeter of this rectangle?*

## Lesson 4

### Introduction
Establish the simple fractions of a metre and a kilometre by question and answer. (Using a metre ruler marked in centimetres may be a useful aid.) *How many centimetres are there in a metre? What fraction of a metre is 1 centimetre? What fraction of a metre are 3 centimetres?* And so on. *What, in centimetres, is $\frac{1}{10}$ of a metre? What, in centimetres, is $\frac{3}{4}$ of a metre?* And so on. Repeat in a similar manner for simple fractions of a kilometre.

### Activities
A whole class or small group game can be made by using a 30 cm or metre rule which is blank on one side. Pupils face each other. The person who can see the scale sets a target length and moves their finger along the ruler until the 'guesser' says stop at what they consider to be the appropriate point. By turning the rule over both players can see how close the estimate from the 'guesser' was. Allow pupils to produce their own system of scoring. (The game allows for estimating at the mm and cm level.)

### Differentiation
Differentiation will be by outcome, although *Low Attainers* may need some support and guidance as to what is expected in some of the activities.

### Plenary
Give pupils the opportunity to share their estimation strategies with the class in a general discussion about estimating length.

## Lesson 5

### Introduction
By question and answer establish situations where the mile might be used as a unit of length, and the fact that 1 mile is greater than 1 km. *Which sort of distances would it be useful to give in miles? What metric measurement of length would be best for these sort of distances? Is 1 mile greater or less a distance than 1 kilometre?* At this point tell pupils that a mile is just over one and a half kilometres. Depending on the class it may be appropriate to state that one way to change from miles into kilometres is to multiply by 3 and divide by 2. *It is about 120 miles from London to Birmingham. Roughly how many kilometres is this? It is about 400 miles from London to Glasgow. Roughly how many kilometres is this?* Some lower attainers will find this challenging, but realising that a mile is longer than a kilometre is a worthwhile achievement in itself.

### Activities
Give pupils Copymaster 14, either as individuals or a small group. Alternatively an OHT of the Copymaster could provide the stimulus for a whole class review session.
When it is clear that most pupils are on the verge of finishing ask them to make up some questions of their own based on the week's work

### Differentiation
*Low Attainers* – Will need help with the reading of Copymaster 14 and should not be expected to complete it.
*High Attainers* – Should be challenged to make up some interesting questions of their own.

### Plenary
Review the theme's content using pupils' responses to Copymaster 14 as the starting point. Take the opportunity to make reference to length measurement in other subjects – for example P.E., science etc. This will provide a realistic scenario in which measurement and the actual instrument used does really matter.
Make use – if suitable – of pupils' own questions.

# Theme 8 Measures problems

### Objectives
- To read the time on a 24-hour digital clock
- To use appropriate notation for 12 and 24 hour clocks
- To be able to estimate and measure time using suitable units
- To solve word problems involving units of time
- To use number operations to solve problems involving time
- To choose appropriate operations and calculation methods and explain the working

### Vocabulary
Analogue clock, digital clock, am, pm, convert, 24 hour clock, 12 hour clock, second, minute, hour, day, week, month, year, decade, century, millennium, estimate, timetable, unit.

### Resources
Clock cards, television programme times, timetables, sunrise/sunset times. Copymasters 15 and 16. Homework Copymaster 8.

### Assessment
*At the end of this theme is the pupil able to:*
- Use the 24-hour clock notation to read and write times for both am and pm;
- Solve word problems involving time and duration;
- Decide on and use a paper and pencil strategy to work out a word problem involving the measurement of time?

### Mental maths starter 21

## Lesson 1

### Introduction
Using clock cards start with quick questions to revise units of time, e.g. *How many minutes in an hour? How many hours in a day?* Then ask the children to show times on their clock cards, e.g. *ten thirty, eleven thirty*.
Show a time on a large clock face and ask the children to show what time it will be a given number of minutes or hours later.

### Activities
Write 5pm on the board.
*What time is this? – 5o'clock in the afternoon*
Explain to the children that there is another way of saying and writing this time. It is called the 24 hour clock. (Ask for examples in everyday life of where the children have seen the 24 hour clock in operation.) *If we use this method there is no need to use am. and pm. How does it work?*
5 o'clock becomes 17:00 using the fact that there are 24 hours in a day. Repeat with a few more example times. Emphasise that am times remain the same for the 12 hour clock and the 24 hour clock. (9.30am becomes 09.30). To convert a pm time to the 24 clock, simply add 12 to the hours.
Write on the board 8 pm = 8 + 12 = 20 = 20:00
*Working in pairs* – Tell the children to draw a timeline on squared paper, with 24 intervals. Explain that you would like them to write am/pm times above the line and the corresponding 24 hrs times below, for each hour of the day.

### Differentiation
*Low Attainers* – Let the children only work with o'clock times.
*High Attainers* – They can practise working out time intervals between key events of the day using the 24 hour timeline, and compare this to calculating with 12-hour clock.

### Plenary
Let the children have copies of the television page of a newspaper and ask them to change the 12 hour clock times into 24 hour time.
*What time is your favourite television programme on in 12 as well as 24 hour clock time?*

## Lesson 2

### Introduction
Rehearse adding pairs of numbers that add up to 60.
*What do I need to add to 26 to make 60? What is 60 − 43?*

### Activities
*What units are suitable for measuring time?*
Work as a class to draw up a list showing all the units of time from smallest to largest.
- *Second*
- *Minute = 60 seconds*
- *Hour = 60 minutes* up to
- *Millennium = 1000 years*

Tell the children that there is no obvious pattern when using units of time, unlike other metric measures that we use (100 cms = 1 metre 1000 m = 1 kilometre). Ask the children what would be a suitable unit for measuring the following –
- *To walk across the playground*
- *To say the alphabet from A to Z*
- *To mow the grass on the school field*
- *To travel to the moon*

*Working in pairs* – Write on the board: A cyclist left home at 08.45 and arrived at her friend's house at 14:35. *How long did she cycle for?* Model from 08.45 to 09.00 is 15 minutes, from 09.00 to 14.00 is 5 hours, from 14.00 to 14.35 is 35 minutes.
Total = 5 hours 50 minutes.
Give out more examples.

### Differentiation
*Low Attainers* – Ask them to explore different time durations of their own choice e.g. *How long is it to lunchtime, hometime etc.*
*High Attainers – How long does it take for your heart to beat 100 times? How long are all the playtimes during the school week added together?*

### Plenary
Use Copymaster 15 and ask the children to answer the questions in 12 and 24-hour clock times.

## Lesson 3

### Introduction
Respond to oral or written questions like –
*Would you expect to roast a chicken in 2 hours, 5 hours, or 10 hours?*
*To walk a mile in 15 mins, 45 mins, or 75 mins?*
*Have you lived more or less than 3650 days?*
*More or less than 100,000 hours?*

### Activities
*Plan a Journey* – Tell the children they are going to use timetables to plan journeys. Look at the part of a timetable on an OHP or the board. Ask questions about it, e.g. *If the bus leaves the church at 08.00, when does it arrive at the High Street?*
*How long does a journey from The Fox Inn to the city centre take?* Ask children to come out and point to the appropriate parts of the timetable to explain how they did it. Then ask each group to come up with a question about the timetable. The groups then pose their questions to the class.
*Working in pairs* – Using a timetable the children pose five questions in their pairs. Then swap questions with another pair to find the answers.

### Differentiation
*Low Attainers* – Answer questions from the teacher about the enlarged timetable extract on the board or OHP.
*High Attainers* – Children write down their own special events (football matches, parties, trips) with times so that others can write down their duration.

### Plenary
Look at a timetable for a bus and a train; ask questions which relate to both timetables, e.g. *If I want to catch the 17:50 train, what is the latest bus I can get from the cinema?*

## Lesson 4

### Introduction
Give each child a digital clockface. Remind them how to convert 12-hour times to the 24-hour clock by adding 12 to the hours of pm times. Ask the class questions that involve conversion and an awareness of time and ordering, and measuring time. Write each time on the board:
*Jane, what time would 5.45pm be on a 24 hour clock?* (17.45)
*Carmen, at which time might you be in a lesson if it was a school day?* (e.g. 09.30) Ask the rest of the class to show you each time with their clockfaces.

### Activities
Ask the class to say where they might see times listed:
- *Cinema Schedules*
- *Sunset and Sunrise Times*
- *School Club Times*

Use Copymaster 16 showing sunrise/sunset times for the first day of each month. Give the children chance to discuss the times in pairs. Then ask such questions as *Which month had the earliest sunrise? On the first of which month was there the least daylight? If you stayed for an after school club until 16:30, on which of these days would you leave for home in the dark?*
1 January, 1 February, 1 November, 1 December. *On which of these days would you wake up in the light? Does school ever start or finish in the dark?*
*Working in pairs* – Give the children chance to calculate how long it is from sunrise to sunset on the days shown. Compile the results in a list on the board from the shortest to the longest day.

### Differentiation
*Low Attainers* – Ask questions such as which month had the latest sunrise and which month had the earliest sunset.
*High Attainers* – Ask for an explanation of why we have different sunrise and sunset times

### Plenary
Look at other 'timed lists' such as school club times and pose questions about, for example, attendance at more than one club at the same time. *Can I play the recorder and play football on Tuesday?*

## Lesson 5

### Introduction
Discuss with the children that when faced with a real life problem we need to select the relevant information and decide on a strategy.
*Which is the best bouncer?*
Drop a tennis ball next to the classroom wall from a height of 1 metre. *How high does it bounce?* Repeat it five times. Find the average height the ball bounces. Enter the information on a graph either by each child or one on the board.

### Activities
Do exactly the same for a selection of balls (tennis ball, table tennis ball, golf ball etc.) Add the results to the graphs drawn by the children. *Which is the best bouncer?*
*Working in pairs* – Repeat the exercise for a paper aeroplane and the average distance it can travel over 5 goes. Use the results of two other pairs and enter them on a graph.

### Differentiation
*Low Attainers* – Find the average shoe size of 5 people in their class.
*High Attainers* – Using the television programme times organise programming a video recorder to record their favourite programmes. They will need to note the start time and finish time and the length of the programme.

### Plenary
Explain Homework Sheet 8.
Answer these questions (with or without the calculator)
- *Can you lift a million pennies?*
- *Can you drink a million cups of tea?*
- *Can you count to a million?*

# Theme 9 Addition and subtraction

## Objectives

- To find differences by counting up through the next multiple of 10, 100, 1000
- To partition into HTU and add most significant digits first
- To use informal pencil and paper methods for addition and subtraction
- To extend written methods of addition and subtraction of two integers less than 10,000
- To check calculations using inverse operation, including with a calculator
- To use all four operations to solve money and 'real life' word problems

## Vocabulary

counting on, shopkeepers' method, add on, next ten, next hundred, hundreds, tens, units, split up, group, digit, method, thousands, inverse.

## Resources

Copymasters 17 and 18. Homework Copymaster 9.

## Assessment

*At the end of this theme is the pupil able to:*

- Find difference by counting up through the next multiple of 10, 100, 1000;
- Partition into HTU and add the most significant digits first;
- Use informal pencil and paper methods;
- Extend written methods +/- of two integers less than 10,000;
- Use all four operations to solve money and 'real life' word problems;
- Choose appropriate operations/calculation methods and explain his/her working;
- Check calculation using the inverse operation, including with a calculator?

## Mental maths starter 14

# Lesson 1

## Introduction

*What do you need to add on to 437 to make the next 10?* Quickly take answers and confirm that all pupils understand the term 'next ten' and that '3' is the answer. Confirm with another one or two similar questions. *What do you need to add on to 670 to make the next 100?* Continue as with the 'next ten'. Finish by asking quick fire questions, such as: *What must be added on to 780 to make the next 100? What must be added on to 781 to make the next 10?* The object of the activity is to increase facility and speed.

## Activities

*You may have heard people in shops counting as they give change: 'seventy, eighty, ninety and one pound' for 40p change. What were they doing?* Allow full discussion and contribution from pupils, but establish the principle of counting on. If real money is available pupils could practise giving change by counting on, either in pairs or demonstrating to the whole class. *Imagine Isha bought a second hand computer for £93. She gave the shop assistant £100. What calculation will tell Isha her change?* Quickly establish it is 100 – 93 and that one way of looking at this is to find what must be added to 93 to give a 100 – which can be found by counting on.

Illustrate this by:

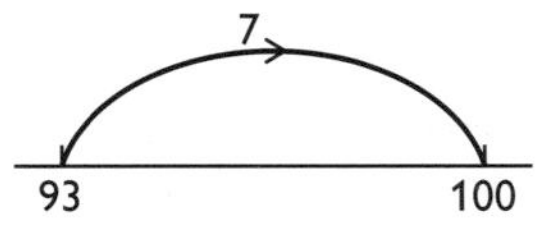


*Counting on can be used for harder subtractions such as 2000 − 1843.* Think "aloud" the step length with each jump on the sketch:

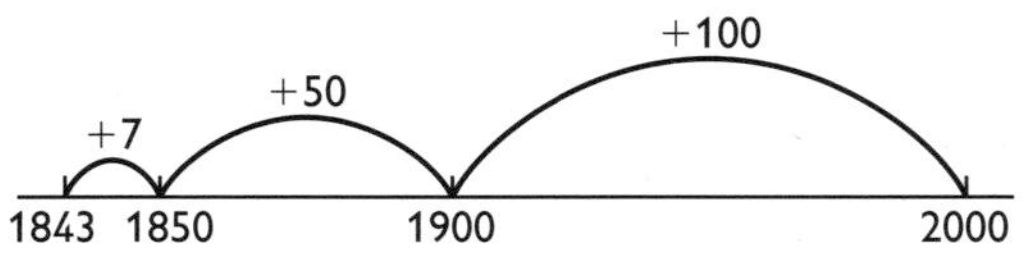


Work through another example to ensure understanding.
*Why is it best to jump to the 'next 10', 'next 100'?*
If necessary illustrate the difficulties that mat arise when this is not done.

## Differentiation

*Low Attainers* – Allow initial use of number line and hundred square. It may also be useful at first to present some of the numbers in HTU format to revise place value informally. Omit the last question.
*High Attainers* – Work independently.

## Plenary

Go through several more examples using the method, e.g. *4629 − 4007, 8124 − 7010*. Involve pupils, encouraging them to 'think aloud'.

# Lesson 2

## Introduction

Quick mental activity – pupils answer (and show these) on whiteboards: *420 take away 50. 560 add 30. What is the sum of 640 and 40? Subtract 40 from 600. Add 260 to 40. How much greater is 540 than 60? What should be added to 340 to make 420? How many 8s are there in 48? What is the product of 5 and 4? What is £60 shared between 6?*
A digit is a single number. 0,1,2,3,4,5,6,7,8 and 9 are digits. 1503 is a 4-digit number using the digits 1, 5, 0 and 3. Check that pupils understand what a digit is. *Write down as many two digit numbers that add to 100 as you can in 1 minute.* Pupils check each other's answers.

## Activities

Without comment write the calculation *428 + 371* on the board.
Again without comment work out the answer writing:

*= 400 + 300 + 20 + 70 + 8 + 1*
*= 700 + 90 + 9*
*= 799.*

Invite the class to explain HOW you did the calculation, insisting on proper mathematical language, to the effect that each number was split into hundreds, tens and units, and each of these added separately. Repeat for *218 + 264*, then invite a pupil to demonstrate *624 + 245* on the board. Jot down about 5 examples on the board and ask pupils to work them out individually, for example:

*324 + 158   371 + 223   516 + 386   732 + 182   613 + 237.*

Quickly work through questions' answers, inviting pupils to participate. *How would you use a similar method for subtractions, for example 438 – 53?*

A possible correct response might be *438 – 53 = 400 + 30 + 8 – 50 – 3 = 350 + 30 + 5 = 385.*
Invite pupils to write their working on the board. Work through an example such as 753 – 71. Jot down about 5 examples on the board and ask pupils to work them out individually, for example:

*862 – 151   428 – 43   859 – 71   965 – 217   915 – 267*

## Differentiation

*Low Attainers* – Begin with (and probably subsequently restrict to) 2-digit numbers *e.g. 54 + 79 and 78 – 51.* This could be put into a more investigative context by asking pupils to investigate the differences between pairs of numbers such as 91 – 19, 32 – 23, 53 – 35 (answers are always in the 9 times table).
*High Attainers* – What is the largest and smallest answer for a 3-digit calculation using only the digits 4, 5, 6, 7, 8, 9?

## Plenary

Display some questions on the board, reading through them if required. Ask pupils for the calculation needed – but without actually working it out. Invite another pupil to talk through the calculation on the board for the whole class. Suitable questions are: *Amy is 181 cm tall. The door to her room is 200 cm high. How much taller is the door than Amy? A small stadium can seat 2000 spectators. For a football match 1273 people sit in the stadium. How many empty seats are there? A plane holds 137 passengers when full. How many more passengers can it hold if there are 95 passengers already on board?* If readily available, use could be made of the school numbers and gender split for each year, such as the total number of boys in Y2 and Y3, the total number of pupils in school.

## Lesson 3

### Introduction

A quick mental activity to practise the skills involved in some informal pencil and paper methods.

*4 + 10 + 300    100 – 75    120 + 12    400 + 150    100 – 64*

Check answers by pupils working on the board.

### Activities

*Here is an addition* [write on board] 587 + 475 *and a particular method to work it out*

| | | |
|---|---|---|
| [write on board] | 587 | |
| | 475 | |
| [write] | 900 | *Adding the hundreds 500 + 400* |
| [write] | 150 | *Adding the tens:* 80 + 70 |
| [write] | 12 | *Adding the units: 7 + 5* |
| [write] | 1062 | *The answer to 587 + 475* |

To reinforce understanding of the method, ask pupils where the various lines of working originated.

*Here is a method of subtracting – remember that when counting on, the answer to the calculation 754 – 286 is the number which when added to 286, makes 754.*

| | | |
|---|---|---|
| | 7 5 4 | |
| | – 2 8 6 | |
| [write] | 4 | *total = 290 (=4 + 286)* |
| [write] | 4 0 0 | *total = 690 (=400 + 290)* |
| [write] | 6 0 | *total = 750 (=60 + 690)* |
| [write] | 4 | *total = 754 (=4 + 750)* |
| | 4 6 8 | *the answer* |

Use questions and answers to probe pupils' understanding.

Give pupils Copymaster 17.

Provide help as and when needed.

### Differentiation

*Low Attainers* – Limited work on Copymaster 17.

*High Attainers* – Should attempt the whole of Copymaster 17.

### Plenary

Give answers and probe pupils' methods for at least questions 1, 2, 3, 6, 7 and 8 for the whole class, and discuss reasons for their choice of methods in questions 7–12.

## Lesson 4

### Introduction

Quick mental activity to practise skills needed in pencil and paper methods, for example:

*10 + 4 – 6    100 + 20 – 60    10 + 1 – 6    100 + 10 – 70*

Quickly revise that, for example, *567 = 500 + 60 + 7*, which can also be written as *500 + 50 + 17 or 400 + 150 + 7* – reinforce with a few more examples. *We can use this to help with subtractions.*

### Activities

*Here is another method of subtraction.* Write the calculation step by step with a commentary and involving pupils by questioning.

$$\begin{array}{rl} 754 & = 700 + 50 + 4 \\ -\ 239 & = \underline{200 + 30 + 9} \\ & = 700 + 40 + 14 \\ & \quad \underline{200 + 30 + 9} \\ & = 500 + 10 + 5 = \underline{515} \end{array}$$

Follow in a similar vein with the harder calculation..

$$\begin{array}{rl} 734 & = 700 + 30 + 4 \\ -\ 239 & = \underline{200 + 30 + 9} \\ & = 700 + 20 + 14 \\ & \quad \underline{200 + 30 + 9} \\ & = 600 + 120 + 14 \\ & \quad \underline{200 + 30 + 9} \\ & = 400 + 90 + 5 = \underline{495} \end{array}$$

Give the class two subtractions to ensure understanding, for example: 865 – 347    976 – 397. Check pupils' progress.

(If pupils are secure in the more direct standard written method allow them to use this.) *Here is another method for addition.* 'Talk' pupils through the calculations but avoid using the expression 'carry 1' etc. when in reality it is 10 or 100 which is being carried. (This may be a convenient point to recap informal place value.)

$$\begin{array}{r} 575 \\ +\,487 \\ \hline 1062 \\ {\scriptstyle 1\,1\ } \end{array} \qquad \begin{array}{r} 3675 \\ +\ 587 \\ \hline 4262 \\ {\scriptstyle 1\,1\,1\ } \end{array}$$

Draw attention to the importance of clear, easy to follow, number work.

### Differentiation

By outcome.

### Plenary

Review the lessons based on pupils' difficulties observed whilst working through the examples.

## Lesson 5

### Introduction

*How many different subtraction and addition problems and their answers can you write down using only the numbers 2, 4 and 6?* Collect in calculations and answers and establish that the only possibilities are 2 + 4 = 6, 4 + 2 = 6, 6 – 4 = 2 *and* 6 –2 = 4. Repeat with 10, 7 and 3 – collect and check. *We can use some of these results to check calculations, for example, if 10 – 7 is then 3, then 3 + 7 must be 10, or 10 – 3 should give 7.* Ensure all understand this by choosing another example, say 20 – 3 = 17 (then 17 + 3 should be 20 and so on). *Phil says that 748 – 215* [on board] *is 543. What calculation can we use to check his answer?*

Collect calculations and establish that if 543 is correct then 543 + 215 should give 748. Ask pupils to do this for themselves (543 is in fact wrong). *Jot down calculations which you could use to check these:*

*[write on the board]    864 – 555 = 319    183 + 361 = 534*

Establish the correct calculations, and then talk them through with the class (both are wrong).

*Can you think of any checking calculations for divisions and multiplications: for example, how could you check that 15 was the correct answer to* 129 ÷ 9*?* Allow discussion but if 15 × 9 = 129 does not emerge, repeat the approach for addition and subtraction i.e. different division, multiplication and their answers from, for example, 24, 8 and 3. *Jot down calculations to check these answers: 1125 ÷ 3 = 385* [385 × 3 which should be 1125], 791 ÷ 7 = 113 [113 × 7 which is in fact 791].

### Activities

Calculators will be needed for the activities on Copymaster 18.

Pupils work through Section A individually, with remediation when needed.

Pupils work through Section B in pairs, with remediation when needed.

### Differentiation

*Low Attainers* – Will need special help with Section A on Copymaster 18.

*High Attainers* – Once Copymaster 18 has been completed ask pupils to make up some questions and try them on each other.

### Plenary

Quickly go through Section A, using the opportunity to informally mention that additions can be checked by subtractions and subtractions by additions; the same applies to divisions and multiplications. Go through Section B with the class ensuring that pupils participate actively. Complete the lesson by formally introducing the term 'inverse': *The word inverse has to do with undoing or reversing.*

*Subtraction is the inverse of addition: for example, when 2 and 5 are added the answer is 7. If 5 is subtracted from 7, the addition is undone and the answer goes back to 2.* Ensure that the class has a firm understanding of this.

# Theme 10 Number sequences

### Objectives
- To recognise and extend number sequences formed by counting from any number in steps of any size
- To extend number sequences beyond zero and counting back
- To recognise square numbers to $10 \times 10$
- To recognise, explain and generalise about properties of numbers
- To identify factors of 2-digit numbers
- To solve mathematical problems

### Vocabulary
Next, consecutive, sequence, predict, continue, rule, relationship, square number, multiple, factor, digit, divisibility, divisible by.

### Resources
Number cards 2–9, pegs, pegboards, squared paper, and counters, negative number numberlines. Copymasters 19 and 20. Homework Copymaster 10.

### Assessment
*At the end of this theme is the pupil able to:*
- Recognise and extend counting sequences;
- Relate square numbers to drawings of squares;
- Find at least two factors of any 2-digit number?

### Mental maths starter 8

## Lesson 1

### Introduction
Start counting round the class in sixes from zero. Then change to sevens, eights and nines. When the children have done this for a while, ask them to continue as before, but start from a number other than zero. Now start from a number, but this time count back. *Will the counting land on 40 or 45 or 52. How do you know? What happens if we keep counting beyond zero?*

### Activities
Write these number sequences on the board:

8, 12, 16, 20, _, _.
111, 113, 116, 120, _, _.
12, 19, 33, 54, _, _.
1.2, 1.3, 1.4, 1.5, _, _.

*Can the children continue these number patterns? Can they explain how they worked it out? Did they look at the difference between two numbers in the sequence?* Explain that to work out a pattern in a sequence you often need to find the difference between two numbers next to each other.
*Working in pairs* – Using a hundred square let one of the pair choose a sequence, say starting at 3 and counting in 5s. Every time a number is said the other partner can mark it on the number square. Swop over and choose a new sequence. Ask the children to describe the patterns they have made.

### Differentiation
*Low Attainers* – Start from a random number between 0–10 and roll a dice (1–6) and count in that number of steps up to 50.
*High Attainers* – Start from a random number between 0–10 and roll a dice and count in that number of steps through zero to −50.

### Plenary
Chanting – Start a sequence; the class join in when they know what
it is. Try sequences starting at a range of numbers (not just zero) with steps of constant size. Let a group start a sequence and other groups take turns to the say the next number.

## Lesson 2

### Introduction
Counting back can be extended into negative numbers. Draw an empty number line on the board. Ask 'John can you continue counting back in the sequence 110, 85, 60, 35?' Demonstrate on the number line. Give the children other sequences with some of the terms missing, tell them to describe the sequence and to fill in the missing terms (some of these should go beyond zero).

### Activities
Count back through zero, for example
*Seven, three, negative one, negative five*
Respond to questions such as
*Put these numbers in order, least first:* −3, −9, −2, −5, −4.
Using a numberline stretching beyond 0 mark on a sequence with arrows and ask the children to mark on where the next number will go.

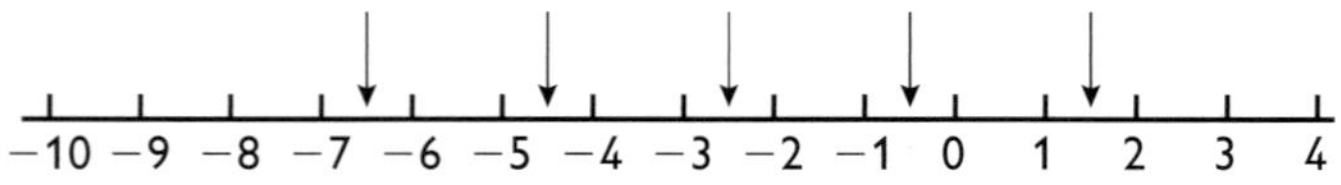


i.e. 1.5… −0.5… −2.5…−4.5… −6.5…

Lay out a row of six cards (or draw on the board), three of them blank.

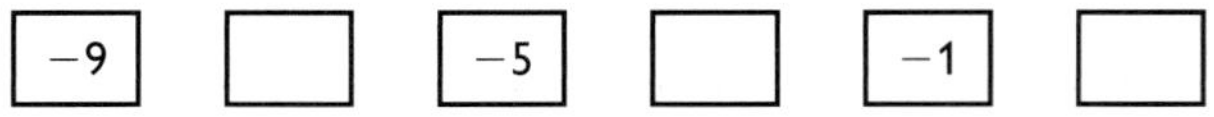


Write a whole number on each so that the six numbers are in order.

### Differentiation
*Low Attainers* – Pick a number card for the starting number and work only with positive numbers.
*High Attainers* – Could invent their own sequences, then swap with a partner and try to extend each other's both ways.

### Plenary
Write on the board some of the sequences that have been generated with some numbers missing. Ask the children to work out the missing numbers. Discuss how they did it and what information they needed.

## Lesson 3

### Introduction
Using a multiplication grid cover over the square numbers with paper and ask the children to work out what these numbers are and the multiplication that leads to them *e.g.* $2 \times 2 = 4$ *and* $7 \times 7 = 49$.

### Activities
'When you multiply a number by itself you get a square number. This means you can arrange these numbers into a square.'
Write the sequence of square numbers on the board, and explain that any number multiplied by itself is called a square number.
Draw out the first three square numbers as an array on the board –

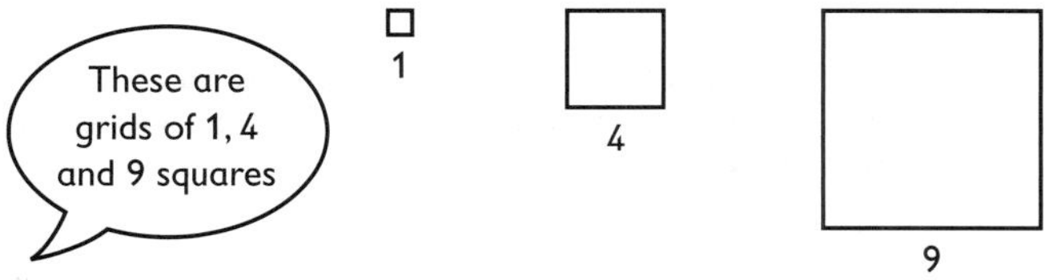


Show how the total number of squares in each array is the same as the square number.
*Working in pairs* – The children could draw these arrays on squared paper up to $10 \times 10$

### Differentiation
*Low attainers* – Respond to questions such as *What is 4 squared? What is the square of 6?*
*High Attainers* – Respond to questions such as *What is the area of a square whose side is 5 cm in length?*

### Plenary
Explain the convention for writing squared numbers: $2^2 = 4$, $3^2 = 9$ etc. Ask the children who is the fastest who can say all their squared numbers up to 100.

## Lesson 4

### Introduction
'Knowing how to generate a sequence allows us to predict how the sequence continues.'
Show on the board how to build up square numbers one at a time, using different colours to represent each new layer

| | | | |
|---|---|---|---|
| 1 | 2 | 3 | 1 = green |
| 2 | 2 | 3 | 2 = red |
| 3 | 3 | 3 | 3 = blue |

Children should build up numbers in the same way using pegs and pegboards or squared paper and counters.

### Activities
Start building up this pattern on the board –

| | | | |
|---|---|---|---|
| 1 ——— | 1 | 2 | 3 |
| 4 = 1 + 3 ——— | 2 | 2 | 3 |
| 9 = 1 + 3 + 5 ——— | 3 | 3 | 3 |

*Working in pairs* – Continue to work out the next number to add to each square number to make the next as far as 10 squared.
Work through Copymaster 19.

### Differentiation
*Low Attainers* – Ask them to describe the patterns they can see. Encourage them to explain them.
*High Attainers* – Can test any patterns/sequences they have found with square numbers over 100.

### Plenary
Invite pairs of children to tell the class what they have found out about square numbers. Build up a list of ideas on the board.

## Lesson 5

### Introduction
Children place their number cards (2–9) face up on the table in front of them. Call out numbers and ask the children to show pairs of factors for that number. Call out random numbers e.g. 14, 24, 50, 34. When the children are confident, call out some prime numbers (37,61) and some square numbers (49, 64.)

### Activities
Revise all the multiples of 3: 3, 6, 9, 12, and the multiples of 7: 7, 14, 21, 28.
12 is a multiple of 3. What are the factors of 12? (A factor is a number that goes into another number without leaving a remainder.) 3 for example is a factor of 12. *What other number goes into 12?*
Use Copymaster 20 to illustrate how numbers can be displayed as rectangles and how by drawing these rectangles to match various numbers it is possible to show their factors.

*Working in pairs* – Find all the factors of these numbers: 18, 24, 30, 42. They can use counters, or pegs and pegboards to set out the rectangles.

### Differentiation
*Low Attainers* – Show the children some numbers and they have to say what they are multiples of.
*High Attainers* – Can look for as many different numbers as they can that make just five rectangles.

### Plenary
Explain Homework 10
Ask the children to suggest numbers that look easy to factorise, such as numbers that you can halve, halve, halve and halve again.

# Theme 1 Comparing and ordering numbers

## Objectives

- To write and read numbers up to nine million; order a set of whole numbers less than 10 million
- To round numbers to the nearest thousand/hundred/ten
- To use and understand the symbols $<, \geqslant, =, >$ and $\leqslant$
- To order positive and negative integers
- To develop calculator skills and use a calculator effectively

## Vocabulary

units, ones, tens, hundreds, thousands, ten thousand, hundred thousand, million, digit, place value, one- two- three- four-digit number, order, maximum, minimum, round up, round down, round to the nearest thousand/hundred/ten, greater than or equal to, less than or equal to, greater/more/larger/bigger than, less/fewer/smaller than, order, positive, negative, integer, display, enter, clear, constant, key

## Resources

Copymasters 21 and 22. Homework Copymaster 11. Calculators – preferably all the same make.

## Assessment

*At the end of this theme is the pupil able to:*

- Use symbols $<, =, >, \geqslant, \leqslant$;
- Order a set of whole numbers less than 1 million;
- Order positive and negative integers (number line, temperature);
- Develop calculator skills and use a calculator effectively?

## Mental maths starter 19

# Lesson 1

## Introduction

Quickly revise the meaning of 'consecutive' as applied to consecutive numbers. *Two consecutive number add up to 21. What are they?* Repeat for 3, 11, 17 etc. Challenge pupils to find a quick way to begin such problems, insist on correct mathematical language. Then issue this challenge for pairs: *Can any number be made by adding consecutive numbers? Which numbers can and which can't? Can you figure out a reason?* (Even numbers cannot be made.) Give pupils a target time in which to finish. Quickly discuss their findings, pointing out the advantages of working systematically.

## Activities

Give pupils a copy of the Place Value table on Copymaster 21 or use an OHT of it. As a whole class activity, point to some of the numbers and ask pupils what they are, one at a time. Explain that the small gap is just there to make reading easier. Remediate any major misconceptions as they arise. Point to a number in consecutive rows, *e.g. 6 000 200 60 5*, and invite the whole class to read the number (in this case six thousand, two hundred and sixty five). Repeat this several times, then extend to pointing to the smallest number first, pointing to the numbers in any order and finally pointing out numbers where there is a zero (i.e. 6065). Involve pupils at the individual level by asking a pupil to point out, for example, 5 717, 500 023. Write down a number and ask pupils to point it out on the Place Value table.

Work in some questions of the type; *Point out a number ten times bigger than fifteen or point out a number which is ten times smaller than six hundred and fifty*. Ensure that pupils have grasped the idea of "times bigger" and "times smaller" by asking them to point out a number that is, say, ten more than fifteen or ten less than six hundred and forty.

## Differentiation

*Low Attainers* – May find a number square a useful visual aid to the introduction.

*High Attainers* – Tackle more challenging questions at an increased pace, including, for the plenary, questions derived from Copymaster 22 such as: *'In which country do almost half the population live in the capital city? Which capital city has a population of just over half a million people?*

## Plenary

Once pupils are secure in writing and reading numbers up to nine million give out (or show on the OHT) Copymaster 22. Take the opportunity to use the word 'database' when describing the sheet to the pupils. A quick question and answer session will establish if there are any serious misconceptions: *What is the population of …? Which country has the longest coastline? Which country has the largest/smallest population?* etc. Where appropriate ask pupils to explain how they arrived at their answers. The copymaster will be needed for the next lesson.

# Lesson 2

## Introduction

Give out, or use an OHT of, Copymaster 22. Quickly recap the last lesson using the data on the copymaster.

## Activities

Draw this number line on the board.

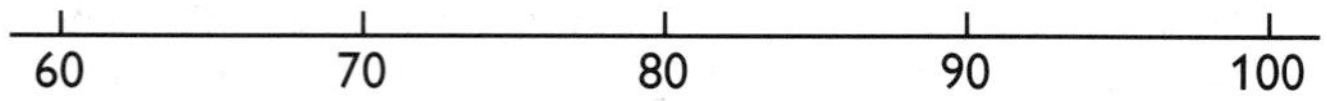


Confirm that each division is 'worth' 10. Invite a pupil to mark where 75 is. *Is 73 closer to 70 or 80?* Quickly establish that the answer is 70. *We say that 73 rounded to the nearest 10 is 70. What is 77 rounded to the nearest 10?* Conclude with: *What is 75 rounded to the nearest 10?* Write down the answers (70 and 80) without comment. Challenge the class to choose between them. Insist on justification. Inform the class that they should round up when a figure is exactly in the middle. Confirm understanding by asking for these rounded to the nearest ten: 37, 137, 145.

In a similar manner round to the nearest hundred, ending with *What is 1559 rounded to the nearest 100*. Conclude in the same way with rounding to the nearest thousand.

## Differentiation

*Low Attainers* – Will need the support of number lines to a greater extent than other pupils.

*High Attainers* – Will need questions of a more challenging nature in the plenary session.

## Plenary

Challenge pupils with *Do you think that the population of Andorra is exactly 72 760?* Guide the discussion into the direction that this is pretty unlikely and that a rounded figure is probably more realistic and easier to handle. Complete the lesson with questions based on the figures presented in Copymaster 22, rounded to the nearest 100 or 1000. Serious misconceptions will become apparent during this exercise and the appropriate steps can be taken.

Pupils could be invited to round some given numbers into suitable headlines, for example a crowd of 24 647 might be reported as 25 000. The complementary activity of giving the 'real' headline and getting pupils to discuss what the 'real' numbers might have been is also useful, especially if genuine news headlines are used.

## Lesson 3

### Introduction

A quick recap of the previous lessons' work with some questions such as these: *Write four six-digit numbers as numbers and in words. Make the largest/smallest number you can using the four digits, 2, 7, 9 and 0. Round your answers to the nearest hundred.*

### Activities

Write on the board or OHT $4 + 7 = 1 + 1 + 9$

*The equals sign shows the connection between $4 + 7$ and $1 + 1 + 9$ – they are equal. Can you give me another symbol to connect $4 + 3$ and $3 + 1$?* Invite suggestions, homing in on $4 + 3 > 3 + 1$. Make a point of verbalising as 'greater/more/larger/bigger than' and 'less/fewer/smaller than'. If appropriate point out to the class that the 'point' of the symbol/inequality always points to the smaller number. *Another pair of symbols we use are* (write) $\geqslant$ and $\leqslant$. *What do you think they might mean?* Allow sensible possibilities, telling pupils what the symbols mean after a suitable time. *Here are three boxes. To be put into a box which conditions must be satisfied?* Draw on the board:

| >3 | =3 |
|---|---|
| | |

| >0 | =2 |
|---|---|
| | |

| =4 | =6 |
|---|---|
| | |

Invite pupils to verbalise each condition (greater than 2, less than or equal to 3 and so on). As a class exercise put the numbers 1 to 6 in the appropriate boxes. *We can sometimes combine statements about numbers, for example $4 <$ a number and a number $< 10$* (on the board but verbalise each statement) *can be combined into $4 <$ a number $< 10$* (on board, verbalising the multiple statement). *If the number is an integer* (some pupils may need reminding as to what an integer is) *what integer values could the number take?* Quickly establish 5, 6, 7, 8 and 9. Write these on the board, asking pupils to find all the integers which will fit in the boxes:

$3 < \square < 5$   $6 < \square < 10$   $3 < \square\ \square\ 5$   $3\ \square\ \square\ \square\ 5$ and so on.

### Differentiation

*Low Attainers* – These pupils will need supporting. Having the numbers, together with the boxes, written on pieces of paper (and thereby moveable) should help. They may have difficulties with the multiple inequalities and should therefore only be expected to solve a few, perhaps with teacher assistance.

*High Attainers* – Invite pupils to write, say, two conditions for each of three boxes to 'catch' all the numbers such as: $\frac{1}{2}$, $1\frac{1}{2}$, $2\frac{1}{2}$, 3, 5, $1\frac{3}{4}$, 10, 20.2, 22.1 – at least two numbers in each box.

### Plenary

Ask the class to put the correct symbol between $-4\ \square\ 3$: quickly establish that it is $<$. Challenge the class as to why.

Guide the discussion into considering the number line: smaller numbers are to the left. With some groups the model of a thermometer scale may be more concrete. Repeat with some more, until the class is secure about using inequalities with negative integers.

## Lesson 4

### Introduction

Quickly remind pupils of the meaning of $<, =, >$ and on the board write some incomplete number sentences such as the ones below. Invite pupils to put in the correct symbols to make the sentences 'true' and to justify their choice.

*$5 + 4 + 3 + 2 + 1 \ldots 6 + 5 + 4 + 3 + 2 + 1$*   *$24 \times 56 \ldots 23 \times 56$*

*$4 \times 4 \ldots 12 + 6$*   *$72 + 8 \ldots 2 \times 5$*

### Activities

*I'm going to read out a list of five numbers. I want you to jot down the smallest (or largest) number.* Read each set of numbers twice – the exercise gives pupils experience at an elementary level of remembering and manipulating numbers in their heads. Initially sets of positive integers like 67, 23, 59, 18, 51 are suitable but when pupils feel secure, add a few negative integers. If necessary mention 'negative integer' to reinforce the vocabulary. Go through the answers and show how the number line can help to order a set of positive and negative integers. Draw this number line on the board:

Invite pupils to mark the positions of $-3, 5$ and so on. Ensure all pupils confidently approach questions like these. Once mastery has been established extend it by asking the class to put lists of numbers such as these into order, smallest first:

$-2, -8, -1, -6, -4$ extending to $-30, -20, -5, -15, 20, -10$.

Working in small groups ask the class to put the correct symbol linking these pairs of numbers, but remind them they will have to convince the class that their answer(s) are correct. (Some may need reminding to use the number line.)

$-7\ \square\ 17$   $-21\ \square\ 0$   $2\ \square\ -2$   $-2\frac{1}{2}\ \square\ 2$   etc.

In the ensuing discussion ensure that the class can locate on the number line points like $-2\frac{1}{2}$. If appropriate, extend to considering the ordering of positive and negative numbers involving decimals.

### Differentiation

*Low Attainers* – These pupils will probably be limited to the ordering of positive and negative integers.

*High Attainers* – Will progress to ordering simple positive and negative decimal fractions.

### Plenary

Recap on the lesson's progress by inviting pupils to find (and justify) appropriate whole numbers to fit into these boxes.

(a) $0\ \square\ 3\ \square\ 78$   (b) $-4\ \square\ -1\ \square\ 10$

(c) $-10\ \square\ \square\ \square\ \square$   (d) $-9\ \square\ -5\ \square\ -1\ \square$

## Lesson 5

### Introduction

To be effective and efficient calculator users, pupils need to be aware of the basic vocabulary associated with the 'calculator'. With this in mind they should begin the lesson with a brainstorming session on calculator words. Collect these on the board without comment and ensure that the class consider at least the key words at the beginning of this theme. Quickly establish that pupils can perform the 4 operations using a calculator. Administer this quick number test, but with the proviso that ALL calculations no matter how simple, are performed on the calculator.

*(a) $5 \times 6$*   *(b) $144 + 3$*   *(c) $150 - 49$*

*(d) $23 + 23$*   *(e) $3 \times 4 \times 2$*   *(f) $24 \div 2$*

Remediate any problems, such as failing to clear the display between calculations.

### Activities

Give pupils one or more of these calculator investigations. Observation of pupils using their calculators should bring to light any serious problems.

(a) Use a calculator to investigate these number patterns:

*$37 \times 3 = 111$*   *$1 \times 13 \times 77 = 1001$*

*$37 \times 6 = 222$*   *$2 \times 13 \times 77$ 2002*

*$37 \times 9 = 333$ and so on*   *$3 \times 13 \times 77 = 3003$ and so on*

(b) Which of these numbers – 17, 19, 23, 29, 31 – are factors of 11339?

(c) Which of these numbers – 3 689, 3 905, 6 293, 88 897 – are multiples of 217?

(d) Line 1  $1 = 1$   Line 3  $1 \times 2 \times 3 = 6$

Line 2  $1 \times 2 = 4$   Line 4  $1 \times 2 \times 3 \times 4 = 24$

On what line will the answer be greater than 10 000?

### Differentiation

*Low Attainers* – The first two investigations should be accessible to all.

*High Attainers* – The later investigations are more challenging.

### Plenary

Pupils report back to the class. Any major problems should become apparent.

# Theme 2 Multiplication and division

## Objectives

- To understand the meaning of division, simple remainders, factors
- To recall answers to divisions presented in various ways
- To perform informal pencil and paper division
- To perform formal pencil and paper division
- To recognise that multiplication and division are inverse operations and use this to check calculations
- To use brackets in calculations involving multiplication or division

## Vocabulary

how many … make/are in …, share equally, remainder, divisor, quotient

## Resources

Copymasters 23 and 24. Homework Copymaster 12.

## Assessment

*At the end of this theme is the pupil able to:*

- Begin to use brackets;
- Use factors;
- Use closely related facts *e.g. derive × 19 from × 20 from × 10 add × 2;*
- Extend written methods to HTU ÷ U (with a whole number remainder)?

## Mental maths starter 9

## Lesson 1

### Introduction

Allow pupils to use their completed table squares on Copymaster 1 to answer these. Remediation, particularly related to vocabulary, can take place in 'real time'. Ask questions of the type: *What multiplied by 6 gives 18? How many 3s make 24?* Encourage pupils to explain how they arrived at their answers. Ask pupils, working in pairs, to complete these table squares (encourage thinking aloud).

| X | 4 | ? |
|---|---|---|
| 3 | ? | 18 |
| 2 | ? | 12 |

| X | ? | 8 |
|---|---|---|
| ? | 21 | 24 |
| 4 | 28 | 32 |

| X | 4 | ? |
|---|---|---|
| ? | 20 | ? |
| 9 | 36 | 18 |

### Activities

Write 12 ÷ 4 on the board. *What does this mean? What do you need to do to work it out?* Encourage whole class discussion, but guide into:
*(a) How many 4s there are in 12?*
*(b) What number makes 12 when multiplied by 4?*
*(c) 12 shared equally by 4.*
*(d) How many times you can subtract 4 from 12?*
The latter, which is not obvious to many pupils, can be illustrated, in steps, as 'sharing out':

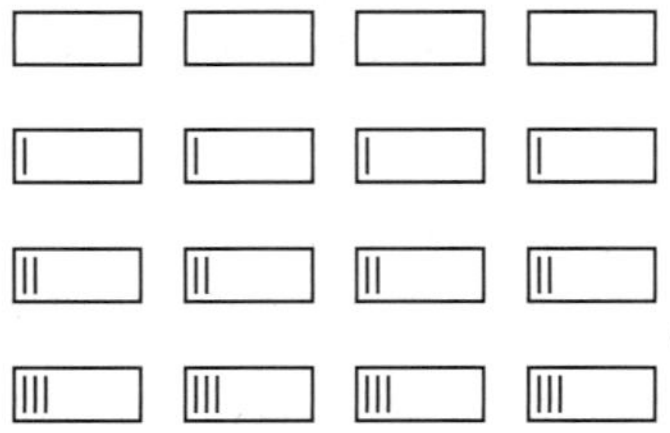

IIIIIIIIIIII
now 12 − 4 = 8
IIIIIIII
8 − 4 = 4
IIII
and now 4 − 4 = 0

Give pupils the opportunity to calculate some simple divisions using at least two of the above ways of looking at division. (The lowest attainers will find access to counters useful.)
*Using just the digit cards 0 to 9, with no repeats in the same calculation, make some divisions which have whole numbers as answers, for example, 30 ÷ 6, 20 ÷ 4 etc.*
*Sometimes a division gives a remainder, for example 27 ÷ 5 gives a remainder of 2.*
*Write down some other divisions that also give a remainder of 2.* Some pupils may need a quick recap about remainders – the method outlined previously lends itself to having 'left-overs'.

### Differentiation

*Low Attainers* – By outcome i.e. number of solutions generated. Ask for stories to fit calculations such as 24 × 3, to probe basic understanding of the division process.
*High Attainers* – Make and test on each other missing numbers in table squares. Find a number which gives a remainder of 1 when divided by 2, a remainder of 2 when divided by 3 and a remainder of 3 when divided by 4.

### Plenary

*Factors are whole numbers which divide exactly into other whole numbers – there is no remainder: for example the factors of 6 are 1, 2, 3 and 6.* Ask the class to give the factors of 8, 20, 24, etc. As a challenge: *find some numbers, under 100, that have an odd number of factors. What is special about these numbers?* (They are always square numbers.)

## Lesson 2

### Introduction

Quick division questions based on table facts e.g. *What is 27 divided by 3? How many 6's in 42? How many lots of 7 are there in 21? Share 48 between 8. Divide 56 by 7. How many groups of 8 can be made from 72? There are several special words we use when using division. Divisor is the number which another in divided by, so for 12 ÷ 3, we say that 3 is the divisor. The quotient is the number of times that one number can be divided into another number, so for 12 ÷ 3 = 4, 4 is the quotient.*
*Jot down a division which has 5 as divisor and a quotient of 3.* (15 ÷ 5 = 3) (One or two more to establish 'divisor' and 'quotient' in the pupils' minds.) Quick set of questions – as above – but involving remainders e.g. *How much is left over when 22 is divided by 5?* Ask pupils how they worked out their answers.

### Activities

*When you have to halve a number, for example 12, what calculation do you have to work out?* Establish that it is 12 ÷ 2. Repeat for some other 'halvings', until the class realises that 'halving' is equivalent to 'dividing by 2'. Extend this to 'one third' is equivalent to 'dividing by 3' and to other unit fractions of quantities – if necessary be prepared to illustrate by dividing up piles of counters on the OHP. *In computers and old books the division symbol '÷' is replaced by the forward slash '/'.* So (on the board) *12/3 is equivalent to 12 ÷ 3, which is 4. 12 ÷ 3 which is equivalent to 12/3 can also be written $\frac{12}{3}$, so $\frac{12}{3}$* = 12 ÷ 3 = 4 (on the board). *In the old days printers found it hard to print fractions so the '/' was often used instead. Jot down the values of these as ordinary numbers.*

$\frac{21}{7}$ $\frac{63}{7}$ $\frac{24}{3}$ $\frac{20}{4}$

Divide the class into groups of four and set them this puzzle to solve for themselves. If at all possible provide 'real' money. Each group of 4 pupils has £1 in these coins: 2 × 20p, 2 × 10p, 4 × 5p, 8 × 2p, 4 × 1p, their task is to share out the money equally.

### Differentiation

*Low Attainers* – May need extra support.
*High Attainers* – Share £3 between 4 people with these coins: 2 × 50p, 5 × 20p, 4 × 10p, 8 × 5p, 9 × 2p, 2 × 1p.

### Plenary

Review the main features of the lesson, invite pupils to explain their thinking to answer questions involving finding the missing numbers in expressions like these:

$\frac{20}{5} = \ldots$ $\quad \frac{20}{\ldots} = 5$ $\quad \frac{\ldots}{2} = 3$ $\quad \frac{\ldots}{\ldots} = 3$ $\quad \frac{\ldots}{\ldots} = 2$ $\quad \frac{\ldots}{\ldots} = 4$

## Lesson 3

### Introduction

Quick start puzzles, allowing all pupils to contribute if possible. There is more than one solution.

*I think of a number and divide it by 7. The remainder is 4. What number could I have started with? The remainder is 3. What could I have divided by? I am less than twenty. When divided by 3 I give a remainder of 2, and when I am divided by 4, I give a remainder of 2. What number am I? I don't give a remainder when I am divided by 2, 3 or 5. What number am I?* Encourage pupils to share their reasons/methods with the group.

### Activities

Write $35 \div 7$ on board and 'instantly' establish that the answer is 5. Now write $350 \div 7$ on board. Depending on the group, 50 will emerge as the answer – if not give the answer. *How could you convince a friend that if 35 ÷ 7 is 5 then 350 ÷ 7 must be 50?* Guide the class into reasoning that 35 shared by 7 is 5, so sharing out 350, ten times more, must result in everyone getting ten times more, so 350 shared by 7 must be 50. Repeat the question/argument sufficiently for all to recall the answers to, say, $180 \div 2$, $360 \div 4$, $400 \div 8$ etc. *You can use what we've just done to work out approximate answers to hard divisions.* On the board quickly convince pupils that the answer to $342 \div 8$ must lie between 40 ($320 \div 8 = 40$) and 50 ($400 \div 8 = 50$). Repeat for some other divisions such as $375 \div 4$, $141 \div 7$, $353 \div 6$. Check that all have a confident grasp by asking for approximate answers to $841 \div 8$, $647 \div 6$, $825 \div 9$, $529 \div 8$, $145 \div 5$. *Now we can do some hard divisions like, for example, 537 ÷ 7. What must the answer lie between?* Establish 70 ($70 \times 7 = 490$) and 80 ($80 \times 7 = 560$). Give a full commentary to the following, if necessary making reference to the 'sharing out' view of division.

$537 \div 7$    537
             – 490        $70 \times 7$
                 47
               – 42        $6 \times 7$

So $737 \div 7 = 76$ remainder 5 (or 76 r5)

On the board work through sufficient examples, such as $553 \div 6$, $256 \div 7$, $382 \div 6$, $595 \div 8$, to ensure understanding, stressing the importance of the initial estimate as a starting point. Invite pupils to work through some on the board. Set pupils sufficient of these for their levels of attainment:

| | | | |
|---|---|---|---|
| $153 \div 7$ (21 r6) | $370 \div 5$ (74) | $158 \div 9$ (17 r5) | $328 \div 6$ (54 r4) |
| $270 \div 7$ (38 r4) | $581 \div 8$ (72 r5) | $501 \div 9$ (55 r6) | $409 \div 5$ (81 r4) |

### Differentiation

*High Attainers* – Make up and test on each other some more 'What number am I?' puzzles. Differentiation by outcome in the case of the last activity.

### Plenary

Talk pupils through (and check) their solutions to the last set of divisions. Encourage pupil participation and explanation wherever possible. Recap progress over the lesson.

## Lesson 4

### Introduction

Some quick fire mental multiplication and division questions up to $10 \times 10$ such as:

$9 \times 7$     $49 \div 7$     $64 \div 8$     $7 \times 8$

*How many different multiplications can you find whose answer is 24? How many different divisions can you find whose answer is 6?*

### Activities

Talk the class through this semi-formal method of calculating $732 \div 9$ – giving a step-by-step commentary and taking care to give numbers their correct names i.e. 'seven hundred and twenty' rather than 'seven two zero'. This will minimise problems later on when the formal method of long division is encountered, since most difficulties in this method arise from a cavalier attitude to place value.

$732 \div 9$    *$720 \div 9 = 80$ and $810 \div 9 = 90$*
*so the answer is between 80 and 90*

9 )7 3 2
    7 2 0     $80 \times 9$
      1 2
        9     $1 \times 9$
        3     Answer = 81 r3

If necessary work through another example or two, such as $509 \div 6$, $493 \div 7$ etc. Give pupils some of these to do in pairs – encourage them to talk through their working. Set a target number to be completed commensurate with levels of attainment:

| | | | |
|---|---|---|---|
| $434 \div 9$ (48 r2) | $169 \div 7$ (24 r1) | $234 \div 4$ (58 r2) | $298 \div 9$ (33 r1) |
| $468 \div 5$ (93 r3) | $749 \div 9$ (83 r2) | $334 \div 7$ (47 r5) | $567 \div 6$ (94 r3) |

### Differentiation

Essentially by outcome i.e. the number of questions successfully attempted.

*Low Attainers* – Could begin with slightly easier questions such as: $241 \div 6$, $153 \div 5$, $87 \div 4$.

### Plenary

Quickly go through the completed work, remediating where necessary. *Here is an easier way to lay your working out.* Work though the example, taking special care over place value language and stressing the importance of lining up numbers of the same place value.

$356 \div 7$
$350 \div 7 = 50$
$420 \div 7 = 60$

       5 0   r6
7 )3 5 6    *Seven into three hundred and fifty*
    3 5 0    *'goes' fifty times.*
       0 6
         0
         6

Repeat with another example if necessary.

## Lesson 5

### Introduction

*Working in pairs, write down, in three minutes, as many division and multiplication calculations and their answers as you can using the facts that 64 ÷ 16 = 4 and 16 × 2 = 32.* Collect and discuss the contributions from as many pupils as possible. Ensure that at least the following cases are covered

$16 \times 4 = 64$ (multiplication is the inverse of division)

$16 \div 2 = 32$ (division is the inverse of multiplication).

Introduce and draw pupils' attention to the word 'inverse'. *We can use inverses to check calculations. If 12 × 3 = 36 then 36 ÷ 3 should be 12 and 36 ÷ 12 should be 3 and if 24 ÷ 8 = 3, then 3 × 8 should be 24.* (Some more examples if necessary.) *How could we use inverses to check if 45 ÷ 5 = 9 or if 7 × 3 = 21?* If appropriate introduce pupils to doubling and halving, for example: *from 64 ÷ 16 = 4, then 128 ÷ 16 = 8, 64 ÷ 32 = 2 and from 16 × 2 = 32, then 32 × 2 = 64, 16 × 4 = 64.*

### Activities

Give pupils, working in pairs, Copymaster 23.

### Differentiation

Differentiation by outcome (*Low Attainers will* not progress as far with Copymaster 23 and may need extra support). Most pupils should be given the opportunity to experience success in all three sections.

*Higher Attainers* – Working in pairs, one player chooses two whole numbers less than 20 and gives their opponent the product of them. The other player has to find the two numbers with as few calculator keystrokes as possible – a combination of trial and improvement and estimation.

### Plenary

Invite pairs to give their answers to Copymaster 23. Insist that pupils explain their decisions.

# Theme 3 Problem-solving

**Objectives**
- To use all four operations to solve word problems involving numbers in 'real life'
- To use all four operations to solve word problems involving money
- To check calculations by equivalent calculation or inverse operation
- To choose and use appropriate arithmetic and calculation methods; explain working and calculation methods
- To choose and use appropriate arithmetic and calculation methods; explain working and calculation methods

**Resources**
Copymasters 25 and 26, Homework Copymaster 13

**Assessment**
*At the end of this theme is the pupil able to:*
- Use all four operations to solve money or 'real life' word problems;
- Choose appropriate operations/calculation methods;
- Explain working;
- Check with inverse operation or equivalent calculation?

**Mental maths starter 15**

---

## Lesson 1

**Introduction**
Write these words on the board: *altogether, amount, change, cheaper, difference, fewer, fewer than, in all, left over, remains, share, share equally, sum, take away, total, twice.* Invite pupils, working in pairs, to make up some word questions using as many of the words as possible. Stress that rough jottings will be sufficient as the questions will be presented to the class orally. After a suitable time, pairs ask their questions to the rest of the class (who then have to solve the problem – the pairs could be grouped into opposing teams). Serious misconceptions will soon become apparent and can be corrected when they arise.

**Activities**
Give pupils Copymaster 25.

**Differentiation**
*Low Attainers* – Should complete Part 1. Calculators available if needed.
*High Attainers* – Should complete both sections of Copymaster 25.

**Plenary**
Go through pupils' work on the copymaster, involving the whole class and making a point that it is important to spend a little time thinking about what the question is really asking (without rushing in) and to lay out their work clearly and check that the final answer fits in with the original question.

---

## Lesson 2

**Introduction**
Set the class, working as individuals or pairs, this challenge.
*On pieces of paper (or number cards if available) write:*
1 2 3 4 5 6 7 8 9
*How many subtractions can be made without using the same card more than once in the same calculation? The number you are taking away from must have at least two digits. For example:*

1 2 – 8 = 4

*More than 10 different calculations is good – don't forget to keep a record of your calculations.*
As a quick warm-up before embarking on the 'money problems' – *Amy has one each of the different coins we use. How much money is this?*

**Activities**
Pupils work on the challenge.

**Differentiation**
*Low Attainers* – Calculators available should support be needed.
*High Attainers* – Do work in pairs.

**Plenary**
Go through pupils' work. How could you check that? Does it seem a reasonable answer? Should circumstances permit, invite pupils to 'come to the front' to show their working to the rest of the class.

## Lesson 3

### Introduction

*Using just the three numbers 3, 8 and 24, make as many calculations and answers as you can.* Quickly establish that the calculations are $3 \times 8 = 24$, $8 \times 3 = 24$, $24 \div 3 = 8$ and $24 \div 8 = 3$. Make an issue of the fact that with multiplication order does not matter as regards the answer – but it does for division. Repeat for some other number triplets *e.g. 6, 8 and 48. Starting with 24, divide it by 3* (write $24 \div 3 = 8$). *How can we get back to 24 again starting with 8?* Establish that $8 \times 3$ will get back to 24. *So to undo 'divide by 3'.* Repeat for some other examples. *How do you think we can, with $6 \times 3 = 18$, get back to the 6 starting with 18 – in order to undo the $\times 3$?* Ensure the whole class realises that '$\times 3$' can be undone by '$\div 3$'.

### Activities

Write this calculation and answer on the board: *$47 \times 11 = 517$. How could we check that this is the correct answer?* Allow a free ranging discussion, but ensure that at least the following are considered:

- repeating the calculation
- estimating by $50 \times 10 = 500$
- using a calculator – but linked to this, repeating the calculation in the form $11 \times 47$ stress that with a calculator we sometimes press the wrong buttons
- use the inverse operation $517 \div 11$ $(=47)$ or $517 \div 47$ $(=11)$ (challenge pupils to explain the term 'inverse', supported with examples.)

Repeat the above for other examples, *e.g. $252 \div 9 = 28$, $23 \times 23 = 529$.* Make reference to the previous term's work on inverse operation with addition and subtractions. Ask the children to work in pairs on two or three examples.

### Differentiation

*Low Attainers* – Extra support may be needed. These pupils should only attempt the first few questions and have calculators available for the checking calculation.
*High Attaining* – Should be able to perform the checking calculation without the use of a calculator.

### Plenary

Go through the answers – acknowledge that there may be several different methods but where possible focus on estimation and the inverse operation. Ensure that pupils are aware of the value of estimating as a check for some of the calculations.

## Lesson 4

### Introduction

Starting with 20, involve the whole class in a counting on in 21s exercise. If there are problems invite successful pupils to explain their strategies to the class. Once a fair degree of success has been experienced, repeat the activity, counting on in 19s.

### Activities

Working in pairs, give pupils Copymaster 26 Part 1 to complete. Make it clear that they may well have to explain their working to the rest of the class.

### Differentiation

*Low Attainers* – By outcome.
*High Attaining* – By outcome.

### Plenary

Go through Copymaster 26, with pupils explaining their methods/working to the class. Challenge pupils on their clarity of explanation if conditions are right. Draw pupils' attention to the desirability of checking their answers against the original problem if appropriate.

## Lesson 5

### Introduction

*Imagine four people have to share these bags of rice.*

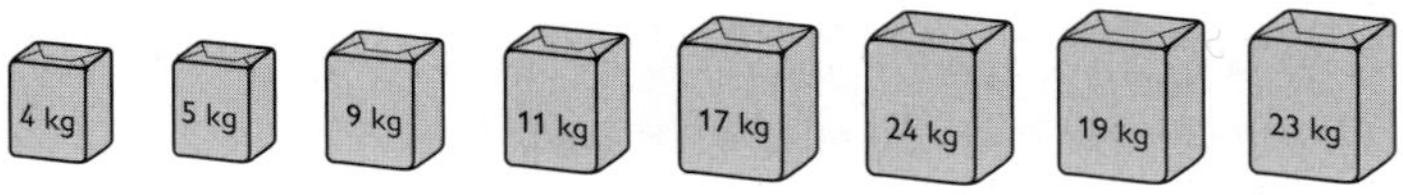


*Each person must get the same weight. The bags must not be opened. How can you do it?* Allow groups a few minutes to get to grips with the problem. Then discuss possible strategies (i.e. first find total weight and divide by 4). Stress the importance of a systematic approach. If there is sufficient time, invite pupils to make up some similar puzzles for themselves.

### Activities

Divide the class into groups of 3 or 4. Depending on the level of attainment, direct or allow a free choice to one of the items on Copymaster 26 Part 2. Explain to the pupils that they will have to make a short presentation to the class on it.
When a group has finished, at an appropriate time, allow them to make their presentation. Encourage positive criticism, with due respect to pupils' sensitivities, by the class after presentation. The whole process will occupy the rest of the lesson.

### Differentiation

*Low Attainers* – Will need extra support. Encourage them to make use of examples rather than to generalise too much.
*High Attaining* – Differentiation by task or outcome.

### Plenary

Continue with the activity above.

# Theme 4 Fractions and decimals

## Objectives
- To order pairs and sets of fractions including mixed numbers
- To order numbers or measurements with up to two decimal places
- To relate fractions to division
- To find simple fractions, including tenths and hundredths, of numbers or quantities
- To use a calculator to work with fractions and decimals
- To round numbers with one or two decimal places to the nearest integer

## Vocabulary
fraction, mixed number, third, half, quarter, eighth, fifth, tenth, hundredth, decimal, place value, order, equivalent, round up, round down.

## Resources
Number lines, number cards, counters, Copymasters 27 and 28, Homework Copymaster 14.

## Assessment
*At the end of this theme is the pupil able to:*
- Position fractions on a number line;
- Give fractional answers to division problems;
- Convert a fraction to a decimal using a calculator?

## Mental maths starter 10

---

# Lesson 1

## Introduction
Write the following pairs of fractions on the board –
$\frac{1}{5}, \frac{4}{5}, \frac{2}{10}, \frac{6}{10}, \frac{1}{4}, \frac{3}{4}, \frac{1}{2}, \frac{1}{4}, \frac{1}{3}, \frac{1}{2}$.
Which is greater, $\frac{1}{5}$ or $\frac{4}{5}$?
*How can you tell?*
*Tell me a fraction that is between $\frac{1}{5}$ and $\frac{4}{5}$. How did you work it out?*
Repeat for the other pairs of fractions.

## Activities
When comparing fractions it is helpful to position them on a number line. Using a number line on the board ask the children to compare pairs of fractions. Encourage them to explain their thinking for example $\frac{1}{3}$ is less than $\frac{1}{2}$ as $\frac{1}{3}$ is nearer to 0 than $\frac{1}{2}$.
Record each answer in words and symbols on the board –
*Which is greater, three quarters or two thirds?* ($\frac{3}{4}$)
*Which is greater, three quarters or two fifths?* ($\frac{3}{4} > \frac{2}{5}$)
*Which is less, one and three fifths or one and one third?* ($1\frac{1}{3} < 1\frac{3}{5}$)
Ask the children to record other comparisons in their books using the number line.

## Differentiation
*Low Attainers* – Give children collections of improper fractions that have the same denominator.
*High Attainers* – Give children a collection of fractions to order, some with same denominator, and some with different denominators. Ask them to discuss strategies.

## Plenary
Use more examples of placing mixed numbers on a number line in order. Away from the number line look at pairs of mixed numbers and decide which is the smaller and which is the larger number.

---

# Lesson 2

## Introduction
Decimal numbers can be ordered by comparing the digits of each, starting with the digits in the highest place value positions. Using the digits 7, 3, 5, make a number which includes tenths and hundredths. Draw a place value table on the board. Ask how 7.35 should be written in the table and write it in.
*Which digit represents ones, which represents hundredths? What does the 3 represent?*
Repeat for other numbers to two decimal places.

## Activities
Ask the children to copy down an empty place value chart and write in the number 5.78 in the first row. Use the same three digits to make five more decimal numbers each having tenths and hundredths, and record their numbers on the chart.
*E.g. 5.87 7.58* 8.57 etc. Complete the chart with the children. Check everyone has all six numbers. Tell them to write the numbers in ascending order in their books. Invite a child to the board to say which is the smallest number.
*Working in pairs* – Work on Copymaster 27 on arranging values in order for different types of measurement.

## Differentiation
*Low Attainers – How many tenths make a unit?* (10) *How many hundredths make a unit?* (100)
*High Attainers – What fraction of one tenth is one hundredth?* ($\frac{1}{10}$)

## Plenary
Write these pairs of numbers on the board and ask in turn for the smaller then the larger number: 12.07 and 12.1; 3.78 and 3.8; 0.09 and 0.3.
*'Carmen can you tell me a number between 1 and 2?'*
*'Hannah can you give a number between 2.7 and 2.8?'*
*'David can you tell me a number between 0.7 and 0.6?'*

## Lesson 3

### Introduction
Practise dividing by single digit numbers. Ask the questions in as many different ways as possible:
*What is 56 divided by 8?*
*How many fives make 25?*
*What is 4 divided into 32?*
Even *I am thinking of a number and multiply it by 7. The answer is 56. What is my number?* (8).

### Activities
Write a set of related calculations on the board, e.g.
$4 \times 5 = 20$  20 divided by $4 = 5$  $20 \times \frac{1}{4} = 5$  $\frac{20}{4} = 5$
Explain that multiplying by $\frac{1}{4}$ is the same as dividing by 4
Put some equations on the board eg.
$? \times \frac{1}{2} = 15$  ? divided by $4 = 20$  $\frac{1}{3} \times ? = 5$
Tell the children to read out the first equation and then try to solve it. 'Something multiplied by half equals 15.' *What must the something be?*
Repeat for other equations. Children can make up some of their own equations involving fractions and write them on the board for others to solve.

### Differentiation
*Low Attainers* – Work on halves and/or quarters only.
*High Attainers* – Include fractions $\frac{1}{5}, \frac{1}{6}, \frac{1}{7}, \frac{1}{8}$.

### Plenary
Write on the board 5 divided 3. The children can decide how to write this division as a fraction, then as a mixed number e.g. $\frac{5}{3}$ and $1\frac{2}{3}$.
Make sure they understand that they can also find this by saying that 3 divided into 5 goes 1, leaving 2 as a remainder, which they also divide by 3, giving $\frac{2}{3}$.
So 5 divided by 3 is $1\frac{2}{3}$.

## Lesson 4

### Introduction
Using number cards ask questions relating to previous work on fractions. *E.g. How many fifths in a whole one?*
*What is a third of 12?* Children hold up number cards to show the answers. Encourage them to explain their methods. Tell the children they are going to find out how to calculate a fraction of a number.

### Activities
*How do we find a half of a number?* Take various suggestions, but focus on the idea of splitting the number into two equal parts.
*How do we find a third of a number?*
Split the counters on the board into groups of 3. *If I divide the counters on the board into 3 groups of equal size, each group is $\frac{1}{3}$ of 9.*
*How many counters would there be in $\frac{2}{3}$ of 9?* (double the total of $\frac{1}{3} = 6$)
Demonstrate with other counters, finding $\frac{2}{3}$ and $\frac{3}{4}$. Ask the children to find $\frac{1}{2}, \frac{1}{3}, \frac{1}{4}$ then $\frac{2}{3}$ and $\frac{3}{4}$ of numbers that are multiples of 2, 3, 4; 12, 24, 36 etc. The numbers and fractions could be written on the board.
Record $\frac{1}{2}$ of $12 = 6$
$\frac{3}{4}$ of $12 = 9$

### Differentiation
*Low Attainers* – Using 12 counters, find out how many make half, how many a third, how many one quarter. Repeat with 24 counters. Record results using pictures or numbers.
*High Attainers* – Pick a 2-digit number and decide whether it can be divided exactly by 3. If so find $\frac{1}{3}$ and $\frac{2}{3}$ of the number. Can it be divided exactly by 4. If so find $\frac{1}{4}$ and $\frac{3}{4}$ of it. Record the answers.

### Plenary
Write some pairs of fraction problems on the board, e.g. $\frac{1}{4}$ of 12 and $\frac{1}{2}$ of 8. Pupils work in pairs to decide which of each pair gives the greater answer. After a few minutes discuss the children's findings.

## Lesson 5

### Introduction
To find the decimal equivalent of a fraction using a calculator we divide the numerator by the denominator using the division key. Name a selection of fractions and mixed numbers and ask the children to firstly work out each fraction as a division sum *e.g. $\frac{3}{10}$ = 3 divided by 10*, as a decimal mental calculation, 0.3, and using the calculator, again 0.3.

### Activities
A number line helps us to estimate the position of a decimal number

*Which whole number is nearest to 3.7 and how can you tell?* (answer 4) Repeat for 3.1 (answer 3). Explain the rule about rounding numbers up or down (1–4 = down 5–9 = up). Explain to the children that rounding a number helps us to check that a calculation is reasonable.
Fill in two empty grids –
1 headed 'Decimals rounded to 5' *e.g. 4.5, 4.7 etc*
2 headed 'Decimals rounded to 6' *e.g. 5.5, 5.7, 6.3 etc*
Draw another sorting grid on the board relating to –
Amounts of money
1 rounded to £6
2 rounded to £7
3 rounded to £8 and ask questions such as *Where will £7.56 be sorted?* and *Where will £7.49 be sorted?*

### Differentiation
*Low Attainers* – Ask questions such as *What is 4.9 rounded to the nearest whole number?*
*High Attainers* – Ask questions such as *What is 3.67 rounded to the nearest whole number?*

### Plenary
As a class, use a calculator to change the mixed number $6\frac{2}{5}$ to a decimal and then round the decimal to the nearest whole number. Record the steps.
$6\frac{2}{5} = 6.4 = 6$
Continue this by completing Copymaster 28.
Explain Homework Sheet 14.

# Theme 5 Shapes, lines and angles

## Objectives

- To recognise the common solids
- To use two-dimensional views of three-dimensional objects
- To recognise nets of cuboids
- To recognise acute, obtuse and right angles and realise that an angle on a straight line is 180°
- To recognise and use the fact that half a turn or a 'straight line' is a rotation of 180°
- To make rough estimates of the size of angles
- To use angle measures/protractors
- To make patterns from rotating shapes

## Vocabulary

polygon, hexagon, cube, sphere, cuboid, cone, congruent, face, vertex, vertices, cylinder, polyhedron, pyramid, hemisphere, octahedron, pentagon, net, turn, angle, degree, right angle, acute, obtuse, angle measurer, protractor, rotate, rotation, half-turn

## Resources

straws cut in equal lengths, about 10 cm, plasticine of two different colours, a set of twelve multicubes for each pupil, squared paper, scissors for making nets, Clixi, Polydron or similar (optional for low attainers), basic set squares, plain paper, rulers, angle measurers/protractors. Copymasters 29 and 30. Homework Copymaster 15. A set of angle cards – several long rectangles cut to show different angles. These can be fitted together again.

## Assessment

*At the end of this theme is the pupil able to:*

- Visualise 3-D shapes from 2-D drawings as identify the nets of an open cube;
- Recognise directions, and perpendicular and parallel lines;
- Understand and use the term 'degrees';
- Identify, estimate and order acute and obtuse angles;
- Use a protractor to measure and draw acute and obtuse angles to 5°;
- Make patterns from rotating shapes;
- Calculate angles in a straight line;
- Recognise and explain patterns and relationships, generalise and predict?

## Mental maths starter 11

---

## Lesson 1

### Introduction

Play 'What's my name?' shape game as in Lesson 3, Theme 6, Autumn term. Two teams can compete against each other against the clock or pupils could play in pairs – high attainers assisting low attainers. Remediate any problems – a set of standard solids is essential here. Keep a record of the times, as these may be needed for the next lesson. Some pupils may not be secure with 'octahedron' but many will be able to work it out – it is a new word.

### Activities

Quickly demonstrate what a skeleton cube is i.e.

Give individual pupils a copy of Copymaster 29 or use the OHP. Encourage pupils to check their answers by making the models. Once they have finished [1] pupils could work in small groups making and testing similar puzzles as indicated in [2]. Encourage pupils at an informal level to explain to each other their strategies.

### Differentiation

*Low Attainers* – May need the support of pre-made models (in order to save time) but should exchange strategies with other pupils. The visualisation process can be a real challenge and many low attainers need to build up this skill.

*High Attainers* – Should attempt the challenge, sketching their different arrangements. These pupils will have less need of concrete models.

### Plenary

Give those pupils who don't already have them 12 multicubes and ask them to make the largest cube they can from them (quickly establish that 8 are needed for the $2 \times 2 \times 2$ cube). *How many more cubes would you need to make the next largest cube?* Recap the lesson's content.

---

## Lesson 2

### Introduction

Depending on the progress in the previous lesson, continue with the cube making activity. As usual invite pupils to share their strategies with the rest of the group. Give each pupil a set of 4 cubes. Pairs of pupils sit back-to-back. One of them makes a solid with their four cubes without the other seeing. The first person then has to explain to the second how to make the solid. Players then swap roles. More confident players may use five or six cubes. Take the opportunity to stress the usefulness of using the correct mathematical language.

### Activities

Quickly recap the meaning of 'net'. It may be useful to illustrate this using Clixi, Polydron or similar materials. Give out Copymaster 30 or alternatively use an OHT of it.

### Differentiation

*Low Attainers* – May need the support of Clixi, Polydron or similar for the whole lesson. They should be given every opportunity to cut out and 'try'. Should there still be difficulties then dismantling a 'real' box might help.

*High Attainers* – Will need little or no concrete materials. As a challenge they could find all the nets of a cube.

### Plenary

Sketch a cuboid with its dimensions on:

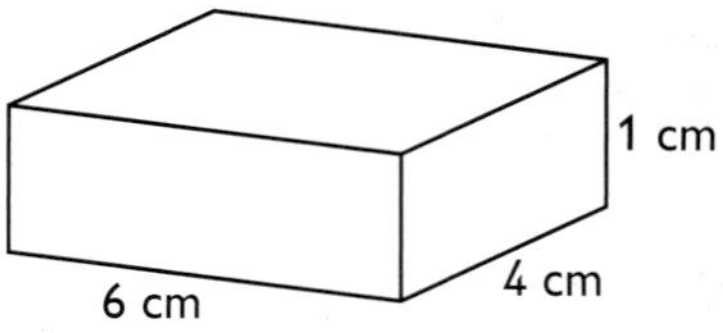


Ask pupils to sketch a net or the cuboid.
Quickly check and remediate.
Recap on progress made over the lesson

## Lesson 3

### Introduction

Invite a pupil to the front to stand with arm outstretched. Ask them to make half a turn clockwise. (Clockwise/anticlockwise may need revising.) Repeat for other simple fractional turns. Probe the group's understanding of turning by questions such as *What fraction of a turn is a right angle?*

### Activities

Quickly brainstorm what the pupils mean by 'angle' – collect their ideas on the board with limited comment. Go through the list, rejecting by 'guided' consent the obviously wrong. Ensure that 'turning', 'rotation', right angle', 'degree' and 'angle measurer' are considered – revise previous encountered vocabulary and introduce the word 'rotation'. Draw pupils' attention to the degree symbol '°'.
Show the class a set square made from multicubes. Point out the 'inner' and 'outer' right angles. A real set square could equally well be used.

*We call angles less than a right angle or 90° acute and angles greater than a right angle or 90° obtuse.*
Spend a few minutes allowing pupils to jot down some acute, right and obtuse angles round the room, thereby establishing that all pupils can recognise these three types of angle. Sketch this quadrilateral on the board.

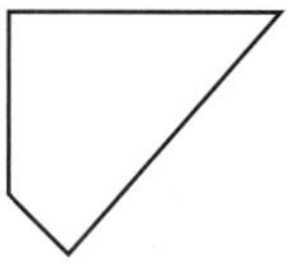

*How many right/acute/obtuse angles does this quadrilateral have?* Establish that the answers are 2/1/1. Set the class the challenge to draw at least one of these if possible (using either squared or plane paper, pencil and ruler):
*A triangle with three acute angles.*
*A triangle with two acute angles and one obtuse angle.*
*A quadrilateral with two acute and two obtuse angles.*
*A quadrilateral with four acute angles.*
*A hexagon with three acute and three obtuse angles.*
What is the greatest number of acute angles a hexagon can have?

### Differentiation

*Low Attainers* – May only consider cases of the types of angles in triangles and quadrilaterals. It may also be worthwhile giving these pupils pre-drawn shapes for them to identify the different types of angle.
*High Attainers* – May experiment with other polygons finding the number of acute, obtuse and right angles – look for general observations about, for example, maximum number of right angles.

### Plenary

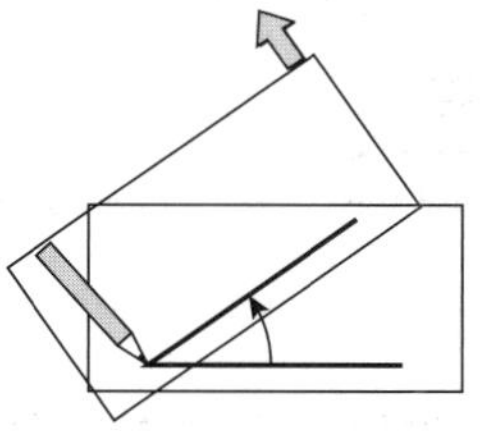

On the OHP show two OHTs with straight drawn on them fixed at one end, using a pencil point. Invite pupils to put their hands up when the angle is 45° and 90°. *The top line has rotated about the pencil point through an angle of 45°/90°*. Pupils could be invited to take the role of 'turner'. Make a particular point of linking turning, angle and rotation. As a final challenge continue the turning until a straight line is made. *What angle has the line turned through?* Accept answers but home in on 'half a turn' leading to 180°. Ensure that all pupils understand 'an angle on straight line is half a turn which is 180°'.

## Lesson 4

### Activities

Quickly recap that there are 180° in a straight line/half turn, then give pairs or individuals a set of angle cards. Pupils then either play solitaire or dominoes making a straight line with the angle cards – with the usual rules of solitaire/dominoes. With the cards turned over pupils can estimate angles, turning the card over to get instant feedback – a worthwhile individual activity allowing pupils to get a 'feel' for the size of angles. After a suitable time set the class some exercises such as these – finding the other angle on a straight line:

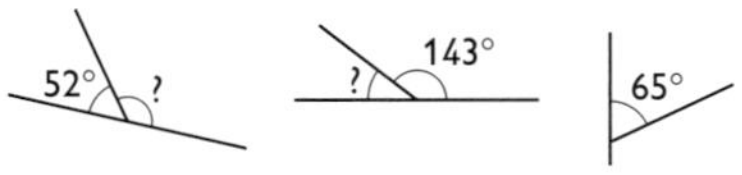


### Differentiation

*Low Attainers* – Will need support and may prefer to work as individuals on the solitaire activity. They may also need calculators to find the other angles.
*High Attainers* – May use a set of angle cards with 'harder' angles such as 37°. Sets of these are easily made – or these pupils could make their own, as this will give practice in angle measuring and drawing.

### Plenary

Quickly recap the lesson's content. Draw several angles such as these on the OHP. Invite pupils to estimate their size and to point to the largest/smallest angle (try to make them equal), leading the class to appreciate the need for some means of measuring angles. Depending on circumstances illustrate on the OHP how to use an angle measurer/protractor – with transparent instruments this is very easily done. Draw some more angles and invite pupils to measure them on the OHP. Encourage them to think aloud and the rest of the class to make constructive comments.

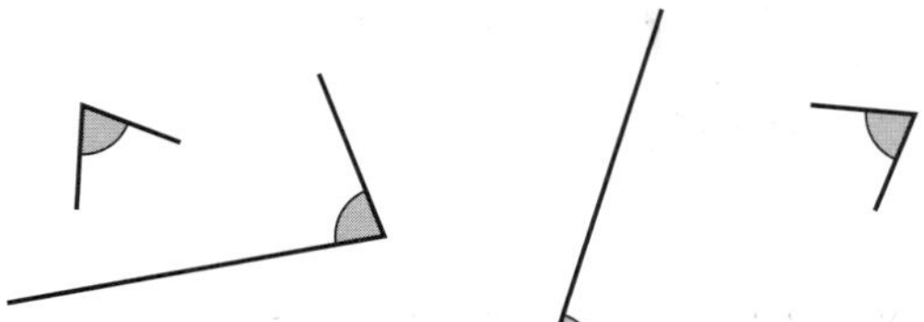

## Lesson 5

### Introduction

Quickly revise how to use an angle measurer/protractor using the OHP as in the previous lesson. *Does anyone remember what a quadrilateral is?* Quickly establish this. Ask pupils to draw a large quadrilateral and then to measure and add up its four angles. Collect in their answers and establish that they are all about 360°. The idea of the activity is to give practice in using protractors rather than establishing the angle sum of a quadrilateral – problems with using a protractor will be made apparent by wrongly answered sums.

### Activities

Demonstrate the rotation of shapes through 90° (always assume that the rotation is clockwise) – use the OHTs as in lesson 3 in this theme. In a similar way shapes on card can be rotated and their shadows cast using the OHP. Invite pupils up to the front to show rotations of various shapes.

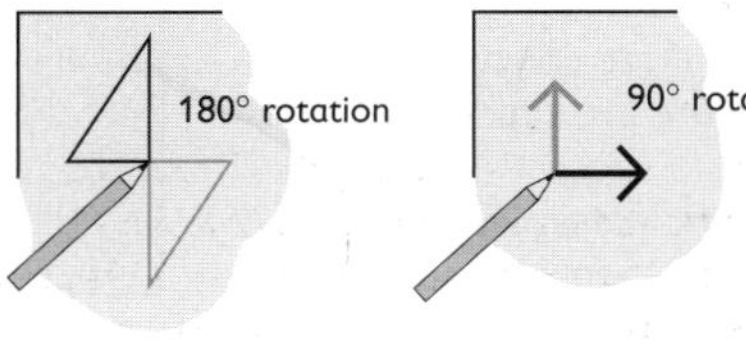


### Differentiation

*Low Attainers* – Will need support using a stencil or cardboard cut outs of the shapes. The provision of pre-drawn shapes would be useful.
*High Attainers* – Can consider rotations of 60° or 30° with more complex polygons.

### Plenary

Ask for examples of rotation patterns in everyday life, *e.g. umbrellas, road signs, logos.*

# Theme 6 Area

## Objectives

- To understand the concept of area
- To use the formula in words for the area of a rectangle
- To understand that area is measured in square metres, millimetres and centimetres
- To use the formula in letters for the area of a rectangle
- To choose appropriate units of area
- To understand that area is measured in $mm^2$, $cm^2$ and $m^2$

## Vocabulary

area, surface, square centimetre, $cm^2$, length, breadth, row, rectangle, grid, word formula, formula, unit of area, approximate area, perimeter

## Resources

A transparent area grid, squared paper (for the homework task), ruler marked in cm, cm and mm graph paper, 4 one metre rules, cm squared paper. Copymasters 31 and 32. Homework Copymaster 16.

## Assessment

*At the end of this theme is the pupil able to:*

- Understand that area is measured in square centimetres;
- Use the formula in words for the area of a rectangle?

## Mental maths starter 12

---

# Lesson 1

## Introduction

As a quick warm-up activity, invite small groups or individuals to complete these calculations using only the numbers 1, 2, 3, 4 or 6. On completion quickly check answers orally.

| | | |
|---|---|---|
| $+ \quad - \quad = 6$ | $- \quad + \quad = 3$ | $+ \quad - \quad = 7$ |
| $+ \quad + \quad = 7$ | $+ \quad - \quad = 9$ | $+ \quad - \quad = 5$ |
| $- \quad + \quad = 5$ | $+ \quad + \quad = 8$ | $- \quad - \quad = 0$ |

Initiate a quick brainstorm asking pupils to share what they know about area. (This will give a useful insight into their retention of any previous work.) Collect these on the board or OHP without comment, ensuring the active participation of as many pupils as feasible. In the light of pupils' input the class discuss those that are useful, but ensure that 'area is how much space something covers' is considered.

Draw a selection of solid shapes and challenge the class to decide which of the shapes has the smallest area and which has the largest area. Encourage discussion and lead the group to consider the use of a grid and square counting as the best strategy. (For most pupils this will simply be a piece of revision but for some low attainers it will be a useful recap.) Take the opportunity to stress the usefulness of square counting to find areas. Mention that if each small square measures 1 cm by 1 cm then each small square has an area of 1 square cm, which is written, for short, as 1 $cm^2$.

## Activities

Give individual pupils Copymaster 31 to do. Low attainers may need support when dealing with curved sides, but should nevertheless be given the opportunity to make an attempt. It may be useful to quickly revise what to do when part filled squares are encountered and to recap 'more than half count as one', 'less than half ignore'. This is met with in 1(e).

## Differentiation

*Low Attainers* – May only complete the first question.
*High Attainers* – Could be invited to find all the rectangles (with whole number length sides) that have an area of 12 $cm^2$.

## Plenary

Go through Copymaster 31 using an OHP, with pupils demonstrating their answers. Some discussion will be needed in order to come to a view on how to deal with 'part squares'. Draw pupils' attention to the importance of units – an area of, say, 16 means nothing, but an area of 16 square centimetres has meaning. Recap the progress made over the lesson.

If appropriate give pupils the homework task of finding (by square counting) the area of their hands. Depending on the group this could be extended into an activity comparing areas of hands and feet. (Some pupils may need a quick recap of when to 'round up' and all will need some squared paper of the appropriate size.)

---

# Lesson 2

## Introduction

Begin the lesson with this short number based game. One person picks a number between 1 and 100. The others have to find out what the number is by asking questions. These can only be questions that give the answer 'yes' or 'no', *e.g. Is the number greater than ten?* and so on. Only ten questions are allowed.

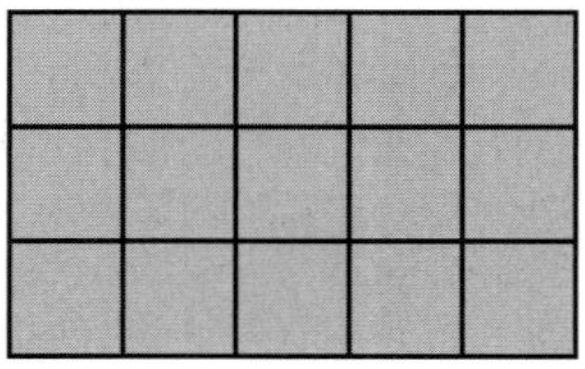

On the OHP show a shape measuring 3 rows by 5 columns.
*As you can see there are three rows of squares. There are five squares in each row.*
*Without counting them jot down the total number of squares in the rectangle.*
Quickly establish that the answer is 15.
*How did you work it out?* Ensure all pupils realise that the appropriate calculation is 3 × 5 (or 5 × 3). *If the small squares are one centimetre by one centimetre, what is the area of the rectangle?*
Insist on the correct units. Repeat with some other rectangles, until an informal feel for 'length × breadth' is achieved. Do not specifically mention 'length' or 'breadth' unless it is pretty certain that this will not confuse pupils and get in the way of their intuitive feel for the calculation of area.

## Activities

Draw further similar shapes. Ask the children to work out their areas, working in pairs. Remediate as and when necessary. Make an issue of the importance of units.

## Differentiation

*Low Attainers* – May only attempt simple shapes and may need help in recognising the link between the number of squares in a row and the actual length of a side.
*High Attainers* – May be challenged to find the area of, say, a piece of paper or the cover of a paperback.

## Plenary

Quickly work through the questions involving pupils as much as possible.

It may be necessary to illustrate several more times the connection between measurements and numbers of squares along a side.

Pose the question: *Can anybody give a word formula for working out the area of a rectangle?*

Collect in suggestions and guide the class into 'length x breadth'.

# Lesson 3

## Introduction

This 'think of a number' activity will give pupils mental arithmetic practice in a 'fun' context.
*Think of a number, add five to it, multiply the answer by four, double the result, divide by eight and subtract your original number. What is your final answer?* (It is always 5!)
*Think of a number, double it, add four to the answer, multiply the result by three, divide by six and subtract your original number. What is your final answer?* (It is always 2.)
Depending on the group this could be a useful vehicle to revise 'doing and undoing'.
Pupils could be asked to write their own similar tricks.

## Activities

*Last lesson we learnt that the word formula length $\times$ breadth gave the area of a rectangle.*
*Use the formula to find the areas of these rectangles.* Draw a few rectangles (with dimensions on). Insist on correct units for their areas. Take the opportunity to remediate.
*Although the word formula area = length $\times$ breadth* (write on board) *is short and easy to remember, we can use algebra to write an even shorter formula using letters. What do you think it might be?* (Allow a few minutes before collecting in answers on the board.) Allow some discussion about the formulae on the board, homing in on 'the correct one(s)' – any form of $a = bc$ will do, providing pupils state what each letter represents. For some groups it may be necessary to give help over 'length' and 'width'.
On the board draw some rectangles with sides in millimetres, centimetres and metres. Invite the group to write down their areas – but at this point do not make an issue about the respective units of area.

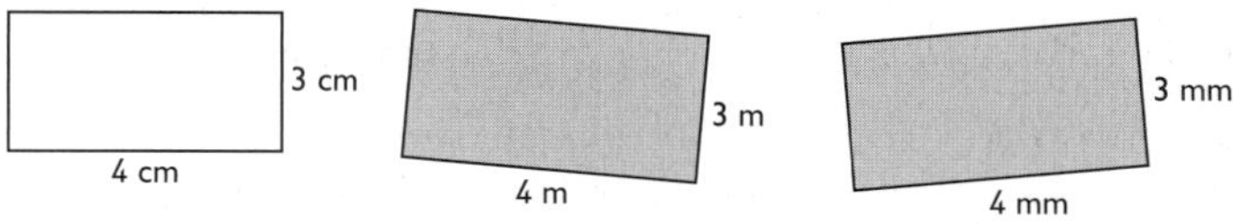


Collect in the answers, making an issue of units and the notation mm$^2$, m$^2$. Follow this up with some more questions on the board.

## Differentiation

*Low Attainers* – May need mm and cm graph paper to draw full-size rectangles on in order to recognise the importance of units. (Square metres will be demonstrated in the plenary.)
*High Attainers* – Will follow the context with few problems. Rectangles with sides given in mixed units should give them sufficient challenge.

## Plenary

Demonstrate to the class (or better still allow pupils to 'see') what 1 mm$^2$, 1 cm$^2$ and 1 m$^2$ looks like. (For the first two use graph paper, for the last make a square of side 1 metre from four metre rules.
Recap the progress made over the lesson.

# Lesson 4

## Introduction

Ensure that pupils understand this sequence: 'four times the units digit plus the tens digit'. *So starting with 27 we get 30 then 3 then 12 then 9 then 36 and so on.* Or write on the board 23 14 17 29 38 and so on. *Working in pairs, you have 5 minutes to find out all you can about this sequence.* Keep to the target time and have a short plenary session in which findings are shared. The time limit is useful as it focuses pupils' minds on the task in hand.

## Activities

Give pupils Copymaster 32 to do, working in pairs. A quick reminder about rounding decimals *e.g. 5.1 $\times$ 6.8 is approximately 5 $\times$ 7* may be needed.

## Differentiation

*Low Attainers* – Will need support and may find question 3 too great a challenge.
*High Attainers* – Should be encouraged to make up and test on each other questions similar to those in question 3. The highest attainers could be asked to check their answers to 3(a) by performing the 'exact' calculation.

## Plenary

Go through Copymaster 32 ensuring full pupil participation and challenging pupils to justify their answers.
Use the ensuing discussion as a means to probe understanding.
In question 1 invite suggestions as to how such areas might be measured in practice, what equipment might be needed etc.

# Lesson 5

## Introduction

Quickly revise perimeter. Then set this problem: *On centimetre squared paper draw some rectangles which have an area of twenty-four square centimetres. Find the perimeter of each rectangle. What sized rectangle has the smallest perimeter?* Set a time limit of 5 minutes, collecting and discussing answers. This should bring to light any serious misconceptions regarding areas and perimeters of rectangles.

## Activities

This activity involves pupils making up questions of their own about area. However the general format could be used with any content, once pupils recognise what is expected from them.
Initially working in pairs pupils make a set of ten game cards. The question is on the front, and the answer on the back, for example:

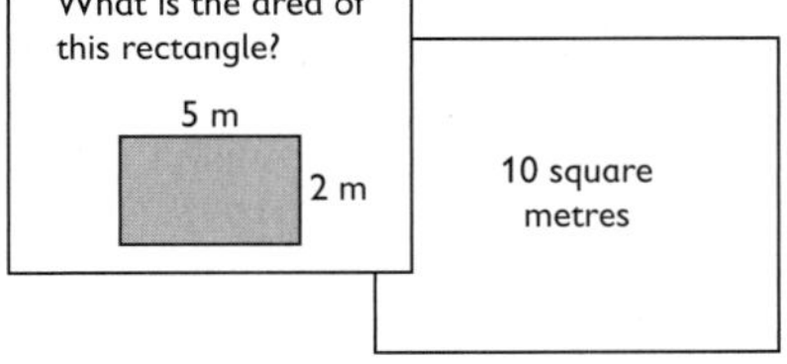


Alternatively sets of game cards could be provided already completed (either by the teacher or by another class of pupils). The actual game is for two or four players. If four, play as two pairs. Cards are placed face up, questions on top. Players play alternatively. They must answer the question, checking against the answer on the reverse side. If the answer is correct they keep the card. If not the card is placed at the bottom of the pile. The game ends when all the cards have been used. The winner is the team or person with the most cards at the end.
An alternative would be to have the questions and answers on two separate sets of cards and to play a game of 'matching pairs' matching questions with answers.

## Differentiation

Differentiation can be achieved by matching of attainment level to card difficulty. In many respects it is self-adjusting.

## Plenary

Review the progress made over the theme on area, using some questions such as these as vehicles: *How could you find the area of the hall/playground? What units would you use? There are 100 centimetres in a metre. How many square centimetres are there in a square metre? There are 100 millimetres in a centimetre. How many square millimetres are there in a square centimetre?* Possible homework activities might involve finding the areas of photographs in different free newspapers or areas devoted to certain advertising *e.g. cars, houses, computer games.*

# Theme 7 Measuring mass

## Objectives
- To use standard metric units of mass and their abbreviations
- To understand relationships between the units
- To be able to convert larger to smaller units of mass
- To be able to read measurements from scales
- To be able to use all four operations to solve measurement word problems. To represent and interpret data in a line graph
- To recognise where intermediate points on a graph have meaning

## Vocabulary
data, graph, chart, tally chart, frequency, bar chart, line graph, interval, database, mass, weight, heavier, lighter, gram, half-kilogram, kilogram.

## Resources
Different size weights, squared paper, various objects to weigh, supermarket carrier bags, scales. Copymasters 33 and 34. Homework Copymaster 17.

## Assessment
*At the end of this theme is the pupil able to:*
- Estimate and record weights to the nearest half, quarter or tenth of 1kg in decimal form;
- Solve measurement word problems using all four operations;
- Estimate intermediate values from a line graph?

## Mental maths starter 13

# Lesson 1

## Introduction
Make sure the children have plenty of experience at handling different weights, *e.g. 1 gram, 5 gram 10 gram, 1 kilogram etc.* Ask them to choose a suitable unit to measure the mass of the following items –
- A small bar of chocolate
- A sack of potatoes
- A postage stamp
- A pencil
- A person

## Activities
*There are 1000 g in a kilogram, so there are 500 grams in half a kilogram. I can use this information to calculate other fractions.* Using Copymaster 33 –
*Can you find one quarter of a kilogram on the sheet?*
*Are there any other amounts on the sheet which are equivalent to three quarters of a kilogram?*
*What are the smallest amounts on the sheet?*
*Which amounts are greater than or equal to ten grams?*

Encourage the children to pose their own similar questions. Then ask the children other questions of equivalence.
*Working in pairs* – Pose questions on the board for the children to answer
3kg = ? grams
$1\frac{1}{2}$ = ? grams
250 grams = ? kg
1250 grams = ? kg etc

Ask the children to find objects which weigh:
(a) less than 100 g
(b) between 650 g and 850 g
(c) about 1 kg 300 g
(d) about 2 kg.

## Differentiation
*Low Attainers – Can you find anything equivalent to half a kilogram?* etc
*High Attainers – How else could we write one gram?* etc

## Plenary
Remind the children that they have been converting between equivalent forms of masses. Give them some quickfire conversions to do, targeting them at particular children.

# Lesson 2

## Introduction
We can write 0.75 kg as 750 g.
Write two sets of masses on the board –
 2 kg – 5 kg – 6 kg – 8 kg – 9 kg
 0.5 kg – 0.75 kg – 0.25 kg – 0.1 kg – 0.01 kg

Ask the children to work individually and make up different amounts by combining a quantity from each set, for example, 6.01 kg or 2.75 kg. Then ask them to convert each amount into grams. Swap their papers with a partner and ask the partner to change the amounts back into kilograms.

## Activities
Tell the class that they can use their knowledge of the masses of familiar objects to help them estimate the masses of other objects.
*Working in Groups of 4 or 5* – Give each group six objects of various masses, ranging from around 100 g up to or beyond 1 kg. As a group without using scales they can order the items from lightest to heaviest. Individually they estimate the mass of the lightest object to the nearest 50 g and write this down. As a group they then weigh the object using the scales and each child calculates the difference between the estimate and the actual weight. Discuss the various ways the children used to make their estimates.
Ask each group to fill a carrier bag with more than three objects to make these weights:
(a) about 400 g
(b) about 250 g
(c) about 700 g
(d) about 900 g.

## Differentiation
*Low Attainers – Can anyone find me something in the classroom that weighs the same as a) a bar of soap or b) a brick or c) a story book?*
*High Attainers – Can anyone find something in the classroom that weighs the same as a) 600 g or b) 900 g or c) 1200 g?*

## Plenary
Ask the children to estimate the masses of different objects in their houses *e.g. television, chair, bed etc.* Discuss how they would go about weighing the objects to check their estimates.

## Lesson 3

### Introduction
Draw this table on the board –

| | |
|---|---|
| Month 1 | 3 kg |
| Month 2 | 5 kg |
| Month 3 | 6.5 kg |
| Month 4 | 7.2 kg |
| Month 5 | 8.3 kg |
| Month 6 | 9.5 kg |

It shows the monthly weights of a new born baby. Ask the children to pose questions about the chart.

### Activities
*How much heavier did the baby become in Month 2?* Ask the class about other ways of showing the information. Suggest a bar line chart. Draw a pair of axes labeled 'horizontal' and 'vertical.' Draw appropriate scales on each axis and decide on the names to go with each axis. Also name the whole graph. Get the children to mark with a cross each weight value that goes with each month. When all the weights have been plotted draw vertical lines between each cross and its marker on the horizontal axis.

### Differentiation
*Low Attainers* – Might well need help with marking out each axis, discussing each scale and how appropriate it might be.
*High Attainers* – Could compare two bar line charts on different subjects.

### Plenary
Return to the bar line chart on the baby's weight. *Can we connect each point with a line?* The answer being yes discuss why we connect the points on the graph with a line and why it makes sense to talk about intermediate values. Draw straight lines to connect each point.

## Lesson 4

### Introduction
Look again at the line graph from Lesson 3. Having connected the points with straight lines the vertical lines to the horizontal axis are not needed so they can be rubbed out. Pose questions about the line graph. *In the middle of Month 3 did the baby weigh more or less than 7 kg?*

### Activities
Draw a line graph by plotting these points on the board (crosses at 100,81,62,45,33,28,26,24,24 degrees centigrade.)

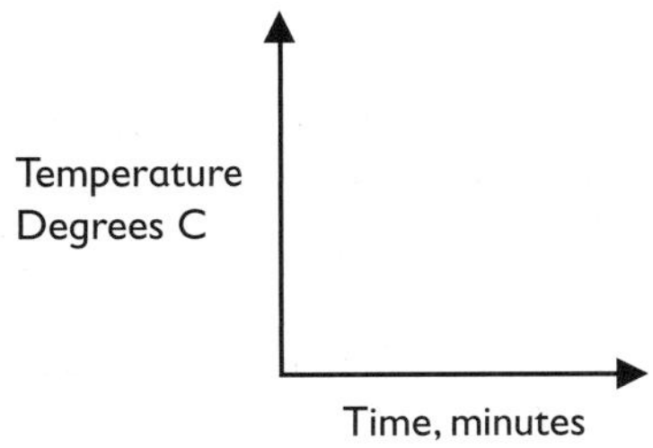


Explain that this data was obtained by measuring the falling temperature of a cup of boiling water that was left to cool. The temperature was measured at 1 minute intervals and the results plotted. Draw a line connecting the points to show the trend which in this case is a fall in temperature as the water temperature cools.
*Working in pairs* –
Draw another line graph:
Time at least five friends on how long it takes them to build a tower of 40 bricks.
Plot each time on the graph.

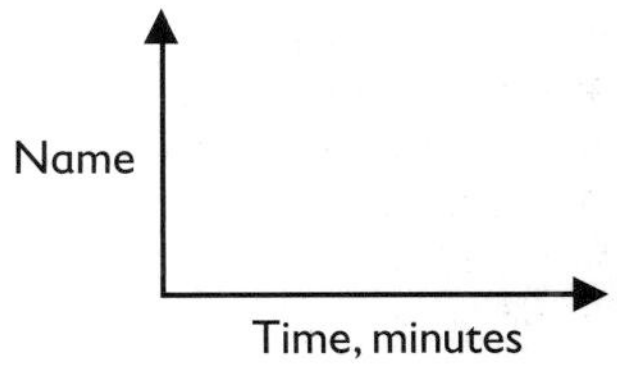


### Differentiation
*Low Attainers – When would the temperature of the water have been about 40 degrees centigrade?*
*High Attainers – When would the temperature of the water have been about 75 degrees centigrade?*

### Plenary
Go through another bar line chart and answer the questions that appear on Copymaster 34.

## Lesson 5

### Introduction
Tell the children they are going to look at word problems that focus on measures. Write on the board: The answer is 500 ml. Ask the children to discuss in pairs what the questions could be. After two minutes, take some ideas and discuss them. Repeat for another answer: The answer is 24 cm squared. Ask the pairs to write a question involving measures. Take some examples to solve as a class.

### Activities
Draw a pair of axes and a table, both labeled with the months of the year and frequency on the board.

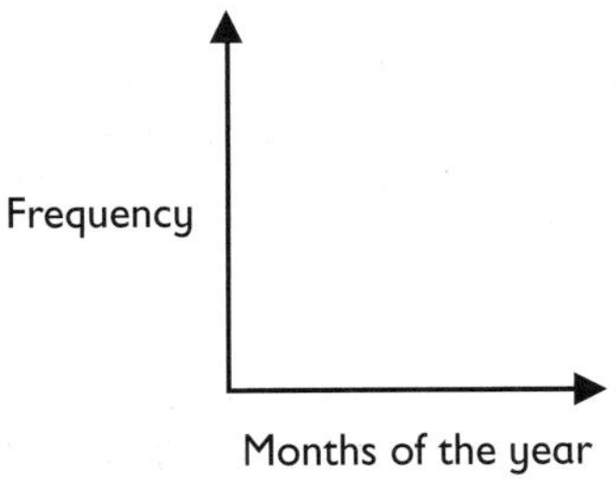


| Month | Number of birthdays |
|---|---|
| Jan | |
| Feb | |
| March | |
| April | |
| May | |
| June | |
| July | |
| August | |
| September | |
| October | |
| November | |
| December | |

Tell the children they are going to collect information to find out when their birthdays are, and discover whether most of the class will be 10 years old by the end of March. The children can then make a bar line chart to record their information.
*Working in pairs* – Carry out a survey on the number of letters in the boys' or girls' names in the class. Which number is the mode? What fraction of the names have 6 letters, 5 letters and 4 letters? What is the range?

### Differentiation
*Low Attainers* – Can complete a chart that has the axes and the first crosses marked on.
*High Attainers* – Write some questions that can be answered using the bar line chart they have drawn.

### Plenary
Remind children about labelling axes and appropriate scales when compiling a graph. Go through Homework 17.

# Theme 8 Addition and subtraction

## Objectives

- To identify near doubles (including decimals with 1 decimal place)
- To add or subtract multiples of 10 or 100 and adjust
- To use the relationship between addition and subtraction
- To extend written methods of addition of more than 2 integers less than 100 000
- To use pencil and paper methods of adding and subtracting decimals both with 1 or 2 decimal places

## Vocabulary

double, near double, multiple, near multiple, compensate, reordering a calculation, decimal, 1-place decimal number, 2-place decimal number.

## Resources

Copymasters 35 and 36. Homework Copymaster 18. Two-digit number cards.

## Assessment

*At the end of this theme is the pupil able to:*

- Identify near doubles e.g. *1.5 + 1.6*;
- Add/subtract multiples of 10 or 100 and adjust;
- Use the relationship between addition and subtraction;
- Extend written methods to addition of more than 2 integers less than 10 000, and + and – of pairs of decimals both with 1 or 2 decimal places?

## Mental maths starter 14

## Lesson 1

### Introduction

Ask the class, with pupils answering on paper, a sample of ten doubles of whole numbers in the range 1 to 100. Invite pupils to explain how they arrived at their answers – did they 'just know' or did they use a method of their own? Follow this by enquiring if any others in the class used another method or perhaps enquire as to how pupils remembered – which doubles do they find hardest? Finish the session by inviting each pupil to give a number from 1 to 100. Write these on the board, then go round the room asking pupils to double one of these numbers, ensuring an equitable matching of pupil with particular double. Stress the importance of knowing doubles by heart.

### Activities

Write the calculation *15 + 16* on the board. Ask class to jot down the answer, then invite pupils to share with the class the methods they used. Guide the class to consider 'double 15 and add on 1'. Repeat the above for *25 + 26 and 27 + 28*. Encourage pupils to use doubling and emphasise the usefulness of the method – if you know your doubles! Ask the class if they can think of another way of using doubling to find *15 + 16, 25 + 26 or 27 + 28* – guide the class into suggesting 'doubling the higher minus 1'. Draw pupils' attention to the expression 'near double'. Ask the class to jot down on their whiteboards the answers to:
*85 + 86 79 + 80 66 + 67 68 + 70 45 + 46 45 + 47.*
The last four show that doubling is useful in cases with a difference greater than 1 – in fact some pupils may spot, that for differences of two, 'doubling the middle numbers' is a useful method.
Write the calculation *1.5 + 1.6* = on the board. Ask the class how they might use 'near doubles' to find the answer – if there is some reluctance or difficulty lead the class by asking: *What is double 15?* 30. *So double 1.5 is …* 3, *we can use this to find that 1.5 + 1.6 is three or three point zero add zero point one, which is … three point one. How could we check this was correct?* Accept any reasonable answer from using a calculator to performing an equivalent calculation. Ask the class to jot down the answers to the previous five questions re-cast as decimals:
8.5 + 8.6 7.9 + 8.0 6.6 + 6.7 6.8 + 7.0 4.5 + 4.6 4.5 + 4.7.

### Differentiation

*Low Attainers* – Will need some initial extra support with decimal work.
*High Attainers* – Calculate, for example, *1.5 + 2.3 + 1.6 or 1.9 + 2.3 + 2.0* – where the 'double' is less obvious.

### Plenary

Invite the class to suggest how near doubles could be used to help with these calculations.
Stress that they should spend some time thinking about the method – although the answer will be needed eventually. If appropriate, invite pupils to talk through their mental calculations on the OHP. (These calculations will also help with decimal work.)

*15 + 12 + 16*    *1.5 + 1.2 + 1.6*
*34 + 35 + 7*    *3.4 + 3.5 + 0.7*
*39 + 15 + 40*    *3.9 + 1.5 + 4.0*

## Lesson 2

### Introduction

Quick whole class chanting activity. Count on or back in steps of tens or hundreds, starting from any two- or three-digit number.
Divide the class into groups. The first group picks a two-digit number at random from a set of two-digit number cards, displays the card and says the number 9 more than it. The next group says the number 9 more than that, and so on. The first team to go over 100 scores a point. Repeat with 11, 21 and 19 …, until all the groups have had the opportunity to start.
Quick discussion with the class: *Was it easier to count on in 10s or 11s or 9s? Is there an easy way to count up in 9s or 11s?* Establish (without forcing the issue) that counting up in 9/11 can be easier if you add 10 then add/take away one.

### Activities

Write *237 + 49* = on the board. Ask the class how they would solve it. Insist on method, not merely the answer. Involve the class in considering all the possibilities, but if it does not arise naturally, guide/suggest: *Round the 49 to 50, 237 add on 50 is 287 and take away 1 gives the answer 286* and also *Take the 49 down to 40, 237 add on 40 is 267, adding back on the 9 gives the answer 286.* Ensure that pupils realise that both methods give the same answer, perhaps by asking them to calculate *716 + 59, 787 – 69* using both methods – encourage pupils to think aloud to the class.
State to the class that the method they have just used, in correct mathematical language, is called *adding or subtracting multiples of 10 or 100 and compensating.* (A useful point at which to use correct language in a real situation and perhaps revise 'multiple').
Write *874 – 48* = on the board. *How could you solve this using multiples of ten and compensating?* Encourage clear exposition of the method used – including jottings on the OHP by pupils. Repeat for the calculation 120 + 490.
Pupils work individually on Copymaster 35. Remind them to use, if suitable, some of the methods they have used during the lesson.

### Differentiation

*Low Attainers* – Complete questions 1–16 on Copymaster 35.
*High Attainers* – Complete questions 15–30 on Copymaster 35.

### Plenary

Review any difficulties emerging from the copymaster.
*This looks very hard* [write 398 + 997]. *How could you reduce it to a far easier problem?*
Guide, if necessary, along the lines *398 + 997 = 400 + 1000 – 2 – 3.*

## Lesson 3

### Introduction

Write on the board the calculation $6 + 13 + 4 + 3 =$.
Invite pupils to write the answer and explain their method – nudge towards (and use the actual word) reordering *i.e.* $(6 + 4) + (13 + 3) = 10 + 16 = 26$. Use the opportunity to bring brackets naturally into play. In a similar way write, invite answers and discuss the reordering of calculations like these:

| | |
|---|---|
| $25 + 73 + 75$ | $17 + 9 - 7 + 1$ |
| $3 + 8 + 7 + 6 + 2$ | $58 + 37 - 38$ |
| $46 - 67 + 54 - 3$ | $85 + 14 + 15 + 26$ |
| $64 + 37 + 46 + 13$ | $10 + 30 + 89 + 5 - 19$ |

Working in pairs, ask pupils to give each other calculations which look relatively difficult but become simpler after reordering. Insist on mathematically correct expressions.

### Activities

Write $1461 + 875 = 2336$ on the board.
*How could you use this number sentence to find 2336 – 875?*
Allow as many pupils as possible to participate.
Ensure this explanation (or similar) : *2336 – 875 means what is added to 875 to make 2336?*
*But as we are told that 1461 + 875 = 2336, this means the answer is 1461.*
Repeat for finding 2336 – 1461.
Write $693 - 517 = 176$
*How could you use this number sentence to find 693 – 176?*

Ensure that as many pupils as possible participate to attempt to give a method.
Guide the class into realising that 693 – 517 = 176 which means that 176 needs to be added to 517 to total 693.
*Using only the numbers 3, 4, 7, 11 and 10, make as many subtraction and addition statements as you can. Here are two:* $3 + 4 = 7$, $10 - 3 = 7$. After several minutes collect pupils' responses on the board, using the class to complete any omissions. Take the opportunity to stress the importance of working systematically and using the relationship between addition and subtraction *e.g. as* $3 + 4 = 7$, $7 - 3 = 4$ *and* $7 - 4 = 3$.
*What subtraction and addition statements can you make from 202, 352, 77, 477 and 125?* This activity will give pupils practice in addition (and perhaps subtraction). [The key expressions are $477 - 125 = 352$ and $125 + 77 = 202$.]

### Differentiation

*Low Attainers* – An easier set of numbers for the last activity would be: 15, 100, 35, 65, and 50
[with key expressions 65 + 35 = 100 and 35 + 15 = 50].
*High Attainers* – Could be asked to make up more challenging activities like the one above, perhaps involving decimals.

### Plenary

Recap the lesson by asking: *given that 3685 – 987 = 2698, how could you straight away know the answer to 3685 – 2698 or 2698 + 987?*
Review the use of this for checking calculations, for example:
*Check 781 – 459 = 322 by calculating 459 + 322 (which should give 781).*

## Lesson 4

### Activities

Tell the pupils they are going to add more than two numbers which may be as large as 99 000.
On the board write $20000 + 6000 + 700 + 80 + 1 =$
Invite the class to jot down the answer (26781) and to explain their reasoning. Repeat if necessary with the calculation $40000 + 3000 + 100 + 30 + 7$. Write the calculation $43 + 309 + 9 + 867 + 1273$ on the board, inviting responses to: *How would you calculate this addition? Think about it for a few minutes*. Ensure that, amongst any others, these two methods are considered:

$43 + 309 + 9 + 867 + 1273$
$= (40 + 3) + (300 + 9) + (9) + (800 + 60 + 7) + (1000 + 200 + 70 + 3)$
$= (1000) + (200 + 300 + 800) + (40 + 60 + 70) + (3 + 9 + 9 + 7 + 3)$
$= (1000) + (1300) + (170) + (31)$
$= (2000) + (400) + (70) + (31)$
$= 2501$

```
    4 3
  3 0 9
      9
  8 6 7
+1 2 7 3
 2 5 0 1
  1 2 3
```

Ensure that pupils use correct language when 'carrying'.
Guide pupils into recognising the advantages of using the standard written method as shown above. Points which might prove problematic are carrying more than the customary 10 or 100 *e.g. 30, 200 in the above example* and the numbers to be added having different numbers of digits – an opportunity to recap on place value.
Divide the class into groups, with each group having to make up one calculation like the previous calculations listed on the board. Each group attempts every other group's calculation. Discuss answers and methods.

### Differentiation

*Low Attainers* – Will progress at a slower rate. Tailor calculations to match their levels of attainment.
*High Attainers* – In pairs ask them to set each other harder examples (but each person must be able to do their own).

### Plenary

Write these sets of calculations on board. Invite pupils to do them, asking what they notice and if they are able to explain it (same answer – 18953; same digits in each column).

| | |
|---|---|
| $85 + 176 + 7 + 864 + 17\,821$ | $17877 + 185 + 6 + 821 + 64$ |
| $10161 + 7074 + 807 + 26 + 885$ | $66 + 825 + 7001 + 874 + 10187$ |

## Lesson 5

### Introduction

*Here are two, 1-place decimal numbers added. How could you find the answer?* Write $3.1 + 2.3 =$. Encourage pupils to talk about their methods, but ensure that a method of the form $3 + 2 + 0.4 = 5.4$ is brought to the class's attention. (If some pupils experience difficulty begin from $31 + 23 = 54$ *and* $31 + 23 = 30 + 20 + 1 + 3 = 54$.)
*Working on your own, write down some additions involving 1-place decimals which have an answer of* 2. Collect these without comment on the board and invite the class to check for any errors. This exercise should bring to the fore any serious difficulties with decimal addition using informal methods as it will force pupils to consider calculations of the type $1.8 + 0.2$. Repeat the investigation, but allowing subtraction rather than addition.

### Activities

Quickly recap the standard written method for addition and subtraction, using examples like these as vehicles: *636 – 229 and 654 + 285.*

Then extend to the money calculations *£6.36 – £2.29 and £6.54 + £2.85.* At a suitable juncture, stress that, although 3.5 is correct when dealing with numbers, with money the correct expression is £3.50. By working through examples like *12.4 + 3.1 or 13.5 – 1.8* ensure that pupils recognise that in using standard written methods for addition and subtraction it is crucial that digits of the same place value must line up. Give pupils Copymaster 36 to work on individually. After completion, pupils check their own solutions on a calculator.

### Differentiation

*Low Attainers* – Complete Copymaster sections A and B (if possible).
*High Attainers* – Complete all the work on Copymaster 36.

### Plenary

Work through – with pupil participation – some calculations of the type: *£5.62 + £6.56 + £2.30  82.5 + 54.3  £9.52 – £4.86  81.5 – 5.8.*

# Theme 9 Money problems

## Objectives
- To use addition and subtraction to solve 'real life' problems
- To use all four operations to solve money problems
- To choose appropriate operations
- To choose appropriate methods of calculation
- To check calculations with inverse operations
- To check calculations using a calculator

## Vocabulary
addition, subtraction, inverse, operation, check, plus, minus, equals, difference, lots of, multiply.

## Resources
Calculators, Copymasters 37 and 38. Homework Copymaster 19.

## Assessment
*At the end of this theme is the pupil able to:*
- Check calculations with inverse operations;
- Check calculations using a calculator;
- Decide whether to work mentally or with pencil and paper;
- Solve two-step problems;
- Describe both mental and written methods?

**Mental maths starter 16**

---

## Lesson 1

### Introduction
Draw a selection of flow diagrams on the board.

E.g. +6 ⟶ +7 ⟶ ×5 ⟶ −9 ⟶

Give children different starting numbers and let them work through each flow diagram as quickly as they can. Discuss the quickest methods of calculation.

### Activities
*Decide the best way of solving a problem before you try to solve it. How long is a trip into town and home again?*
What do the children need to know before they start? Sensible estimates first. Decide what unit the answer should be in. Work out a procedure to use. *E.g. Leaving home to the car park is 25 minutes depending on the weight of traffic. Time spent in the toy shop is 5 minutes. Time spent in the café is 30 minutes. Time spent in the library should have been 50 minutes but it was closed so the total time is 50 minutes less etc.* Encourage the children to work out the problem in sections, making notes as they go.

*Working in pairs* – Estimate how long it should take for, *e.g., registration + assembly + break + everyone hanging their coats up.* Was the estimate correct? What took a longer or a shorter time?

### Differentiation
*Low Attainers* – Let the children work with a short timed period *e.g. the school morning.*
*High Attainers* – Let the children work with a longer period of time which requires more information.

### Plenary
Compare the children's results to their trips into town and check their answers. They should have reached the same conclusions.

---

## Lesson 2

### Introduction
*Sometimes, it is best to write down the result of each stage in solving a problem.* Pose this question.
The Scout Group organised a 'Bring and Buy Sale'. Four stalls collected £5.50 each. Three stalls collected £4.50 each. How much did they collect all together?
*Working in pairs* – Discuss how to work out the problem.

### Activities
Bring the ideas from the introduction together –
- *What do we need to find out?*
- *What calculations do we need to make?*
- *What can we do mentally and what with pencil and paper?*

Ask the children for their thoughts and persuade them that it makes sense to work out and write down the answer to both parts separately, then add the two answers together. Children should now answer the problem and others written on Copymaster 37.
Remind the children of two important questions
1) *Can it be done in stages?*
2) *Do you need to write anything down?*

*Working in pairs* – Ask the children to compose their own two- and three-stage problems using everyday situations and money and to exchange them with other pairs.

### Differentiation
*Low Attainers – What are two lots of £3.50? How could you work out four lots of £3.50 from that?*
*High Attainers – What is the least amount of information you need to write down to solve any problem on the Copymaster?*

### Plenary
Encourage the children to write up any notes they make on the board. Demonstrate any methods the children didn't use. Ask the children for any methods they used for checking their answers.

## Lesson 3

### Introduction
*Different operations can be used to solve the same problem.*
'The class gets a new set of 136 reading books.'
Give children different problems related to this statement, and discuss how they solved them. Then make points about each calculation.
*The teacher gives out 66 reading books how many books are left?*
*How many books would be left if the teacher gave out 99?*
*How many books would fit equally on 4 shelves?*

### Activities
*It is important to decide whether to use mental, written, or calculator methods to solve a problem.*
*Examples*
1) 30 + 60 + 70 = (add 30 and 70 to make 100, then add 60)
2) 257 + 399 = (add 257 and 400 subtract 1)
3) 384 + 672 =
4) 564 divided by 7 =
5) 24 × 12 =

Ask the children to make decisions about the methods they would use.

### Differentiation
*Low Attainers – How would you work out 4 times by 16. Etc.*
*High Attainers – How would you work out 180 times by 19. Etc.*

### Plenary
*A man goes into a shop and buys the following*
A saw £6.78
A hammer £4.23
A set of spanners £3.78
3 screwdrivers at £1.25 each
30 nails at £2.00 per 100
Total the bill. What methods of calculations are the best?

## Lesson 4

### Introduction
*You can check addition with subtraction, and you can check subtraction with addition.*
Write on the board: 245 + 456 = 701 and other similar examples.
Ask children what other number sentences it is possible to write just with those numbers.
701 – 456 = 245, 701 – 245 = 456,
456 + 245 = 701.
Repeat with other statements.

### Activities
Remind the children of the meaning of 'inverse' and that subtraction is the inverse operation to addition. That is subtraction 'undoes' addition, and addition 'undoes' subtraction.
*Working in pairs* – Make as many subtraction and addition statements as possible from the following numbers.

123, 453, 330
167, 569, 402
325, 165, 160
536, 243, 293
634, 142, 492

Invite some children to report back on what they have found, writing the statement on the board.

### Differentiation
*Low Attainers* – Use tens and units to illustrate the 'inverse' operation.
*High Attainers* – Choose their own numbers over 1000 to illustrate the 'inverse' operation.

### Plenary
Gather all the suggestions worked on by the class. Focus on the

## Lesson 5

### Introduction
*When you check a calculation using a calculator, use the inverse calculation as a double check.*
The children are going to practise checking addition and subtraction, using the inverse operation on a calculator. Remind the children about how to use a calculator and how it is important to use the clear key before undertaking another operation. When working with money, a display of, for example, 3.5 means £3.50.

### Activities
Ask the children to look at Copymaster 38. Read through the questions there and then set them to work in pairs to find the answers. They should make an estimate of each first. As they complete these problems, ask the pairs to make up one or two similar problems of their own to share with the rest of the class.

### Differentiation
*Low Attainers* – Get them to put each piece of information (item and price) on a separate slip of paper and use these as aids when answering the questions.
*High Attainers* – They can answer questions set by other children.

### Plenary
Remind the children that using the memory on the calculator can be helpful but that they may also want to jot down intermediate steps in their working as a check. Finish the lesson with some calculations for them to work on that require the use of the memory, for example:

4578 + (325 divided by 5)
2368 + (522 divided by 3)

Explain Homework Sheet 19.

# Theme 10 Properties of numbers

## Objectives
- To recognise multiples of 6, 7, 8, 9 and 11
- To extend number sequences by adding 6, 7, 8 or 9 to any number
- To know and apply tests of divisibility by 2, 4, 5, 10 or 100
- To make and investigate general statements
- To suggest extensions by asking 'What if …'

## Vocabulary
multiple, digit, divisible, divisibility, factor, constant, strategy, reasoning.

## Resources
100 square. Copymasters 39 and 40 and Homework Copymaster 20.

## Assessment
*At the end of this theme is the pupil able to:*
- Describe and explain patterns of multiples on a number grid;
- Use their knowledge of divisibility to work out the factors of numbers;
- Explain a general statement by giving an example that illustrates it?

## Mental maths starter 15

---

# Lesson 1

## Introduction
Write the numbers 6, 7, 8, and 9 on the board and ask the children to list the multiples of each number as far as they can go in 45 seconds. Remind them that multiples are the same number repeated. Also remind the children that (up to the tenth multiple) they are the answers to their tables.

## Activities
Complete these number lines:

24, 30, _____, 42, _____, _____.
28, 35, _____, 49, _____, _____
24, 32, _____, 48, _____, _____
54, 63, _____, 81, _____, _____ etc.

Do these addition sums as multiplication sums;
$8 + 8 + 8 = (3 \times 8) = 24$
$8 + 8 + 8 + 8 = \square$ $8 + 8 + 8 + 8 + 8 = \square$
Repeat for multiples of 6, 7, and 9.

Compose a series of small multiplication grids involving the 6, 7, 8, 9 and 11× tables. These should be no larger than $4 \times 4$ and can be put on the board and copied onto squared paper and completed by the children.

## Differentiation
*Low Attainers – Can you work out the patterns of the three and four times tables?*
*High Attainers – Can you find a multiplication table where the tens go up by 1, and the ones go up by 2?*

## Plenary
Discuss the patterns the children have discovered. Ask if any of the children have found an interesting pattern for the multiples of 9.

- 9-digit adds up to 9
- 18-digits add up to 9
- 27-digits add up to 9
- 36-digits add up to 9 etc

---

# Lesson 2

## Introduction
'When you add the same number repeatedly, you get repeating patterns in the ones digits.' Set the constant function on your calculator to add 6, then set the display to show 3(6 + = 3) and ask the children to predict the numbers that will appear when you press = again. Write them on the board:

15 21 27 33 39.

Draw children's attention to the repeating pattern of the one's digit
(5, 1, 7, 3, 9).

## Activities
Adding 6 starting at 3 gives a repeating cycle of five digits. (5, 1, 7, 3, 9) *Does this always happen when you keep adding 6 to a number?* (try adding 6 to 5, pattern is 1,7,3,9,5) Do the same for adding 7 (7 times table, 7, 4, 1.8.5.2, 9, 6, 3, 0 gives you every digit in the same repeating order) Add 8 to any number and look for a pattern. What happens when you add 9 (9, 8, 7, 6, 5). Using a 100 square, divide each square into 4 ⊠ and ask the children to colour in the multiples of either 2, 4, 6 and 8 or 3, 5, 7 and 9 using each triangle. *Can the children display their results in different forms, charts, circles etc?*

## Differentiation
*Low Attainers* – Let them use a 100 grid to record the patterns.
*High Attainers* – Explore and describe the patterns of a family of tables such as 7, 17, 27.

## Plenary
Ask the children to report back on the work they have done, adding the same number repeatedly to one starting number. Encourage them to describe the patterns they have discovered, and if possible explain them.

## Lesson 3

### Introduction

*Group Counting* – Tell the children they are going to count up in sixes. Start as a class, then point to particular groups. Say that if you clap your hands, the count will change direction and go down in sixes. Repeat with counts of sevens, eights and nines, starting from 0 each time.

### Activities

Ask the children what they remember about patterns of multiples, and how they recognise, for example, even numbers. Ask them to look at this list of statements and decide if they are true or false or 'in between.'

*The sum of three even numbers is odd.*
*The sum of three odd numbers is odd.*
*The difference between one odd and one even number is odd.*
*The difference between two odd or two even numbers is even.*
Continue this work, using Copymaster 39

*Working in pairs* – Explore the answers to the times tables. Are there rules? *E.g. answers to the 4× table are always even. Answers to the 9× table are alternate odd/even.*

### Differentiation

*Low Attainers – What happens when you multiply a number by 2? Does it become odd or even? How do you know?*
*High Attainers – Why can multiples of six never end in 3?* (They always end in 6, 2, 8, 4 or 0.)

### Plenary

Discuss the results with the class, going through each statement in turn. Emphasise the statements that are always true, because they are helpful in understanding how numbers work.

## Lesson 4

### Introduction

Investigate this Venn Diagram:

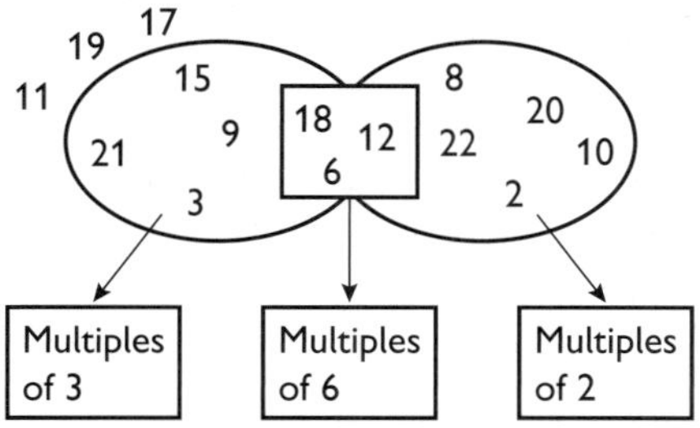


Recognise multiples of more than one number, for example multiples of both 2 and 3.

### Activities

*A quick way of adding* – Three numbers increasing by one:
3 + 4 + 5 = 3 × 4 = □ *What do you notice? Note the middle number.*

Three numbers increasing by two 3 + 5 + 7 = 3 × 5 = □
*What do you notice? Note the middle number.*

*What if ???* – We used five numbers increasing by one –
2 + 3 + 4 + 5 + 6 = 5 × 4 = □
Can the class come up with their own statements about these numbers and test them out on other numbers? (They should find that they can use this method of addition when the numbers increase by the same amount each time.)
*Working in pairs* – Children can compose their own Venn diagram around multiples of 4, 8 and 10.

### Differentiation

*Low Attainers* – Make a problem up about odd and even numbers. (*How do you know a number is odd?* – 'It does not divide by 2'.)
*High Attainers* – Can they extend their statements to include a different problem? (Does this make the overall problem more understandable?)

### Plenary

Take one of the invented problems (or make one yourself) and solve it as a class. Ask the children to suggest the best ways of tackling them.

## Lesson 5

### Introduction

Tell the children to write out the multiples of 2, 4 , 5, 10 and 100 in columns –

| Multiples of 2 | Multiples of 4 |
|---|---|
| 2 | 4 |
| 4 | 8 |
| 6 | 12 etc |
| 8 | |
| 10 | |

Ask them to investigate how you can tell if a number is divisible by 2, 4, 5, 10, and 100.

### Activities

*Rules of Divisibility* – If a number is divisible by 2 it means 2 can go into it exactly, leaving no remainder. Ask the class to chant in twos again and as they chant, write the numbers on the board up to the tenth multiple. *What do you notice about those numbers?* – They are even and all end in 0, 2, 4, 6, or 8. Repeat for 4, 5 and 10 – They should conclude that: Numbers divisible by 5, all end in 5 or 0. Numbers divisible by 10, all end in 0. Numbers divisible by 4, are all even and if you halve them they still remain even.
Look at Copymaster 40

### Differentiation

*Low Attainers* – Give them a list of random numbers and ask them to work out from what they have learned which are divisible by 2, 5 or both.
*High Attainers* – Give them a list of random numbers and ask them to sort them into numbers divisible by 2, 4, 5 and 10.

### Plenary

Give each table a number 2, 4, 5 or 10. Ask the children to stand up if you say a number which is divisible by that number. Discuss why the twos are standing up a lot. *How would we recognise a number divisible by 100?*
Go through Homework Sheet 20

# Theme 1 Multiplication and division

## Objectives

- To express a quotient as a fraction, or as a decimal when dividing a whole number by 2, 4, 5, or 10
- To divide £ and pence by 2, 4, 5 or 10
- To use the relationship between multiplication and division
- To use known facts and place value to multiply and divide mentally
- To round up or down depending on the context
- To make rough estimates of multiplications and divisions
- To extend written methods to TU × TU (long multiplication)

## Vocabulary

round up, round down

## Resources

Copymasters 41 and 42. Homework Copymaster 21. Calculators.

## Assessment

*At the end of this theme is the pupil able to:*

- Express a quotient as a fraction, or as a decimal when dividing a whole number by 2, 4, 5, 10 or when dividing £ and pence;
- Round up or down depending on the context;
- Use the relationship between × and ÷;
- Use known facts and place value to multiply and divide mentally;
- Extend written methods to TU × TU (long multiplication)?

## Mental maths starter 15

# Lesson 1

## Introduction

Write the calculation *24 ÷ 6 = 4* on the board. *Using this division and its answer I can make up other divisions and their answers:*240 ÷ 6 = 40, 240 ÷ 60 = 4. *Jot down some divisions and their answers which can be made from* 35 ÷ 7 = 5. Quickly establish that all pupils are aware of the underlying mathematics, using more examples and/or a calculator if necessary.

Write ____ ÷ ____ = *6.*Working in pairs invite pupils to jot down as many divisions as they can which have 6 as an answer, in two minutes. Collect the divisions on the board, remediating or recapping as necessary.

## Activities

Write the calculation *17 ÷ 5* on the board. Quickly establish that the answer is '3 remainder 2': *What does '3 remainder 2' tell us? Is there another way of writing the answer to 17 shared by 5?* Two different courses are possible – some pupils will benefit from exploring both of them. Guide the class to consider *17 ÷ 5* as $\frac{17}{5} = 3\frac{2}{5}$. The last step will require care as not all pupils will be able to recall previous informal work on improper fractions. Another possible/additional path is: *17 shared by 5 will be 3 each with 2 left over. In other words we still need to share 2 between 5. How do we write this division?* Ensure all pupils grasp that the correct way is 2 ÷ 5 not 5 ÷ 2.This may be an appropriate point at which to touch upon the non-commutative nature of division. *You may remember that we can write divisions as fractions so 2 ÷ 5 is the same as* $\frac{2}{5}$. *So that* (writing on board) 17 ÷ 5 = . Some low attainers may find counters to illustrate sharing out (fractions of a counter) useful.

Repeat with another example if required.

Consolidate this piece of content by asking pupils to give the answers to these, using fractions rather than remainders.

*7 ÷ 2    21 ÷ 2    11 ÷ 5    13 ÷ 4    15 ÷ 4*

extending to more difficult divisions such as *49 ÷ 4   102 ÷ 5   122 ÷ 4.*

*Which of these divisions has the greater answer: 32 ÷ 5 or 27 ÷ 4? Show some figures to support your answer.* Allow all pupils sufficient time to grapple with the problem. Establish that the two answers are $6\frac{2}{5}$ and $6\frac{3}{4}$ and that $\frac{2}{5}$ is less than $\frac{3}{4}$.

*Sometimes it may be difficult to compare fractions – changing the fractions into decimals helps. Here is a fraction and decimal line.* Give individuals (or use the OHP to show) the top half of Copymaster 41. Give practice in using the lines *e.g. what is three quarters as a decimal?* Some pupils may need extra support initially in using the fraction and decimal lines. Once pupils are secure in the fraction/decimal conversions they should be able to tackle the copymaster questions.

## Differentiation

*Low Attainers* – Complete just (initially at least) section (A).

Give calculators out and allow discussion, after which establish the method which is accessible to all. Then use a calculator and, working in pairs, investigate the remainders when you divide one or more of 5039, 2519 or 2520 by each number from 1 to 10 in turn.

*High Attainers – How can you use your calculator to find the remainder to, say, 567 ÷ 17?*

## Plenary

Go through Copymaster 41, involving pupils as much as feasible.

# Lesson 2

## Introduction

As appropriate divide the class into two groups and play a division 'circle' game using mental division *e.g. 160 ÷ 80.*

## Activities

Write the calculation *£22 ÷ 4* on the board. Invite pupils to invent a story to fit and to share it with the class.Ask pupils to estimate an answer; accept reasonable answers. *How could you work out the exact answer?* Ensure that at least following are explored: Use a calculator – (make an issue of 5.5 on a calculator meaning £5.50);

Change to ps and calculating 2200 ÷ 4 (remembering to change back to £s); Share out the £s (£5 each) then the remainder of £2 (50p each) giving a total of £5.50 each.

*What would be an estimate of the answer?* £20 ÷ 4 is £5, so a good estimate would be a bit more than £5.

*How could you check your answer?* Use the inverse operation i.e. answer × 4; some pupils may need reminding of the meaning of 'inverse'.

Repeat the above, with increased pupil participation, for: *£32.60 ÷ 4, £32.60 ÷ 5 and £32.60 ÷ 10.* For each one stress the importance of making a rough estimate to check the answer.

On the board set these 'pure' money division questions – to be done without a calculator. Insist that pupils jot down a rough estimate before attempting each one.

*£13 ÷ 5    £19 ÷ 4    £15.50 ÷ 5    £33.50 ÷ 5    £54.80 ÷ 4*

## Differentiation

*Low Attainers* – Provide extra support and initially ask questions involving whole numbers of £s.

*High Attainers* – Use problems with 'harder' numbers.

## Plenary

Collect answers and go through the set questions, ensuring that all pupils have estimated answers.

*Jen and three of her friends have been car cleaning. They collected a total of £17.70. They share this equally between themselves. How much should they each get?*

Ask the class to solve this working in pairs. Make calculators available to those who want to use them. Collect in the answers and initiate a discussion as to how best to give each person £4.475!

## Lesson 3

### Introduction

As appropriate divide the class into two groups and play a multiplication and division 'circle' game using mental calculations. *Using only the numbers 3, 5, 7, 9, 21, 45 make up as many calculations and their answers as you can in three minutes, e.g. 5 + 7 + 9 = 21* (5, 7, 9 and 21 were all used). Quickly collect in a sample of the answers for other pupils to check.

### Activities

Write $2 \times 3 = 6$ on the board. *Using this fact, jot down three other multiplications or divisions and their answers which can be made from 2, 3 and 6.* Quickly establish that these are $6 \div 3 = 2$, $6 \div 2 = 3$ and $3 \times 2 = 6$. Some pupils may need convincing that $2 \times 3$ and $3 \times 2$ equal the same. This would make a suitable point to informally touch upon commutativity showing that order does not alter the answer in addition and multiplication, but that it does in subtraction and division. Use the numbers 15, 20 and 300 to jot down four different multiplication or division statements. (Quickly establish that these are $15 \times 20 = 300$, $20 \times 15 = 300$, $300 \div 15 = 20$ and $300 \div 20 = 15$.)

Write these statements on the board:
*Doubling the numbers on each side of a division does not alter the answer. The same is true if the numbers are halved.* Invite a pupil to read out the statements and others explain what they mean by examples.
Repeat for halving one and doubling the other one of the two numbers in a multiplication. *You will need these results to help you multiply and divide mentally.* Now challenge pupils to construct some calculations of their own where this is so.

### Differentiation

*Low Attainers* – Should only attempt simple calculations.
*High Attainers* – May be given harder calculations to time themselves against the clock.

### Plenary

Go through the calculations, involving pupils and asking supplementary questions where necessary. Make up 'number stories' to fit calculations such as: *11.3 × 24 = 271.2 and 284 ÷ 8 = 35.5.* Activities such as this give valuable insight into pupils' understanding.

## Lesson 4

### Introduction

Ask the class to jot down rough answers to the following calculations, stress that the answers must not be guesses but genuine approximations using what they know. (The activity may need to be repeated to ensure that all pupils have grasped what is expected from them.)

*32 × 6 (30 × 6 = 180)* | *870 ÷ 29 (900 ÷ 30 = 30)*
*65 × 9 (70 × 9 or 60 × 10 – good discussion point)* | *37 × 7 (40 × 7 = 280)*
*126 ÷ 42 (120 ÷ 40 = 30, 120 is easier than 130)* | *399 ÷ 21 (400 ÷ 20 = 20)*
*237 ÷ 45 (240 ÷ 45 or 250 ÷ 50 – discussion needed)* | *99 × 9 (100 × 10)*
*507 ÷ 54 (500 ÷ 50)* | *94 × 6 (100 × 6)*

Discuss the answers, allowing pupils to put their cases. Stress than simply rounding up or down may not always be the answer – the idea is to end up with a simple calculation close to the original. Some pupils may need reminding of the meaning of 'rounding up' and 'rounding down'.

### Activities

Work through Copymaster 42 as a class. The focus is on rounding and choice of operation so calculators may be made available. Ensure as much pupil participation as possible. If there are some insecure readers then ensure that reading aloud is done by more secure readers.
Divide the class into groups of two or three pupils and ask each group to make up at least two problems involving choosing whether to round up or round down. These may then be shared with the whole class.

### Differentiation

By outcome. *Low Attainers* may need significantly more help.

### Plenary

Review the progress made over the lesson.
A quick 'no frills' tables 'test' involving multiplication and divisions up to $10 \times 10$.
Invite pupils to share their deductive processes when solving puzzles to find the missing operation, such as 319 □ 272 = 47, 18 □ 10 = 1.8, 228 □ 38 = 6. Pupils could be invited to make up their own puzzles.

## Lesson 5

### Introduction

*The order in which we do a multiplication does not matter* (write $3 \times 4 = 12$, $4 \times 3 = 12$).
*In the same way* (write $2 \times 3 \times 4$, $3 \times 2 \times 4$ and $4 \times 3 \times 2$) *all equal 24.*
*It sometimes helps to use brackets to see what we are doing .*
$(2 \times 3) \times 4 = 6 \times 4 = 24$ $\quad 2 \times (3 \times 4) = 2 \times 12 = 24$.
*The order in which we do a multiplication can make a calculation easier.*
$2 \times 17 \times 5 = 2 \times 5 \times 17 = (2 \times 5) \times 17 = 10 \times 17 = 170$
*Splitting up a number into its factors can also help.* (Chance to recap on factors.)
$12 \times 20 = 12 \times (2 \times 10) = (12 \times 2) \times 10 = 240$
Invite pupils up to the board to explain to the rest of the class how to calculate, for example,
*12 × 20 30 × 40 40 × 60 35 × 20 90 × 90 2 × 3 × 4 × 5 etc.*
Confirm mastery by a quick fire mental activity: jot down answers to all the possible products involving 3, 20, 30 and 300 (i.e. $3 \times 20 = 60$, $3 \times 20 \times 30 = 1800$ etc.). Remediate or extend where necessary.

### Activities

Before the lesson, draw a square of 306 triangles on the board. *What calculation will give you the total number of triangles here?* Establish that it is $17 \times 18$. *Is there any way, using the diagram, of making the multiplication simpler?* Guide the class into considering splitting up the grid into four simpler multiplications (using brackets to make this clearer) $(10 \times 10) + (10 \times 8) + (10 \times 7) + (8 \times 7)$. Allow pupils to draw on the board to make this clearer – should other valid methods arise give them due consideration. Rather than draw a grid of spots or triangles each time, it is easier to draw a grid, like this one.

$17 \times 18$
$\approx 20 \times 20 = 400$

| × | 10 | 8 |
|---|---|---|
| 10 | 100 | 80 |
| 7 | 70 | 56 |

180
+ 126
306

Show the working step by step and stress the importance of the approximation as a check.
It may be necessary to recap on the symbol ≈ and to discuss why $20 \times 20$ is a reasonable approximation. Work through another example if necessary. Ask pupils to talk through how they solve puzzles involving finding missing digits, such as

□2 × 4 = 32□ $\quad$ 1□ × □2 = 35□
*1□ × □7 = 855* $\quad$ □□ × 7 = 4□5

### Differentiation

*Low Attainers* – By outcome.
*High Attainers* – By outcome.

### Plenary

Recap the progress over the lesson. Encourage pupil participation.

# Theme 2 Money problems

## Objectives
- To use all four operations to solve money or 'real life' problems
- To use all four operations to solve money or 'real life' problems, including percentages
- To choose and use appropriate arithmetic and calculation methods
- To choose and use appropriate arithmetic and calculation methods; explain working and calculation methods

## Vocabulary
Hong Kong dollar, exchange rate

## Resources
Copymasters 43 and 44, Homework Copymaster 22. Money cards – different amounts from 5p to £2.50 in multiples of 5p. Multiple copies of the same shopping catalogue e.g. *Argos, Index.* Photocopies of itemised supermarket receipts.

## Assessment
*At the end of this theme is the pupil able to:*
- Use all four operations to solve money or 'real life' problems, including percentages;
- Choose appropriate operations/calculations methods;
- Explain working?

**Mental maths starter 16**

---

## Lesson 1

### Introduction
*Amy has a 2p coin, a 5p coin, a 10p coin and a £1 coin. What different sums of money could she make by taking just two of these coins?* (The lowest attainers could use 'real' coins.) Collect answers on the board. Be prepared to remediate the odd place value error. Encourage pupils to explain their approaches, systematic or not. Guide the class into appreciating the virtue of a systematic approach.

### Activities
Give each pair of pupils a copy of the same shopping catalogue. Depending on the group's level of attainment spend a little time getting used to the catalogue, for example finding and using the index, finding the correct page in the fewest tries (good informal practice in trial and improvement and 'number sense'). A quick question and answers session will show how competent pupils are at using the catalogues and provide useful practice: *On what page are the calculators? On what page do the rings start? How many pages have rings on? Which is the cheapest hairdryer?* Calculators may be useful for the next two activities. *Imagine that you have £50 to spend on anything you want! Make a list of what you might buy from the catalogue. How much change will you have? Your school has collected £200 for the local children's hospital. Use the catalogue to make a list of things the school would be able to buy.*

### Differentiation
*Low Attainers* – Reduce the sums of money to 'spend' and perhaps reduce extent of choice.
*High Attainers* – For the introduction extend to 3 coins at a time.

### Plenary
*When you go shopping it's a good idea to keep a rough total of how much you've spent. Turn to page XX in the catalogue. If you were silly enough to buy all the items on the page, about how much would it cost?* Give pupils an opportunity to discuss this amount amongst themselves. Then discuss the possible strategies with the whole class. Ensure that at least the following are considered 'above 50p round up to next £, otherwise round down … always round up to be on the safe side.'

---

## Lesson 2

### Introduction
An activity for the whole class. Cut out and shuffle the set of money cards you have made. Show a single card one at a time to the class (keep these cards in their correct order). Pupils keep a running total of the money and decide for themselves when this total is closest to £5 but not over £5 and 'stick'. Pupils jot down the card when they 'stuck'. After all have 'stuck' collect the answers and discuss their strategies, then give the 'right' answer. Play the game several times, adjusting the speed of showing cards to best suit the attainment level of the group.

### Activities
Recap on simple percentage work with this simple question and answer activity, remediating when problems become apparent: *What is 50% as a fraction? What is 50% of £4? What is a quarter as a percentage? What is a quarter of £8? What is 25% of £8?* Give pupils, working in pairs, Copymaster 43 Section A. (Some higher attainers attempting Section B may need some help over the meaning of 'profit'.)

### Differentiation
*Low Attainers* – These pupils should do 1–3 on Copymaster 43.
*High Attainers* – Do numbers 4, 5, 6 and Section B.

### Plenary
Go through the appropriate parts of Copymaster 43, challenging the pupils to describe how they worked out their answers and how they should have checked them.

## Lesson 3

### Introduction
On the board or OHP show pupils this table.

| coin | 1p | 2p | 5p | 10p | 20p | 50p | £1 | £2 |
|---|---|---|---|---|---|---|---|---|
| weight (g) | 3.56 | 7.12 | 3.25 | 6.5 | 5 | 8 | 9.5 | 12 |

Pupils jot down their answers and working to questions such as these:
*Which coin weighs almost 10 g? How much would two £2 coins weigh? Some 20p coins weigh 40 g. How much money are they worth? How much will £5 worth of 50p coins weigh? Which is the lightest/heaviest coin? Which weighs more: £5 worth of 20p coins or £10 worth of 50p pieces?*
Challenges: *What would a kilogram of 20p coins be worth? Roughly, what would a kilogram of £1 coins be worth?*
On completion ask pupils to 'talk through' their answers. Pupils could be invited to make up their own problems. If appropriate, questions could be opened out to involve measures to a greater extent e.g.: *If you were weighed in … coins. How much would this be?*

### Activities
Give out Copymaster 44 Part 1. Pupils work through in pairs, calculators freely available if needed. Remediate as and when needed, but expect lower attainers to experience difficulties with place value and money.

### Differentiation
*Low Attainers* – Pupils will need to be asked about their answers.
*High Attainers* – Should not necessarily need the help of a calculator.

### Plenary
Hand out the till receipts, with the totals erased. Pupils work in pairs: one estimates, the other uses a calculator. How close were they? Repeat for several different receipts. In a plenary session discuss the methods of estimation employed by pupils.

## Lesson 4

### Introduction
Write this on the board:

*Exchange rates for £1 are 11 Hong Kong dollars*
*1.5 US dollars*
*1.6 Euros*

By questions and answers determine and remediate any misconceptions regarding exchange rates and foreign currency. (The idea of buying money can be very confusing to some pupils.)
Extend to questions of the type: *A CD costs 22 dollars in Hong Kong. How much is this in pounds? A CD cost £4 in England. What is this in Hong Kong dollars? Dina is going on holiday to Germany. She has saved up £10. How could she work out how many Euros this is worth?* Ensure pupils have a grasp of the idea of changing money.

### Activities
On the board, write some money calculations with numbers missing, e.g.

```
  £
  2.63
+ 1.5
  4. 7
```

Tell pupils to work them out in pairs and that they may have to explain how they arrived at their answers. Challenge pupils to explain their methods in, where realistic, correct mathematical language.

### Differentiation
*Low Attainers* – By outcome.
*High Attainers* – By outcome.

### Plenary
Write some calculations involving money on the board:
*£2.05 + 50p + £9 + 20p* (*approx. £2 + £9 + £1 = £12 – stress the usefulness of regrouping as a strategy*)
*47p + 15p + £1.40* (*approx. £2*)
Invite pupils to quickly estimate a sensible answer, stressing that the activity is about estimating not getting THE answer. Collect in the estimates and discuss how they were arrived at. If appropriate the till roll exercise of the previous lesson could be repeated.

## Lesson 5

### Introduction
Quick no-frills percentage and fraction questions such as:
*50% of £12 half of 24 50% of £7 a quarter of 12 half of 101 three quarters of £8 a quarter of £5*
Discuss pupils' methods with the group.
As a challenge: 10% of £30.

### Activities
Give pupils, working individually, Copymaster 44 Part 2 – stress the need to check calculations and to give the correct units in the answers. Just a number without £ or p is not sufficient.

### Differentiation
*Low Attainers* – Should complete, with help, the first part, but may need support for this.
*High Attainers* – Should complete all of Copymaster 44 Part 2.

### Plenary
Collect answers and discuss the whole of Copymaster 44. Discuss which calculations merit using a calculator and the methods used for the others, and how the answers may be checked.

# Theme 3 Fractions, decimals and percentages

## Objectives
- To figure out simple percentages of quantities, including money
- To find percentages using halving and quartering
- To recognize equivalencies between percentages, fractions and decimals

## Vocabulary
fraction, decimal, percentage, equivalent, per cent, %, halve, quarter.

## Resources
Place value grids. Copymasters 45 and 46. Homework Copymaster 23.

## Assessment
*At the end of this theme is the pupil able to:*
- Move between equivalent fractions, decimals and percentages;
- Without a calculator find answers to questions like 25% of £200 or 30% of 100 g;
- Answer $\frac{1}{4}$ of 240 and $\frac{1}{2}$ of 500 etc?

## Mental maths starter 17

---

# Lesson 1

## Introduction
Explain and revise that fractions can be changed into decimal form. A place value grid will help introduce this part of the theme. Give the children plenty of practice at putting fractions such as $3\frac{1}{2}$, $4\frac{1}{4}$, $5\frac{1}{10}$ and $3\frac{1}{100}$ on the grid. Also practise reversing the process.

## Activities
Write $\frac{34}{100}$ on the board. Divide 34 by 100 and write 0.34 also on the board. Ask the children to use this information to convert other fractions of 100 without using the calculator. The children then pick a 2-digit number card, write the number over 100 in fraction form, then write the decimal equivalent. They repeat to make ten decimals, then swap with a partner to convert back to fractions.

## Differentiation
*Low Attainers* – Convert tenths to decimals and vice versa initially.
*High Attainers* – Work with help on writing the fractions of 100 in their simplest form.

## Plenary
Key 70 divided by 100 into the calculator. Discuss what it shows ie. 0.7.
*Is this correct?* Discuss the fact that $0.7 = \frac{7}{10} = \frac{70}{100}$.
Repeat for other examples.

---

# Lesson 2

## Introduction
Ask lots of questions relating to fractions of different amounts. *E.g. $\frac{1}{4}$ of 16, $\frac{1}{3}$ of 15, $\frac{1}{2}$ of 40.*
Also $\frac{1}{3}$ of £30 or $\frac{1}{4}$ of £24 or $\frac{1}{2}$ of 100 g or $\frac{1}{5}$ of 50 kilograms.
Discuss what you actually do to get the answer.

## Activities
Make sure the children understand that to find a fraction of any amount you must divide by the denominator of the fraction, so dividing that amount into so many equal parts. *E.g. $\frac{1}{4}$ of 28 = 28 divided by 4 = 7.*
If you have to find a multiple fraction of an amount then divide by the denominator and multiply by the numerator. *E.g. $\frac{2}{3}$ of 18 = 18 divided by 3 then times by 2 = 12.*
Look at Copymaster 45.

## Differentiation
*Low Attainer* – Find halves, quarters and thirds of small amounts.
*High Attainer* – Find more complicated fractions of larger amounts.

## Plenary
Offer questions like:
*If I know the answer to a fraction question is 5, what could the question be? If I know the answer to a fraction question is 10 what could the question be?* Ask the children to make up their own similar questions.

## Lesson 3

### Introduction

*Percentages, fractions and decimals are ways of expressing the same number.* Ask the children to share examples of where they have seen percentages before in everyday life. Remind the children that the % sign is read as 'percent.' This means 'out of 100.'
Use a 100 grid with some squares shaded in that represent a percentage. If necessary repeat this for other percentages.

### Activities

Draw three number lines on the board:

| | | | | | | | | | | | | |
|---|---|---|---|---|---|---|---|---|---|---|---|---|
| 0 | 0.1 | 0.2 | 0.3 | 0.4 | 0.5 | 0.6 | 0.7 | 0.8 | 0.9 | 1.0 | 1.1 | 1.2 |
| 0 | $\frac{1}{10}$ | $\frac{2}{10}$ | $\frac{3}{10}$ | $\frac{4}{10}$ | $\frac{5}{10}$ | $\frac{6}{10}$ | $\frac{7}{10}$ | $\frac{8}{10}$ | $\frac{9}{10}$ | 1.0 | $1\frac{1}{10}$ | $1\frac{2}{10}$ |
| 0 | 10% | 20% | 30% | 40% | 50% | 60% | 70% | 80% | 90% | 100% | 110% | 120% |

Decide how they can be used for finding equivalent fractions, decimals, and percentages. Invite a pair to explain what they decided. (If no one suggests it, use a ruler or a straight edge to show how 0.1, $\frac{1}{10}$ and 10%, align vertically and are equivalent numbers.) Explain that 10% means 10 parts in a hundred, which is written as $\frac{10}{100} = \frac{1}{10} = 0.1$. Work through Copymaster 46.

### Differentiation

*Low Attainers* – Repeat questions such as $0.4 = \frac{4}{10} = 40\%$, $0.7 = \frac{7}{10} = 70\%$.
*High Attainers* – Ask questions about 25% equivalent to ? equivalent to ? Also 50% and 75%?

### Plenary

Draw this 'triangle trio' on the board.

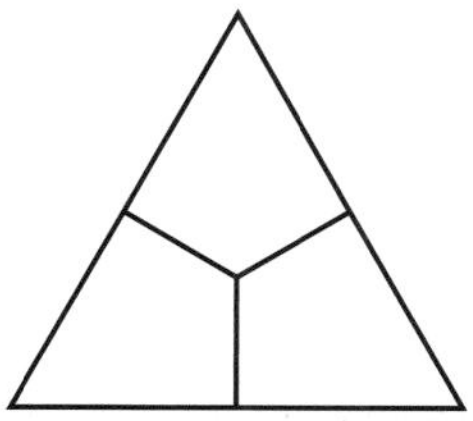

Write one tenth in the top section. Fill the other sections with equivalent numbers i.e. 10% and 0.1. Repeat for other triangle trios.

## Lesson 4

### Introduction

Write on the board these fractions: $\frac{4}{5}, \frac{5}{10}, \frac{3}{4}, \frac{2}{5}, \frac{9}{100}$. Then these quantities: £200, 5000 km, 700 g, 4000 kg. Underneath write a template for the children's calculations:

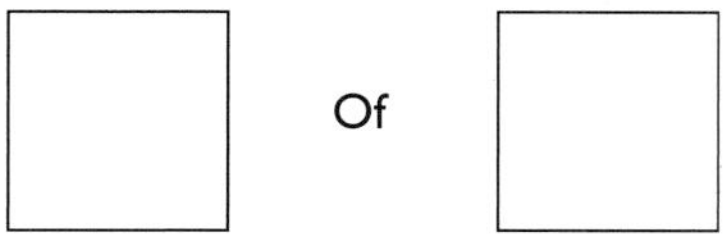


Ask one child to choose a fraction for the first box and another child to choose a quantity for the second box. *E.g.* $\frac{4}{5}$ *of 4000 kg*. Let the children work out the calculation. Remind them to divide by the denominator and times by the numerator. *E.g. 4000 divided by 5 and times by 4 = 800 × 4 = 3200 kg*. Repeat for other quantities.

### Activities

On the board write this calculation involving percentages 20% of £400. Show the children how to work out the answer, explaining that the method is similar to the one they have used when calculating a fraction of a quantity. 10% is equivalent to 1\10, so 10% of £400 is £40, so 20% of £400 is £40 × 2, which equals £80.
*Working in pairs* – Practise further calculations including 10% of 5 kg which should be broken down into 5 kg = 5000 g, so it becomes 10% of 5000 g = 500 g.

### Differentiation

*Low Attainers* – They could draw a diagram splitting the amount of money into ten parts (10%) and then collecting together the required number of 10%'s, or parts of 10%.
*High Attainers* – Looking at an itemised list of prices, they could work out how much cheaper each item becomes if the price is reduced by 35%.

### Plenary

Work out these percentages of £500 – 10%, 20%, 25%, 90%, 75%, with the whole class.

## Lesson 5

### Introduction

*We are going to find percentages using halving and quartering.*
Working out 75% of quantities is sometimes made easier by finding first 50% by halving, then 25% by halving again. The two amounts, the 50% and the 25% can be added to give 75%. Work through one example: 75% of 1000 g = 50% × 1000 g = 500 g + $\frac{1}{2}$ of 500 g = 250 g = 750 g

### Activities

Write these quantities on the board :

| | |
|---|---|
| £300 | £100 |
| 70 km | 150 km |
| 140 g | 200 g |

Ask the children to come out to the board to show how to find 75% of each amount by halving and quartering. Then progress to asking questions such as
*If 75% of £100 is £75 what is 25% of £100 (£25).*
*If an item normally costs £100 but in the sale it is reduced by 25%, how much will it cost?*
*If an item cost £50 in a sale and normally costs £200. How many percent was it reduced by?*

### Differentiation

*Low Attainers* – Find 25%, 50%, 75% of multiples of £100.
*High Attainers* – Find 75% of 1.5 kg in grams or 75% of 10 metres in centimetres.

### Plenary

Reiterate that to find a percentage of a quantity we change the percentage to an equivalent fraction. Remind the children to write the units at each step. Go through a final few examples.
Go through Homework Sheet 23.

# Theme 4 Ratio and proportion

## Objectives
- To discuss the language of 'for every' and 'in every'
- To solve simple ratio problems
- To solve simple proportion problems

## Vocabulary
for every, in every, equivalent, ratio, proportion

## Resources
Interlocking coloured cubes. Copymasters 47 and 48. Homework Copymaster 24.

## Assessment
*At the end of this theme is the pupil able to:*
- Discuss statements such as 'there is 1 boy for every 2 girls at the disco' and solve related problems?

**Mental maths starter 18**

## Lesson 1

### Introduction
The difference in the language used to express proportion (in every) and ratio (for every) is subtle, and children need constant practice of both concepts to consolidate their knowledge.
Choose two girls and four boys to stand at the front of the class in two groups, each of one girl and two boys. Ask the class to suggest how we could use a diagram to represent the information, and draw it on the board.

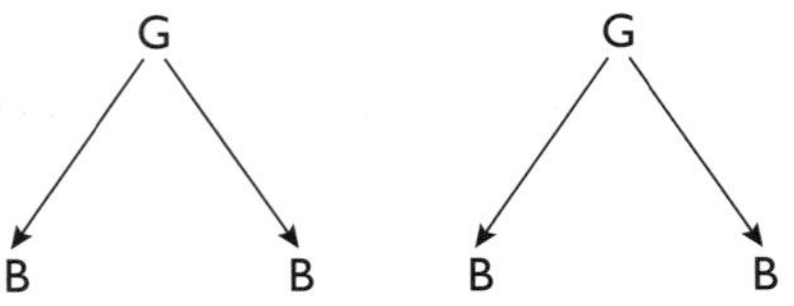


### Activities
Ask the question: *What is the ratio of girls to boys?* (2 girls for every 4 boys or 1 girl for every 2 boys).
*What is the proportion of girls to children?* (2 girls in every 6 children or 1 girl in every 3 children). List both statements under the headings:

RATIO STATEMENTS and PROPORTION STATEMENTS.

*Working in pairs* – Children think of another way of describing the diagram, either as a ratio or a proportion. Invite the pairs in turn to tell you their statement and how it relates to the diagram. Write it on the board and discuss with the class whether the statement is correct and whether it is a ratio or proportion statement. When everyone agrees write it under the appropriate heading.

### Differentiation
*Low Attainers* – They could use black and white cubes to represent each person.
*High Attainers – Do all the statements remain true if you add more groups of boys and girls to the diagram?*

### Plenary
Draw more boys and girls in the diagram to show that all of the statements remain true if more groups of 1 boy and 2 girls join those at the front.

## Lesson 2

### Introduction
*We can use multiplication and division facts and strategies to solve ratio problems.*
Pose this problem:
*I am thinking of a group of children who will come to the front. The ratio will be 1 boy for every 4 girls. How many boys and girls could there be in the group?*
*If 12 girls come to the front, how many boys will come to the front?* (3 boys) *How do you know? Did you multiply or divide?*

### Activities
Make a table of children's answers in a pattern, and talk about the pairs of numbers stressing that:
- The ratio is 1 for every 4
- The number of boys is always $\frac{1}{4}$ of the number of girls
- The number of girls is always four times the number of boys

| Table | 1 boy for every four girls | |
|---|---|---|
| | Boys | Girls |
| | 1 | 4 |
| | 2 | 8 |
| | 3 | 12 |

Use Copymaster 47 to continue.

### Differentiation
*Low Attainers – If 4 boys come to the front, how many girls will come to the front?*
*High Attainers – If 25 children come to the front, how many are boys? How many are girls?* (5 boys, 20 girls)

### Plenary
Emphasise how it is possible to find other ways of saying a ratio or a proportion by multiplication or division. Repeat for other simple ratios. Stress that *ratio* compares two separate quantities and *proportion* compares one part of a quantity with the whole quantity.

## Lesson 3

### Introduction
Write this statement on the board:
'Sally has 1 sweet for every 2 that Mike has.'
Ask children about their understanding of this statement:
- Sally has half as many sweets as Mike
- Mike has twice as many sweets as Sally
- Sally has one third of the total number of sweets and Mike has two thirds.

### Activities
*Part 1*
Ask questions such as: *If Sally has 3 sweets, Mike has ? sweets? If Mike has 40 sweets, Sally has ? sweets? If Sally has 12 sweets Mike has ? Etc.*

*Part 2*
If 1 in every 4 bulbs doesn't flower, and 5 of my bulbs don't flower, how many bulbs did I buy.
Build up the solution step by step:
*What do I know? Proportion* is 1 in every 4.
*What do I want to find out? How many bulbs were bought if 5 didn't flower?*
*What do I do?* Change the proportion sentence to talk about 5 bulbs instead of 1 by multiplying by 5.
For 5 bulbs not to flower I would have needed to buy:
$5 \times 4$ bulbs $= 20$ bulbs
Ask the class to look at Copymaster 48

### Differentiation
*Low Attainers* – Examine *If 1 in every 2 bulbs doesn't flower, and 5 of mine don't flower, how many bulbs did I buy?*
*High Attainers – If one in every 4 doesn't flower, how many bulbs are there for every 6 that don't flower?*

### Plenary
Work through some more examples as a class, explaining what is happening and, where necessary, modelling the situation with counters or cubes.

## Lesson 4

### Introduction
Ask two boys and a girl to come to the front. *What is the ratio of boys to girls?* Answer 2:1. Write it on the board. Add a girl to the group.
*If I want the ratio to be the same as before, how many boys do I need to add?* Answer another 2 boys to make the ratio 4 : 2. Continue with different groupings and ratios.

### Activities
*Ratios in the room* – Say that in this lesson, you will be looking at different ratios in the classroom. For example: The ratio of adults to children is 1 to 30. The number of chairs to tables in that group of tables is 6 to 3 or 2 to 1. Ask someone to explain what that means. (For every single table there are two chairs.) Point to other groups of tables. *If I add another table what would the ratio be then?* Continue with other examples.

### Differentiation
*Low Attainers* – Work with help, using interlocking cubes to show groupings.
*High Attainers* – Write some ratios to do with their group or the class, using their own criteria.

### Plenary
Hold up a tower of interlocking cubes, 2 red and 3 yellow. *What is the ratio of red to yellow?* (2:3). *What fraction of the tower is red?* Explain that there are 5 equal parts in the tower, and 2 out of the 5 are red;Therefore $\frac{2}{5}$ of the tower is red.

## Lesson 5

### Introduction
*Ratio Race* – Roll two dice to generate ratios *e.g. 1 : 5*. Groups hold up a tower of interlocking cubes with the correct ratio of colours. Discuss different responses, *e.g. why some groups might hold up 1 : 3 to show 2 : 6.*

### Activities
*Ratios as Fractions:* Look at different ratios of cubes, *e.g. red : yellow 2:1, green : blue 1 : 3*. Build the towers. *What proportion of this tower is red? What fraction of the tower is green?* Go straight from a ratio to a proportion, *e.g. Blue : yellow is 3 : 5*. There are 8 parts in the whole, 3 are blue, so $\frac{3}{8}$ is blue.
*Working in pairs* – The children roll a 6-sided dice twice to generate a ratio, then write it in fraction form.

### Differentiation
*Low Attainers* – Always use interlocking cubes to help create an image of the ratio/proportion.
*High Attainers* – Use a 10-sided dice to generate ratios.

### Plenary
Use cubes to convert fractions to ratios, *e.g.* $\frac{2}{3}$ *are green*. There are 3 parts in total, so 2 are green and the ratio is 2 : 1. Continue with other examples. Go through Homework Sheet 24.

# Theme 5 Handling data

## Objectives

- To solve a problem by representing and interpreting data in bar line charts
- To find the mode and range of a set of data collected
- To interpret and draw line graphs and discuss cases where intermediate points may have no meaning and cases where points may be joined to show a trend
- To use a computer to compare different representations of the same data

## Vocabulary

mode, range, maximum, minimum, recognise the 'story' behind a graph, bar chart, line bar chart, line graph, line chart

## Resources

Copymasters 49 and 50, Homework Copymaster 25. One 6-sided die per child. Some dice made from different solids *e.g. 'Cliki'*. Matchboxes.

## Assessment

*At the end of this theme is the pupil able to:*

- Solve a problem by representing and interpreting data in bar line charts: axis in 2s, 5s, 10s, 20s, 100s;
- Discuss cases where intermediate points have no meaning and cases where points may be joined to show trend;
- Find the mode and calculate the range of a set of data;
- Use a computer to compare different presentations of the same data?

## Mental maths starter 19

# Lesson 1

## Introduction

Give each pupil a 'normal' 6-sided die. Ask them to look for anything interesting about it. Collect these observations on the board, ensuring that pupils of all attainment levels contribute. Ensure that at least the following are noted: numbers on opposite faces add to 7, the dice has 6 faces and 8 vertices, edges are equal in length, there are 12 edges. Some of the vocabulary may need revising. *What is the total of the six numbers on a dice? What's the rule for finding the number on an opposite face? Can you see the faces marked 1, 2 and 3 at the same time? Can you see the faces marked 6, 5 and 3 at the same time? When you throw a dice is one number more likely to come up than any other?* Allow sufficient discussion to establish that the answer is no.

## Activities

Have sufficient match boxes or similar small cuboids for each pair to have a cuboid like this die (the numbers may be fixed on using sellotape).

Invite each pair to make a tally of how many times each number comes up when the die is thrown.

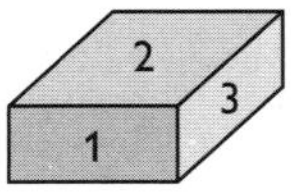


When each pair has generated about 30 results collect them all on the board.

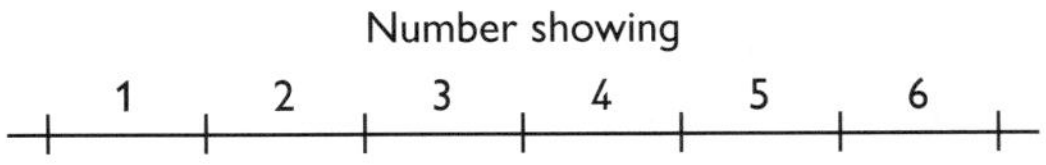


Establish that although there is some variation, the results are sensibly similar. Draw pupils' attention to the advantages (and legitimacy) of combining the results. Assign groups columns to add up – a chance to discuss methods of checking. Write the grand totals on the board. *Would your cuboid make a fair dice? Explain why.* Give each pair some graph paper and invite them to show the cuboid results in a bar line graph. Provide minimum help – let the pupils make their own decisions about scale – but provide support where pupils are really struggling. When pairs have finished, comment on their completed chart, correcting any errors. Make reference to the mode being the most frequently occurring result.

## Differentiation

*Low Attainers* – Use ordinary dice.
*High Attainers* – Use dice made from different solids.

## Plenary

Quickly share with the class some of the common errors observed. Recap the essential features of any chart – clear labels, sensible scale etc.

# Lesson 2

## Introduction

Invite pupils (or employ 'guided choice') to select one of these problems to solve. Remind pupils that they may need to talk the class through their solution and their thinking.

- *Josh buys an orange drink. It costs him 85p. He pays with a £2 coin. He receives 6 coins for his change. What coins could they be?*
- *A farmer grows 450 kg of pears. He sells them in 3 kg and 2 kg bags. He uses the same number of 3 kg bags as 2 kg bags. How many bags does he use in all?*
- *Three ducks and two ducklings weigh 11 kg. Two ducks and two ducklings weigh 8 kg. All the ducks weigh the same. All the ducklings weigh the same. How much does a duckling weigh?*
- *A 800 seat multi-screen cinema has three screens. There are 270 seats in Screen 1, and 150 more seats in Screen 2 than in Screen 3. How many seats are there in Screen 2?*
- Invite pupils to share their thinking with the class. Ensure that even partial solutions are received positively.

## Activities

*Here is the number of goals scored by a team in its last ten games.*
Write: 1 3 2 4 3 4 2 0 1 2
*What is the mode number of goals scored by the team?* Collect in answers and establish that the answer is 2. Challenge pupils as to how they found the most common (mode) score. *Another interesting way to describe a set of data is the range. This is the difference between the highest value and lowest value. What was the maximum number of goals scored?* Quickly establish it is 4. *What was the minimum number of goals scored?* Quickly establish it is 0. *So what is the range?* Quickly establish it is 4 – 0 which is 4. Repeat with this set of data: *1 3 1 2 5 1 9 3 5 2* (mode 2, range 8). As a challenge invite pupils to jot down a group of ten results which have a mode of 4 goals and a range of 3 goals. Continue until all pupils are secure with 'mode' and 'range'. Quickly check these, taking the opportunity to use 'maximum value' and 'minimum value'. Invite the pupils, working in pairs, to collect (and record), from ten pupils in the class, data about: the total number of children in their families, shoe sizes, number of pets. If a previous Sunday's or Monday's newspaper is available, home, away or total goals scored in the weekend's football matches might appeal to some pupils as a suitable source of data. From their data each pair should find the mode and range. Pupils needs to keep their data for Lesson 5.

## Differentiation

*Low Attainers* – Will need a directed choice and some support to finish the task.
*High Attainers* – Should be encouraged to compare the mode and range from two sets of data.

## Plenary

Discuss pupils' results: *Did sets of the same type of data have the same mode and range? Would plotting the results in a bar line chart have helped? Did you use a tally to help collect in the original results? Does putting the results in order make things easier?*

## Lesson 3

### Introduction

Draw this on the board: 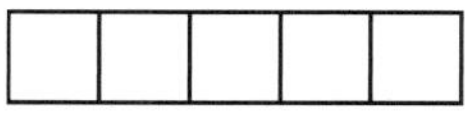

*Using squared paper how many different arrangements can you make by shading in two squares? Here are two:*

(There are a total of 10.) *What about when three squares are shaded?* (There are 10 again – the patterns are just the complement of previous.) Quickly discuss pupils' strategies, if any, making a point of the advantages of being systematic. The problem may be extended to six squares with two squares shaded (giving 15 possibilities).

### Activities

Give out or use an OHP of Copymaster 49. Explain to the pupils the purpose of the broken scale on the temperature axis. With the whole class draw attention to the main features for example: *What is the temperature at 10 am/2 pm? What is the temperature at noon?* (To involve a half division.) *What do you estimate the temperature to have been at 9 am/3 pm?* (Ensure all understand what is involved here.)
*We can make clear what is happening over the whole day by joining up the points in order.* Invite pupil(s) to do this either on their paper or on the OHT. *We call this chart a line graph or chart. We can use the lines to estimate the temperature at times in between the ones we know.* Invite pupils to fill in the temperatures on the second graph – preferably in turns on the OHT – then join up the points to form a line graph. Use the line graph as a source of similar questions as for the first graph.

### Differentiation

*Low Attainers* – Will need support and may only cover the first part of the copymaster.
*High Attainers* – May be ready to plot their own line graphs involving temperatures over several days using information already collected from newspapers (or teletext).

### Plenary

Recap on the lesson content. Discuss with the class the difficulties of estimating, for example, the temperature at 6 pm by finding the temperature between that at midnight and midday. A sketch graph on the board will help. Depending on the attainment level of the group ask for further examples.

## Lesson 4

### Introduction

Give the class sufficient time to answer some 'extended' mental questions such as: *The sum of two numbers is 20; their product is 36. What are the numbers? Write down a number which is a multiple of 3 and a factor of 48. Write down two divisions that have a quotient of three. The sum of two numbers is 17; their difference is 11. What are the numbers? The product of two numbers is 54; their difference is 3. What are the numbers?* Give answers to the class, but involve pupils – make the point that in questions like these it is a very good idea to check answers by feeding them back into the original question.

### Activities

Make OHTs or copies of Copymaster 50. Ensure that the general nature of the axes, i.e. not marked in specific units, is understood. Discuss what is happening at the lettered points or line segments. Invite pupils to pose questions of their own to the class. However, always insist on reasons to support answers.

### Differentiation

*Low Attainers* – Increase the number of questions for each graph, and so by limiting the scenarios increase understanding of a few cases.
*High Attainers* – Invite these pupils to make up a story and draw the appropriate graph for themselves.

### Plenary

Review the main points of the lesson.

## Lesson 5

### Introduction

Depending on the number of computers available it may be useful if some pupils worked on paper whilst others were working at the computer(s). Depending on circumstances discuss answers with small groups.

### Activities

On the database software available, invite pupils to display their data from Lesson 2 using the software. Alternatively pre-prepared data (sometimes provided in the software package) may be used. To avoid drifting make it clear that pupils will need to report back to the class during the plenary session.

### Differentiation

*Low Attainers* – May need a high degree of support.
*High Attainers* – May use their own data to input and view in different chart forms.

### Plenary

Initiate a general discussion about anything of interest pupils discovered or observed. Emphasise that charts and graphs are meant to make things easier rather than complicate them: unless a graph tells a story clearly, it makes no difference how 'fancy' it looks.

# Theme 6 Reflections and symmetry

## Objectives

- To draw and recognise mirror images
- To recognise reflection symmetry in regular polygons, and know that in the case of regular polygons the number of lines of symmetry is equal to the number of sides
- To test for lines of symmetry using folding or a mirror
- To recognise and identify lines of symmetry in polygons
- To complete symmetrical patterns with two lines of symmetry using a square grid
- To complete symmetrical patterns with a line of symmetry not necessarily parallel or at right angles to the axis of the pattern
- To identify lines of symmetry in patterns and shapes
- To recognise where a shape will be after a translation or reflection
- To identify lines of symmetry

## Vocabulary

mirror image, mirror line, reflection, symmetry, line of symmetry, symmetrical, regular polygon, translation

## Resources

Class set of mirrors, scissors, OHT with grid on it, including thick vertical and horizontal lines to indicate lines of symmetry, counters, square spotty or squared paper, thin cardboard, squared and triangular dotty paper. Copymasters 51 and 52. Homework Copymaster 26. A square, pentagon, triangle, octagon, and hexagon drawn on a page and photocopied. A large square made from display backing paper.

## Assessment

*At the end of this theme is the pupil able to:*

- Recognise reflective symmetry in regular polygons;
- Complete symmetrical patterns with two lines of symmetry at right angles;
- Reflect shapes in a mirror parallel to one side;
- Recognise where a shape will be after translation;
- Make and investigate a general statement about shapes?

## Mental maths starter 20

## Lesson 1

### Introduction

Quickly revise what a net is. Draw these nets on the board/OHT:

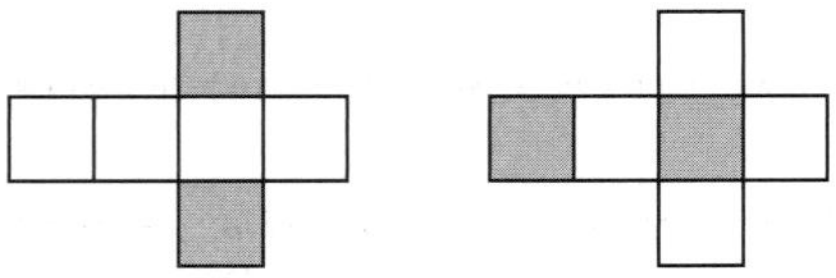

*When folded up to make a cube the shaded faces will be opposite each other.* Ensure that pupils understand the situation – in a few instances an actual demonstration may be needed. *Draw some other nets where this is also true.* Set a target time for this of five minutes. Invite pupils to sketch nets on the OHP – resolve any problems. As a quick fire activity ask pupils to write down the names of polygons that have four/six/five/three/eight/seven sides. Quickly check and give the correct answers and move on.

### Activities

Give out the mirrors and Copymaster 51. The object of this activity is to give pupils the opportunity to experiment with mirror images and to use the terms 'mirror image' and 'mirror line'. Provide help when necessary.

### Differentiation

*Low Attainers* – Will need support in order to complete up to [3] on Copymaster 51.
*High Attainers* – Will be challenged to complete [4] on Copymaster 51.

### Plenary

Give some higher attainers the opportunity to explain how they went about [4]. Finish the lesson with a series of drawings on squared paper, with mirror lines, inviting pupils to draw in the mirror image. Then invite the class to check using their squared paper and mirrors. Here are some suitable shapes – take the opportunity to use the appropriate vocabulary.

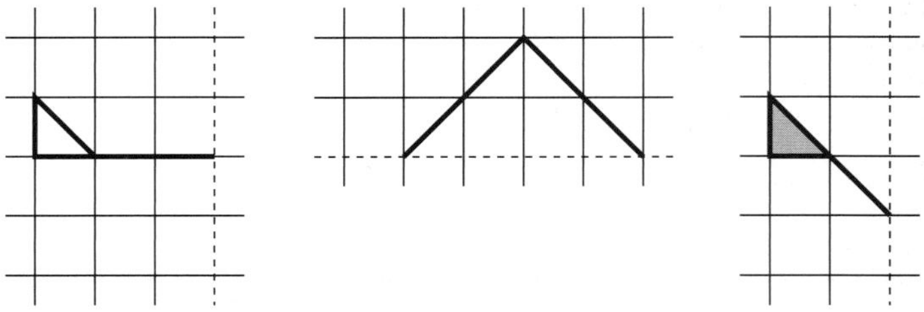

## Lesson 2

### Introduction

Write these numbers on the board or OHP:
*37 102   3725   3752   3720   37 021   3750   7570*
Ask questions of the form *What is the largest/smallest number? What number does this represent/stand for?* Indicate a digit. Invite pupils to write inequalities involving the number, for example:
$3752 > 3720$ or $3720 < 101$
(Use the opportunity to revise place value and the inequality symbols.)

### Activities

Show the class the paper square and without comment fold the square in half and open it out. *This shape is symmetrical: what does that mean?* Give pupils the opportunity to air their views – correcting, with sensitivity, the more outlandish. *We call this a line of symmetry* – indicate the fold line. *We can fold the shape along this line so that each half is the mirror image of the other half. We call a line like this a mirror line.* Quickly invite one or two pupils up to the front to demonstrate this. Invite a pupil to the front to fold the shape another way to show a line of symmetry. Continue until all the lines of symmetry have been found. When the two diagonal lines are offered make a point of mentioning that the line of symmetry is along a diagonal. Reiterate that a square has four lines of symmetry. Repeat the process with an oblong – make an issue of the fact that for an oblong the diagonals are not a line of symmetry and illustrate this by folding and using a mirror if necessary. Give pupils, working in pairs, the page of shapes. On each shape, ask them to write the number of sides, number of lines of symmetry and name of the shape. Encourage them to check their answers by cutting and folding or using a mirror. Ensure that the three-sided shape is called an equilateral triangle (opportunity here for protractor revision and ruler measuring to convince pupils that polygons are regular – the term itself may need revision).

### Differentiation

Differentiation will be by outcome.
*Low Attainers* – May not necessarily complete the activity on their own and will need support to do so.

### Plenary

Can you see any connection between the number of lines of symmetry a regular polygon has and its number of sides? Allow a free discussion – although the actual answer should not take too long to emerge.

## Lesson 3

### Introduction

*A mistake a lot of people make when first using coordinates is to get them the wrong way round. Remember, starting from the origin it is first number across then second number up.* Illustrate this for four points, written on the board (1, 4), (1, 2), (2, 2) and (2, 4) – on a pre-drawn grid. Join them up to make a rectangle. *What shape would you have got if you had plotted the coordinate the wrong way round. When you have done this, experiment with some other simple shapes.* Give squared paper (pre-drawn with a grid would save time) and set a time target. At the end discuss findings – challenge pupils to use correct mathematical language *e.g. two shapes are congruent.*

### Activities

On the OHP show partially completed sets of counter patterns having vertical and horizontal lines of symmetry on a grid. Show the class where to add the extra counters, involving the class as actively as possible. For example:

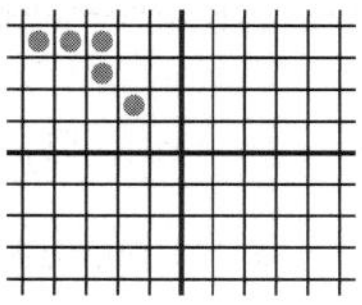

Becomes this when completed…

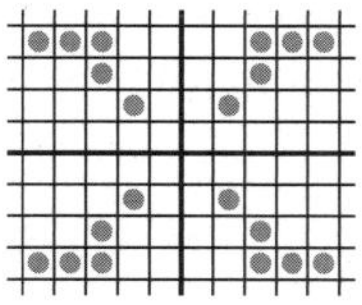

Make a similar partially completed counter pattern and invite pupils to individually add one or two counters until it is complete – encourage these pupils to give their method/rationale. Repeat this several times. Ask pupils, in pairs, to play this game with each other.

### Differentiation

*Low Attainers* – Could make symmetrical shapes using elastic bands on a pinboard, showing lines of symmetry with an elastic band of a different colour.
*High Attainers* – May be asked to draw polygons for themselves.

### Plenary

*Jot down a list of four objects which have reflection symmetry and four objects which look as if they might at first but don't really. Compare your list with the person setting next to you.* Quickly collect a whole class list – encourage discussion by challenging pupils' choices.

## Lesson 4

### Introduction

Give each pupils Copymaster 52 and a mirror (to check their answers) and work through the sheet as a class, taking the opportunity to use and reinforce the appropriate vocabulary. Challenge pupils to justify their answers. (Some of the questions could be used for homework.)

### Activities

Using an OHT and a cardboard triangle ask pupils how the shape was moved 'from here to here'. Allow a free ranging discussion. Should it not arise (which is unlikely) guide the class into four squares to the right and one up. Consolidate with some other moves, then invite pupils to show translations such as 'three squares to the right and one down' by drawing on the OHP. *When we move a shape into a straight line without any change to the shape itself we call this a translation.*

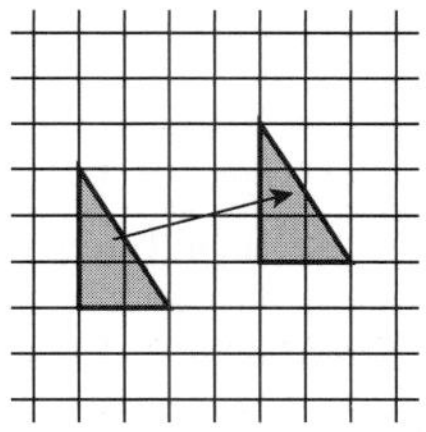

Pupils can then either repeat the above working in pairs or play this 'hunt the treasure game': each player has a grid of squared paper and one buries the 'treasure' in a square 2 by 2. Starting at the bottom left hand corner the 'seeker' tells the first person where to translate a 2 by 2 square. This person tells the 'seeker' how many squares of the treasure are covered, if any, then they give another translation and so on until the treasure is found – a record of the number of translations moved is recorded. Players then swap roles – the least number of moves wins.

### Differentiation

Differentiation will be by outcome, with *Low Attainers* needing support with the game.

### Plenary

Quickly recap on translation.

## Lesson 5

### Introduction

Counting activity with decimals with whole class or large groups – counting in steps of 0.1, 0.2 and 0.5, changing 'direction' on command. Solve any problems as they occur. The exercise may bring to light misconceptions about place value.

### Activities

Very quickly recap the content theme – reflection in mirrors, lines of symmetry and translations. Divide the class into pairs. *In your pairs make up three or four questions (and answers!) about reflections, line of reflection symmetry and translations, use paper for drawing and so on. You will be swapping questions with another pair so make sure your diagrams are neat.* After a suitable time pairs swap questions and do them. Encourage discussion between pairs. Novel questions could be banked for another group.

### Differentiation

Ensure that pairs are matched in terms of attainment so that each pair is given a realistic challenge.

### Plenary

Recap on the main activity sharing some of the more interesting questions with the whole class. A suitable homework task would be to invite pupils to draw and note the symmetry of 2 by 2 squares made from individual tiles like these:

# Theme 7 Time

## Objectives
- To become used to using timetables
- To use the 24 hour clock in timetables
- To understand and use the relationships between units of time
- To be able to use all four operations to solve measurement and time word problems

## Vocabulary
timetable, interpret, data, how long, am., pm., 24 hour clock, second, minute, hour, day, week, month, year, decade, century, convert, appropriate.

## Resources
Assorted timetables. Information about currency conversion (Euros). Holiday brochures. Copymasters 53 and 54. Homework Copymaster 27.

## Assessment
*At the end of this theme is the pupil able to:*
- Read and use a train timetable;
- Give an accurate estimate of how they spend their time during the week;
- Solve multi–step problems involving time and measures?

**Mental maths starter 21**

---

# Lesson 1

## Introduction
Ask the children some conversions from 24 hour to 12 hour clock and the reverse. Remind them to always add 12 hours onto the p.m. time after midday. Individual children could be timed to see how fast they can convert 5 or 10 'times'.

## Activities
*Timetables are useful for organizing and presenting information clearly.*
Draw this simple bus timetable on the board:

| | | | | |
|---|---|---|---|---|
| WELBOURN | 11:05 | 12:35 | 14:05 | 15:35 |
| NAVENBY | 11:15 | 12:45 | 14:15 | 15:45 |
| COLEBY | 11:25 | 12:55 | 14:25 | 15:55 |
| LEADENHAM | 11:40 | 13:10 | 14:40 | 16:10 |

Ask the class *working in pairs* questions about the timetable. *E.g.*
*Which buses leave Welbourn in the morning?*
*How long is the journey from Welbourn to Leadenham?*
*Which is the longest part of the journey?*
*How many buses leave Navenby in the morning? Etc.*
Now ask each pair to examine their own daily timetable of lessons and total how much time is spent on each subject during the week.

## Differentiation
*Low Attainers* – Make a shorter timetable of their lessons during the day and compose some questions about it.
*High Attainers* – Supply them with more detailed timetables with questions about them.

## Plenary
Ask more questions about the original timetable.
*How often do buses leave Welbourn?*
*If you arrived at the bus stop in Coleby at 3:15 p.m., how long would it be before a bus arrives?*
*If there were a bus that left Welbourn at 14:35, what time would you arrive in Leadenham if the journey time was the same?*

---

# Lesson 2

## Introduction
Timetable information is often presented in 24-hour clock time.
How many minutes are there between these times:
- 12:35 and 13:15
- 16:50 and 17:20
- 18:50 and 22:50
- 14:50 and 16:30 etc

## Activities
Write this timetable on the board and fill in the gaps:

| | Train Departs | Train Arrives | Time of Journey |
|---|---|---|---|
| 1) | 10:30 | 12:15 | ? |
| 2) | 11:30 | 14:02 | ? |
| 3) | 07:35 | 09:05 | ? |
| 4) | 07:10 | ? | 2hrs 5 min |
| 5) | 15:05 | ? | 1 hr 10min |
| 6) | ? | 10:20 | 1hr 55min |

Extend this.
Ask the children to look at their personal timetable and total how much time is spent:
(a) washing
(b) eating
(c) sleeping
(d) playing
(e) working.

## Differentiation
*Low Attainers* – They could make a list of the times of important events during their week and the duration of *e.g. going to the swimming pool.*
*High Attainers* – They can investigate whether timetables use the 12 or 24 hour clock most often, using examples from school, from newspapers, and local events.

## Plenary
Discuss with the class the reasons for using the 12 or 24 hour clock in timetables.
*Does it matter which we use?*
*Which do you find easier?*
Ensure the children are clear that whichever is used, a timetable must be consistent.

## Lesson 3

### Introduction

Write on the board

| | | | | |
|---|---|---|---|---|
| 60 | ________ | in a | ________ |
| 24 | ________ | in a | ________ |
| 7 | ________ | in a | ________ |
| 52 | ________ | in a | ________ |
| 10 | ________ | in a | ________ |
| 365 | ________ | in a | ________ |

What words will fill the spaces?
Work with the class to revise the relationships between units of time, noting that there is more than one answer to some of the questions.

### Activities

Ask these questions: *How many seconds are there in 5 minutes?* (300)
*How many years is 5 decades?* (50)
*How many years in a century?* (100)
Estimate the answer to *How long do you think you have slept so far in your life?* Ask if the children would estimate in hours, days, weeks or years.

Model each step on the board:
*Average sleep in our class = 10 hours per night*
*× 7 days a week = 70 hours per week.*
*70 hours × 52 weeks in a year = 3640 hours per year.*
*3640 hours × 10 years = 36400 hours in a lifetime so far.*
*Is this more than a month? More than a year?*
*Working in pairs* – Ask the children to estimate how long they have spent cleaning their teeth and watching TV in their lifetime.

### Differentiation

*Low Attainers* – They can decide whether a half- term lasts more than 10,000 minutes.
*High Attainers* – They can estimate, then work out, how old they will be by the time they have slept for 20 years.

### Plenary

Suggest that the children use a strategy to make an estimate of how their answer to the 'sleep' problem in hours relates to days or years.
24 hours = 1 day, so 240 hours = 10 days, 2400 hours = 100 days.
State that 10 hours per day is more than a third of a day, so if they are 10 years old, they must have been asleep for more than a third of 10 years.

## Lesson 4

### Introduction

*Do you think you could run 1,000,000 millimetres in half an hour?*
Break this down using the children's knowledge of the relationships between units of measurements.
1,000,000 mm = 100,000 cm
100,000 cm = 1000 m
1000 m = 1 km
*Can I run a kilometre in half an hour? Is it easier to work with kilometres in this context?*

### Activities

*To decide which number operation to use, we must pay close attention to the problem?*
Use Copymaster 53 *Plan a holiday!*
Tell the children they are going to plan a holiday. They will need to work out the time for their journey, and the costs in pounds and in the currency of the country they are travelling to. Go over how to change one currency to another, e.g. *If there are $1\frac{1}{2}$ Euros to £1, how many Euros are there in £2? How would we calculate £50 worth of Euros? (Multiply $1\frac{1}{2}$ by 50)*
TO BE CONTINUED IN LESSON 5.

### Differentiation

*Low Attainers* – Concentrate on times and total cost rather than currency conversion.
*High Attainers* – Extend the holiday to a second destination.

### Plenary

Discuss what the children have done. *How much money have you spent so far in pounds and in Euros?*

## Lesson 5

### Introduction

Ask questions related to foreign currency, e.g. *There are 1.6 Euros to the pound. How many Euros do you get for £12?* Then extend your questions.

### Activities

Continue with Lesson 4 after recapping what information the children need and what they have done so far.
Using the holiday brochures and *working in pairs*, the children can plan the cost of holidays, including flights, accommodation and car hire.

### Differentiation

*Low Attainers* – Concentrate on timetables and total cost rather than currency conversion.
*High Attainers* – Extend the holiday to a third destination.

### Plenary

The groups describe their planned holiday, where they are going, when, and how much it will cost (in both pounds and foreign currency/*Euros*.)
Go through Homework Sheet 27.

# Theme 8 Capacity

## Objectives
- To be able to use standard metric measures of capacity including abbreviations and relationships, and reading scales
- To be able to relate the pint and gallon to their approximate metric equivalents
- To be able to use the relationship between units of capacity
- To covert larger to smaller units of capacity
- To choose appropriate operations and calculation methods, and explain working
- To use all four operations to solve capacity word problems

## Vocabulary
metric unit, imperial unit, pint, gallon, approximately, equivalent, convert,
litre, half-litre, millilitre.

## Resources
Various containers for measuring capacity, including cups, shampoo bottles and containers to measure imperial as well as metric units. Copymasters 55 and 56. Homework Copymaster 28.

## Assessment
*At the end of this theme is the pupil able to:*
- Estimate capacities of containers such as 1000 ml, 500 ml, or 250 ml;
- Convert, for example, 25 litres into millilitres;
- Solve a capacity word problem and explain how they did it?

## Mental maths starter 22

# Lesson 1

## Introduction
Hold up a litre jug and ask the children to name something else that is about 1 litre in capacity, e.g. a bottle of drink. Ask them to name something that holds ten times as much, then ten times as much again etc. Return to the litre jug and ask the children to name something that holds one tenth of the capacity, then one tenth of the capacity again etc.

Record the results
100,000 litres = swimming pool
10,000 litres = oil lorry/ tanker
1,000 litres = domestic oil tank etc.

## Activities
Write on the board that there are 1000 millilitres in a litre. Remind the children of the standard abbreviation for litres and millilitres.
1 l = 1000 ml
*What do we measure smaller capacities in?*
*How many millilitres in half a litre? A quarter of a litre? A tenth of a litre? A hundredth of a litre?*
*Working in pairs* – Produce a table showing each $\frac{1}{10}$ of a litre and its millilitre equivalent, including 0.25 l, 0.5 l and 0.75 l.

## Differentiation
*Low Attainers – Which containers hold less than one litre?*
*High Attainers – Approximately how many of these containers would it take to make a litre?*

## Plenary
Using the selection of containers ask the children to estimate the capacity of some of them and fill them with water to check if they are right, and that the measurement on the container is correct.

# Lesson 2

## Introduction
Explain that we now use the metric system to measure capacity but that two imperial measures, the *pint and the gallon* are still in use today. *Ask the children what sort of things do we measure in pints or gallons?* (milk, beer, petrol).

## Activities
Hold up a full pint container and ask several children to estimate its metric capacity. Pour the liquid into a measuring cylinder calibrated in millilitres. Write on the board 1 pint = 568 ml (approx. 570 ml) which is approximately just over half a litre.
Explain to the class that 8 pints make one gallon. This means that a gallon is equivalent to
8 × 568 ml = 4544 ml or 4.544 litres.
A gallon is approximately 5 litres. Ask:
*If petrol costs 70p per litre about how much is that per gallon (£3.50).*
Use Copymaster 55 to continue asking questions.
Ask the children to estimate the capacity of a series of containers in metric and imperial measurements.

## Differentiation
*Low Attainers* – Convert gallons by multiplying by 10 and then halving the answer.
*High Attainers* – Taking an average of 70p per litre, they could work out how much petrol would have to go up per litre, before it costs £5 per gallon.

## Plenary
It is useful to have a clear idea of what a given capacity looks like. Show the children a fruit juice carton which would be an example of 1 litre. Show a medicine spoon as an example of 5 millilitres. Then hold up a bucket and ask the children to estimate in litres its capacity. Do the same for a standard size mug.

## Lesson 3

### Introduction
Show the class all the containers that have been collected for the theme. Then ask them to put them all in order from the smallest to the largest. Suggest that they could first of all estimate the capacity of each one, then measure it.

### Activities
*Capacity can be expressed as fractions of a litre or in millilitres.*
Hold up a measuring container that holds 1 litre and another that holds 250 millilitres. Ask the class the following questions:
*How many small containers can be poured into the larger container?* (4)
*What fraction of the larger container is the smaller one?* ($\frac{1}{4}$).
*Can anyone estimate the capacity of each container?*
Repeat with a variety of containers, asking questions in both millilitres and fractions of a litre.
*Working in pairs* – Examine the capacity of containers that are showing 500 ml, 750 ml etc. Are they correct?

### Differentiation
*Low Attainers – If I poured 500 ml into a litre container, how many more millilitres would fill it?*
*High Attainers – If I poured 20 lots of 10 ml into a 1 litre container, how many lots of 100 ml would fill it?*

### Plenary
Ask the children to bring in empty shampoo bottles and investigate the prices and capacities of each .

## Lesson 4

### Introduction
*Because there are 1000 millilitres in a litre, parts of a litre can be expressed as decimal fractions.*
Hold up a 1.5 litre bottle containing 1 litre of water and ask for estimates of the amount of liquid. Then tell them that it contains exactly a litre, and ask them to use this knowledge to estimate the capacity of the bottle.
On the board:
Express 1.5 litres in millilitres (1500 ml)
2.5 litres in millilitres (2500 ml) etc.

### Activities
Question (hold up the plastic cup): we need to estimate how many 1.5 litre bottles of drink we need for the next Christmas party. Each person will drink about 2 of these cups. Using approximation ask the children to estimate how many cups you will get out of each 1.5 litre bottle. Ask a child to measure its capacity by pouring. *If the bottle has a capacity of 1.5 l, what is the approximate capacity of this cup if I can get 10 cups out of a bottle?* (150 millilitres). *So allowing 2 cups per person, how many bottles will I need to buy for the class?*

*Working in pairs* – Help the children to order their work:
1) *How many children are in the class?*
2) *How many millilitres of drink will they use?*
3) *How many bottles will they need?*
4) *Will there be any spare drink?*

Extend to other situations e.g. *How much drink is consumed in one week at home? How much drink is consumed by the whole class in one week? In one year?*

### Differentiation
*Low Attainers – Allowing 1 cup per person, how many bottles do I need to buy?*
*High Attainers – Allowing 3 cups per person, how many bottles should I buy.*

### Plenary
Ask the children how their calculations worked out and go over any difficulties that they had.

## Lesson 5

### Introduction
List amounts of litres and millilitres on the board. Fill in the spaces with the class:

| | |
|---|---|
| 2 l 400 ml | 2400 ml |
| 3 l 200 ml | ? |
| 4 l 350 ml | ? |
| ? | 1300 ml etc. Make the lists as long as time permits. |

### Activities
Emphasise that you can add and subtract measurements just like normal numbers.Eg. Hannah drank 300ml of cola followed by 450ml of orange juice and then 800ml of water. Work through Copymaster 56 reminding the children to record their calculations carefully and not to forget to put the proper units in place at the end.

Using information gathered on the children's drinking habits, compose questions e.g. *How much did John, Jane and Beth drink in one week?*

### Differentiation
*Low Attainers* – Work with measured containers to enable them to estimate larger capacities accurately.
*High Attainers* – Prepare a sheet to take home to measure the amount of liquid used in a kitchen e.g. during meal preparation.

### Plenary
*Find the weight of a litre of water. How can it be done?*
*Using only a large plastic bottle, funnel and scales, discuss with the class how you can measure out exactly half a litre of water?*
Go through Homework 28.

# Theme 9 Addition and subtraction

## Objectives

- To mentally add several numbers
- To use known facts and place value for mental subtraction and addition
- To extend written methods
- To perform addition and subtraction of integers less than 10 000, and decimals with up to two decimal places
- To use all four operations to solve money or 'real life' word problems, including percentages
- To choose appropriate operations/calculation methods
- To explain working
- To check using sums/differences of odd or even numbers
- To make decisions
- To check results, including through use of a calculator

## Vocabulary

consecutive, sum, difference, odd, even, target, operation, round, calculator, display, key, enter, clear, approximate

## Resources

Copymasters 57 and 58. Homework Copymaster 29.
Sets of number cards from 1 to 30.

## Assessment

*At the end of this theme is the pupil able to:*

- Add several numbers;
- Use known facts and place value for mental addition and subtraction;
- Extend written methods;
- Perform addition and subtraction of integers less than 10 000, and decimals with up to two decimal places;
- Use all four operations to solve money or 'real life' word problems, including percentages;
- Choose appropriate operations/calculation methods;
- Explain working;
- Check using sums/differences of odd or even numbers?

## Mental maths starter 23

## Lesson 1

### Introduction

A quick 'no frills' block of mental additions and subtractions, for example:

| | | | | |
|---|---|---|---|---|
| $4.3 + 2.5$ | $6.8 - 3.2$ | $3 + 7 + 5 + 3$ | $680 - 320$ | $80 + 40 + 60$ |
| $27 + 13 + 7$ | $570 + 35$ | $400 + 500 + 700$ | $638 + 400$ | $1263 - 400$ |
| $2.3 + 2.3$ | $300 - 247$ | $6.2 - 4.0$ | $6.2 - 3.8$ | $2.5 + 2.5 + 1.5$ |
| $4 + 25 + 1$ | $3.8 + 3.9$ | $501 - 297$ | $460 + 518$ | $503 - 247$ |

Invite pupils to say how they arrived at their answers – encourage critical evaluation by pupils as well as the sharing of methods. At an informal level, enquire how answers might be checked. Write this problem on the board and ask pupils for their ideas about how best to solve it:

$3 + 9 + 7 + 5 + 4 =$ *[Rearranging is a useful strategy]*

*Challenge the class with* $1 + 2 + 3 + 4 + 5 + 6 + 7 + 8 + 9 = ?$

### Activities

Remind the pupils of some of the methods to work out additions and subtractions mentally. Include examples of the following – as usual, ensure that the pupils are active rather than passive learners during this process, but do not make an issue over the names of the methods.

| | |
|---|---|
| $580 + 300$ $\quad 960 - 500$ | (counting forwards and backwards) |
| $4.6 + 3.8 + 2.4 = (4.6 + 2.4) + 3.8$ | (reordering) |
| $43 + 38 + 61 = (40 + 30 + 60) + (3 + 8 + 1)$ | (partitioning using |
| $5.6 + 3.7 = 5.6 + 3 + 0.7 = 9.3$ | multiples of 10) |
| $4.7 - 3.5 = 4.7 - 3 - 0.5 = 1.7 - 0.5 = 1.2$ | |
| $3.8 + 2.6 = 3.8 + 0.2 + 2.4 = 4 + 2.4 = 6.4$ | (bridging through |
| $5.6 + 3.5 = 5.6 + 0.4 + 3.1 = 6.0 + 3.1 = 9.1$ | multiples of 10) |
| $138 + 69 = 138 + 70 - 1 = 208 - 1 = 207$ | (compensating) |
| $405 - 399 = 405 - 400 + 1 = 6$ | |
| $1.8 + 1.7 = (2 \times 1.7) + 1 = 3.4 + 1 = 3.5$ | (near doubles) |
| $1.8 + 1.7 = (2 \times 1.8) - 1 = 3.6 - 1 = 3.5$ | |

Should pupils use hybrid methods which are equally efficient, react positively. Stress that the purpose of each method is to reduce the calculation to a simpler one. They are not merely tricks.
Give pupils Copymaster 57 to do as individuals.

### Differentiation

*Low Attainers* – Tackle Copymaster 57, section A and some of section B.
*High Attainers* – Tackle Copymaster 57, sections B and C.

### Plenary

With the aid of jottings on the board, talk through Sections A and B of Copymaster 57 with pupils.

## Lesson 2

### Introduction

Begin this segment with a quick recap on the meaning of consecutive, sum and difference, perhaps on the lines of: *What's the special name for numbers which follow on, for example 4, 5, 6? What's the mathematical name for the result of adding two or more numbers? What's the special mathematical word for the amount by which one number is greater or less than another?* To give practice in using consecutive, sum and difference set the class some puzzles of the type: *I'm thinking of two numbers. Their sum is 9 and their difference is 1. What are the numbers?* Other sums and differences are: 11/3 and 13/7 – for high attainers 8/1 (for decimals 4.5 and 3.5). *The sum of two consecutive whole numbers is 21. What are the two numbers?* Pupils should be encouraged to look for patterns and describe these to others.

### Activities

Recap the standard pencil and paper methods for addition and subtraction, working through some examples (with pupil participation) including those involving money, for example:
*£7.62 + £5.86 + £3.20 and £9.52 − £6.87.*
For additions and subtractions involving whole numbers ensure that pupils are able successfully to manage calculations involving numbers with different numbers of digits and also multiple 'borrowing' within a single calculation. Suitable examples would include:

| | | | |
|---|---|---|---|
| | $4598 + 564$ | $692 + 560 + 781$ | $54.6 + 72.5$ |
| and | $855 - 386$ | $754 - 286$ | $72.5 - 4.6$ |

Wherever possible elucidate from pupils their reasoning so that it can be understood by the rest of the class.
Extend the addition and subtraction of decimals to include the handling of mixed units, for example, *5.6 m − 350 cm, 5.6 m + 250 cm, £2.69 + 78p and £4.67 − 78p*, again using question and answer to draw out and explain their working.
With pupils working in pairs, write some pencil and paper calculations similar to those below on the board. Ask pupils to do the calculations, but stress they will have to show their working to the whole class – so it will need to be clearly laid out. (Alternatively the class could be split into groups and groups show their working to each other.)

| | | |
|---|---|---|
| $11 + 920 + 835 + 76$ | $3352 - 782$ | $1058 - 773$ |
| $54 + 2226 + 156 + 26$ | $5.93 + 38.5$ | $1.6 + 0.82$ |
| $7.19 - 5.2$ | *£11.50 − 85p* | *£7.70 + 85p* |

### Differentiation

*Low Attainers* – Direct these pupils (or groups) to work on problems of an appropriate challenge.

### Plenary

Recap on the progress made over the lesson, emphasising pupils' own explanations.

## Lesson 3

### Introduction

Pupils, in groups, play the game *Answer Snap*. Each group picks, at random, five number cards from the set 1 to 30. Ask a quick-fire question e.g. *How many 20p pieces will make £2?* A group which has a 10 card can turn this. Play until a group has turned over all their cards. The game can be revisited with pupils compiling their own questions.

### Activities

Working in pairs, give pupils Copymaster 58 or display a copy on the OHP. Go over the Copymaster with pupils showing their working out on the board. Encourage discussion to highlight (and resolve) any problems.

### Differentiation

*Low Attainers* – May need some support with the reading. Pairing good and less good readers could help. Select appropriate questions from the Copymaster.

### Plenary

Write some calculations on the board, e.g. $6 \times 7$, $45 \times 9$, $17 + 15 - 12$ Invite pupils to make up interesting storylines to fit the calculations.

## Lesson 4

### Introduction

Target number: Write four one-digit numbers and two 2-digit numbers on the board. Then invite groups to form in as many ways as possible the target number, using any of the six numbers once only in a calculation involving any operations. Allow an initial time limit of 2 minutes A good starter is 1, 2, 5, 6, 8, 45 and 20 with target number 60 *e.g.* $(1 + 2) \times 20$ $(45 - 20 + 5) \times 2$ $3 \times 20$ $20 \times (8 - 5)$. Give the groups an initial free hand, but take the opportunity during the collecting of results to illustrate the use of brackets to remove ambiguity (this may well arise naturally when groups have to justify their results and methods to others). Repeat the activity for other target numbers. Depending on the group, 3-digit target numbers may make realistic challenges.

### Activities

Ask the class: *What are even and odd numbers?* Allow free discussion but nudge towards an agreed definition that even numbers are multiples of 2, but odd numbers are not. *Give me some examples of even numbers – as big as you like!* Collect these on the board without comment. *How can we test that these are even numbers?* If it does not arise from pupils, suggest using a calculator. *How could a calculator help?* Lead the class to appreciate that when dividing by two, even numbers give a whole number result but odd numbers give a decimal. *Give me some odd numbers.* Collect these on the board. Write on the board:
[odd number] + [odd number] = [even number] or [odd number]
*Which one of the statements on the right is wrong? Remember you only need a single example which does not fit to prove it wrong.* Ensure that all pupils recognise that 'odd' + 'odd' cannot be 'odd' (giving examples where this is false) and so
[odd number] + [odd number] = [even number].
Divide the investigation of the following up between groups of about 4 or so:

[even number] + [odd number]　[odd number] + [even number]
[even number] + [even number]
and [even number] – [even number]　[odd number] – [odd number]
[odd number] – [even number]　[even number] – [odd number]

Set pupils a time limit of about 10 minutes for these investigations – stress the importance of collecting examples. Collect in the results, encouraging critical pupil participation, and clarify the results. *What would be the result of adding three or more even numbers?* With active pupil participation establish that the result will be even. *What would be the result of adding three odd numbers?* With active pupil participation establish that the result will be odd. *How could you use the above results to check additions and subtractions?* Establish how this may be done. Depending on the group enquire as to how useful such tests are.

### Differentiation

Divide the investigation out to give a reasonable level of challenge for all levels of attainment.

### Plenary

Invite a pupil to write a number on the board. The rest of the class makes up calculations which have this number as their answer. Encourage pupils to be adventurous, but also encourage them to challenge each other if they think a calculation does not fit (but insist they show where the error is).

## Lesson 5

### Introduction

Write these on the board.

*3318 ? 21 = 158　672 ? 391 = 281　569 ? 198 = 767　915 ? 53 = 950*
*19 ? 7 = 133　948 ? 487 = 461　317 ? 185 = 132　329 ? 274 = 603*
*228 ? 38 = 6　29 ? 13 = 377*

Invite pupils to decide which operations are represented by ?, after ensuring that all pupils know the meaning of 'operation'. Go through the answers, asking pupils to explain how they arrived at them. Suggest that it sometimes helps to round the numbers into easier ones, *e.g. 569 ? 198 = 767 can be rounded to 600 ? 200 = 800, so ? is probably '+'* (recap meaning of 'round/rounding' and '~'). Make an issue of the fact that approximation to an 'easy number' is a useful means of checking a calculation.
*Use approximation to find which of these answers must be wrong:*

*367 + 158 = 425　924 – 687 = 137　984 + 498 = 1482*
*731 – 397 = 134　239 + 684 = 923　292 – 103 = 189*

Invite pupils to show their working on the board, for example, with $367 + 158 = 425$, $367 + 158 \sim 400 + 200 = 600$, but $425 \sim 400$ so answer must be wrong. Bring out the discussion that we can improve on the approximation a bit because the exact answer must be less than 600, as 367 is less than 400 and 158 is less than 200.

### Activities

In pairs pupils play *Call my Bluff*: they have to bluff their opponent with the answer to a calculation. The bluffer shows the other player a calculation and its answer. The answer need not be correct, but the bluffer should have worked out the correct answer. Without actually working out the answer in full, the other player must say if the answer is correct or not and say why. If they are correct they win a point. (The bluffer must show how they worked out the correct answer.) Players take it in turns to be the bluffer. (The activity forces pupils to approximate and to justify their approximations and correct answers.) As an initial sub-activity, the teacher could play the part of the bluffer. Write this calculation on the board $15 \times (121 + 17)$. *Can you say this calculation in words?* Accept: '15 times the sum of 121 and 17' or '121 add 17 all times 15' or similar – ensure that pupils recognise the 'grouping job' of the brackets. Repeat for other expressions such as: $(343 - 143) \times 56$　$2 \times (1 + 2 + 3 + 4)$ Then, working in pairs, *Use the bracket keys on your calculator to help you investigate these number patterns. Jot down anything interesting you notice.* Write on the board:

$(9 \times 9) + 7 = 88$　$1 + (7 \times 1) = 8$
$(98 \times 9) + 6 =$　$2 + (7 + 12) =$
$(987 \times 9) + 5 =$　$3 + (7 \times 123) = 8$
$(9876 \times 9) + 4 =$　$4 + (7 + 1234) =$

### Differentiation

Low Attainers – Pair pupils of similar attainment in *Call my Bluff*.
High Attainers – Consider other number patterns such as:
$(8 \times 1) + 1$　$(8 \times 12) + 2$　$(8 \times 123) + 3$　$(8 \times 1234) + 4$
$(1 \times 2) + 2 = 2 \times 2$　$(2 \times 3) + 3 = 3 \times 3$　$(3 \times 4 + 4 = \ldots$　$\ldots$

### Plenary

*Calculators are only as good as the person using them. What mistakes are easy to make when you use a calculator?* Collect these on the board. Ensure that (informally) the following are included: digit in wrong order, wrong operation key pressed, not clearing the display
*How can you check the answer to a calculator calculation?*

# Theme 10 Properties of numbers

## Objectives
- To be able to find all the pairs of factors of numbers up to 100
- To explore the properties of odd and even numbers
- To make general statements about the sums and differences of odd and even numbers
- To explain a generalised relationship in words

## Vocabulary
factor, divisible by, product, multiple of, odd, even, equation, sum, difference, reasoning, pattern, sign, rotation.

## Resources
100 grids, Copymasters 59 and 60. Homework Copymaster 30.

## Assessment
*At the end of this theme is the pupil able to:*
- Find all the factors of 24 and use this knowledge in mental calculations;
- Use his or her understanding of odd and even numbers to solve problems;
- Make and explain a general statement that describes a relationship between numbers?

## Mental maths starter 5

---

# Lesson 1

## Introduction
Remind the children that factors are whole numbers that go into other whole numbers without leaving a remainder.
*Make a factor chain:*
Start with 12: Find its factors, excluding the number itself:
1, 2, 3, 4, 6. Add these up = 16
Find the factors of 16 excluding the number itself:
1, 2, 4, 8. Add these up = 15
15 ___ 1, 3, 5. = 9
9 ___ 1, 3. = 4
4 ___ 1, 2. = 3
Factors of 3 = 1

## Activities
*Some numbers have many factors. It is useful to know these because it helps with mental calculations.*
The factors of 30 are 30, 1, 6, 5, 3, 10, 15, 2. Ask the children to work with a partner, looking at the multiplication grid if necessary, to find the factors of 24. Remember that 1 and the number itself are always factors of a number. Try this with other numbers and remind the children of factors they will not find on the multiplication grid, *e.g. 32 has 16 as a factor.*

## Differentiation
*Low Attainers – Which numbers are divisible by 2? How do you know?*
*High Attainers – Can you work out any of these mentally?*

## Plenary
Work through the factorizing that the children have done. Discuss numbers that have just two factors (apart from the number itself an 1) and those that have many factors. Look at how children have simplified the calculations by using factors. Emphasize the easiest methods that the children have found.

---

# Lesson 2

## Introduction
Odd and even numbers behave in predictable ways when you add and subtract them.
Ask the children to write pairs of odd numbers like this-
19 + 1 = 20. They must add up to 20.
Also write pairs of even numbers which add up to 20. Do the same for other numbers. Do the children notice anything?

## Activities
*Working in pairs* – Play the following game:
Each player decides who will play first.
*Player 1* secretly writes down any 2-digit number.
*Player 2* does the same.
The two players show each other their numbers and write down the sum of the two numbers
If the total is even player one scores one point.
If the total is odd player two scores 1 point. The first player to score 10 points wins.
*Is it better to be player one or player two? Or doesn't it matter? Do any strategies help you to win? Or not to lose?*

## Differentiation
*Low Attainers – I'm the first player and I have written down an even number. Will you write down an odd or an even number to win?*
*High Attainers – Does it make a difference to the game if you add three or four numbers? Do your strategies change?*

## Plenary
When the children have played a few rounds begin a table on the board to summarize their findings.

| Player 1 | Player 2 | Result |
|---|---|---|
| Even | even | even |

To be continued in Lesson 3.

## Lesson 3

### Introduction
Make sure the children have completed the table from Lesson 2. Then ask the children to modify the rules and try variations:
The two numbers are subtracted to find the difference. The same rules for winning apply.
The children can make tables of the results.

### Activities
*When you check the results of a calculation, it helps to know that the sum of two odd numbers is an even number, and so on.*
Discuss the tables that the children have drawn up, and establish general statements about the sums and differences of odd and even numbers. Use Copymaster 59 and look at the addition and subtraction calculations. Children should work in pairs to decide whether these equations are true or false, using their knowledge about how odd and even numbers work together.

### Differentiation
*Low Attainers* – They can play the game in the introduction with single digit numbers.
*High Attainers* – They can try multiplying the two numbers instead of adding.

### Plenary
Draw together children's findings and encourage them to say things like – 'It can't be an even number because you're adding an even and an odd number together.' Remind children that this is another good way of checking a calculation.

---

## Lesson 4

### Introduction
Write on the board—1, 2, 3, 4, 5, 6, 7, 8, 9.
1) Make the largest odd number you can
2) Make the largest even number
3) Make the smallest odd number
4) Make the smallest even number
5) Make the number nearest to 200
6) Make the number nearest to 222

### Activities
When you tackle a problem look for patterns and connections.
Write three 'mystery number' descriptions on the board:
- I am a multiple of 6 between 40 and 50, and the sum of my digits is 6;
- The product of my digits is 2, and I am a multiple of 7;
- I am an even 2-digit square number over 50.

Continue with these sorts of questions by tackling Copymaster 60.

### Differentiation
*Low Attainers* – Work on simpler problems, e.g. *I am a number in the 5 times table between 20 and 30. What am I?*
*High Attainers* – Write their own clues and swap with a partner to work out the mystery numbers.

### Plenary
Go through some of the problems on the sheet together. *What do you think the mystery number is? Why?* Discuss methods.

---

## Lesson 5

### Introduction
Tell the children they are going to investigate patterns in number sequences. Do some counting in steps of 0.1 using calculators and the 'constant' function. Repeat, going up in steps of 0.2 from a decimal number. Think about why there are ten steps of 0.1 from one whole number to the next. Repeat for steps of 0.3, 0.4, 0.5.

### Activities
Using a 100 grid choose a number. Find two numbers that add up to that number and draw a straight line to join them up. Find other pairs of numbers that add up to the same number. Keep going until there is a symmetrical pattern.
*How many pairs are there? Where do the lines cross over? Why?*
Draw a rectangle on the 1–100 grid. Add the pairs of numbers in the opposite corners to get two sums. (These totals will be the same.)

### Differentiation
*Low Attainers* – They can shade in the numbers on the grid to help see the patterns.
*High Attainers* – *Which other pairs of numbers in the rectangle add up to the same total? Does this help find the sum of all the numbers in the rectangle? Which rectangle has opposite corners that add up to 99?*

### Plenary
Discuss all the children's findings from the main activity. The children should be able to explain all the extension and variation work they have done on the grid. Go through Homework Sheet 30.

Copymaster 1

# Multiplication and division

| X | 1 | 2 | 3 | 4 | 5 | 6 | 7 | 8 | 9 | 10 |
|---|---|---|---|---|---|---|---|---|---|---|
| 1 | | | | | | | | | | |
| 2 | | | | | | | | | | |
| 3 | | | | | | | | | | |
| 4 | | | | | | | | | | |
| 5 | | | | | | | | | | |
| 6 | | | | | | | | | | |
| 7 | | | | | | | | | | |
| 8 | | | | | | | | | | |
| 9 | | | | | | | | | | |
| 10 | | | | | | | | | | |

You will need this multiplication square later on.

Write down three different calculations to find all the hearts in this pattern.

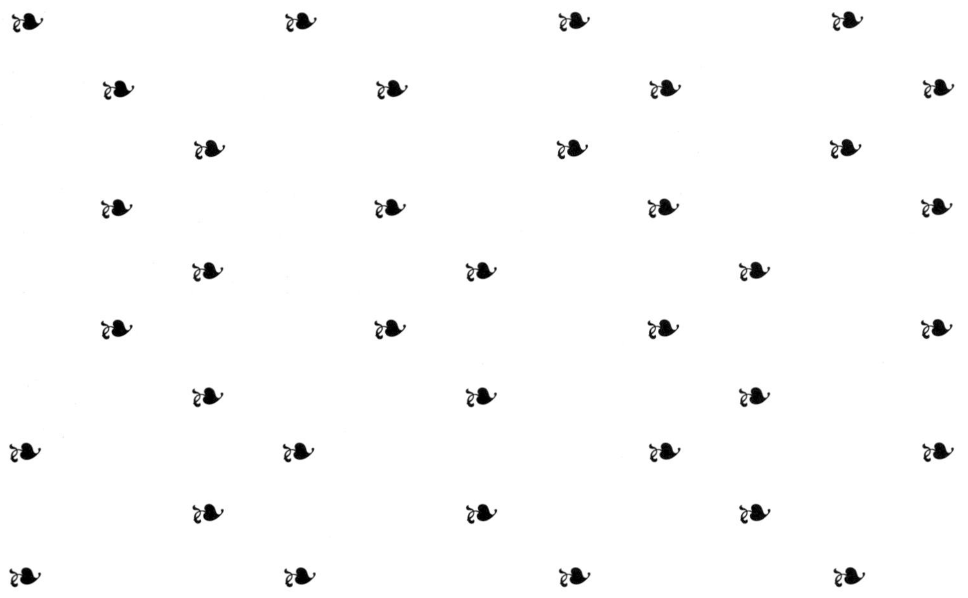

# Multiplication and division

THIRTEEN TIMES FIVE

NINE FIVES

HALF OF ELEVEN

$5\frac{1}{2}$

DOUBLE FORTY-NINE

505

45

60

65

A TENTH OF SIX-HUNDRED

10

HALF OF 160

FOUR MULTIPLIED BY SEVEN

A QUARTER OF FORTY

98

28

9

80

32

MULTIPLY EIGHT BY FOUR

MULTIPLIED BY THREE GIVES 27

PRODUCT OF 31 AND 3

16

HALF OF THIRTY-TWO

DIVIDE THIRTY-THREE BY THREE

SIX MULTIPLIED BY ZERO

0

130

93

5 TIMES 101

DOUBLE SIXTY-FIVE

11

Draw a line to link the correct answers (small circles) to the questions (large circles).

# Problem solving

## Section A

1) A bus seats 52 people. No standing is allowed.
   a) 8 people get off a full bus. How many are left on? ____________
   b) How many people can sit on 6 buses? ____________
   c) How many buses are needed to seat 300 people? ____________
2) There are 12 eggs in a box.
   a) How many eggs in 8 boxes? ____________
   b) How many boxes will 182 eggs fill? ____________
3) I have read 34 pages of the 128 pages of my book.
   How many pages must I read to reach the middle? ____________
4) I think of a number, then divide it by 15. The answer is 20.
   What was my number? ____________
5) There are 4 stacks of plates. Three of the stacks have 10 plates each.
   One of the stacks has 11 plates.
   How many plates are there altogether? ____________

## Section B

1) Grandad was 11 in 1956. When was he born? ____________
2) A bus has 34 passengers. Ten get off and 12 get on.
   How many passengers are there now? ____________
3) Golf balls are packed in boxes of 8.
   How many boxes are needed for 21 golf balls? ____________
4) A crate holds 24 milk bottles.
   How many bottles can 3 crates hold? ____________
5) A pencil costs 11p, and a crayon costs 8p.
   What do 2 pencils and 4 crayons cost? ____________
6) When Ben posts a parcel it needs two 35p stamps and three 20p stamps.
   How much is this in total? ____________
7) If I double a number, then subtract 5, the answer is 7.
   What is the number? ____________
8) How many 4 cm lengths of ribbon can be cut from 38 cm of ribbon?
   ____________

# Problem solving

## Section A

Find the missing digits in these calculations.
You may use a calculator.

1) 27 × 13 = __51
2) 69 × __ = 276
3) __45 × 52 = 49 140
4) 243 ÷ __ = 27
5) 21 × __9 = 819
6) __67 × 47 = 40 749
7) 5_7 × 14 = 8190
8) 4__ × 21 = 1008
9) 31 × __46 = 452__
10) 4__ × __ = 129

*Challenge:* 64_ × 5_ = 3_17_

## Section B

Find the correct operation (=, −, ÷ or ×) to fit these number sentences.
Check your answers with a calculator.

1) 57 __ 5 = 285
2) 285 __ 57 = 5
3) 285 __ 5 = 57
4) 159 __ 159 = 318
5) 851 __ 315 = 536
6) 536 __ 315 = 851

## Section C

Choose from 'in your head', 'pencil and paper' or 'use a calculator' as the best method for YOU to find the answers to those. Use your choice of method to find the answers.

1) 19 + 1 ____________
2) 63 × 10 ____________
3) 486 − 244 ____________
4) 63 × 12 ____________
5) 120 ÷ 3 ____________
6) 711 − 12 ____________
7) 146 − 20 ____________
8) 40 + 30 + 10 + 20 ____________
9) 88 ÷ 4 ____________
10) 600 − 5 ____________

# Fractions and decimals

## Cakes on plates

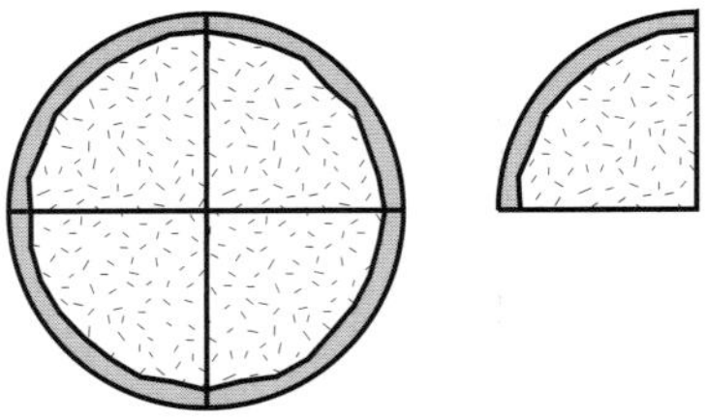

$= 1\frac{1}{4}$ or $\frac{5}{4}$

1. 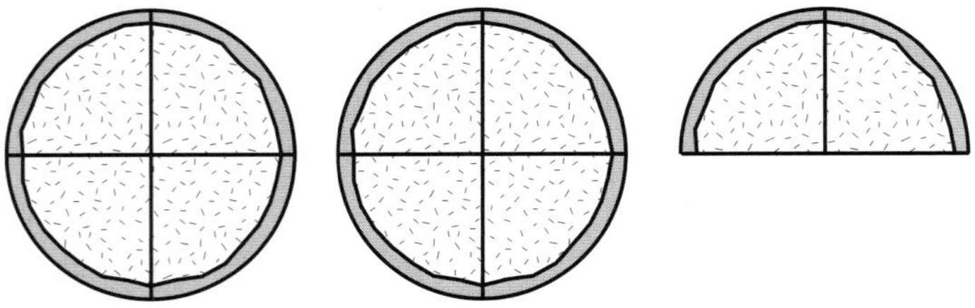

Mixed number =

Improper fraction =

2. 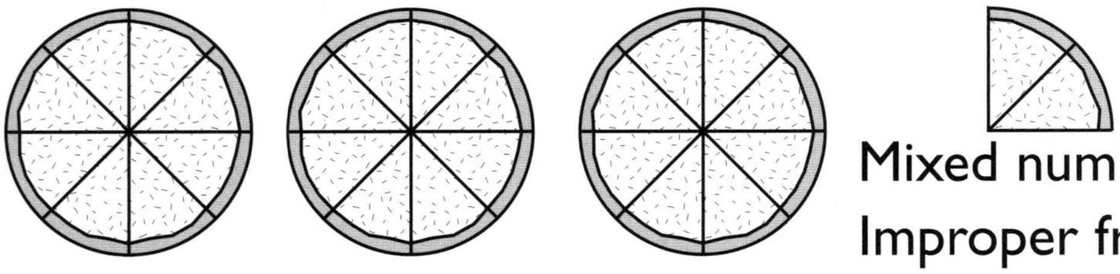

Mixed number =

Improper fraction =

3. 

Mixed number =

Improper fraction =

4. 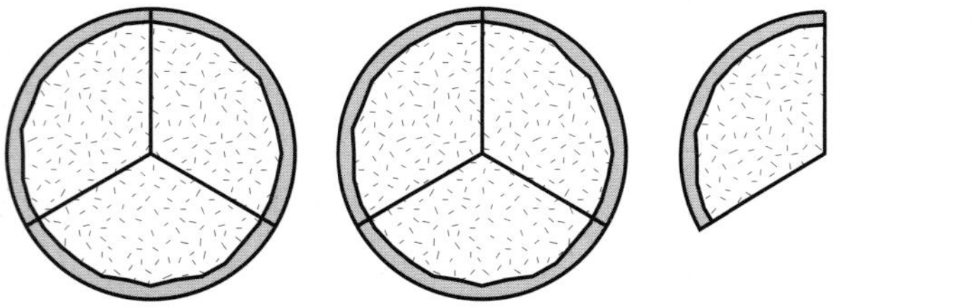

Mixed number =

Improper fraction =

5. 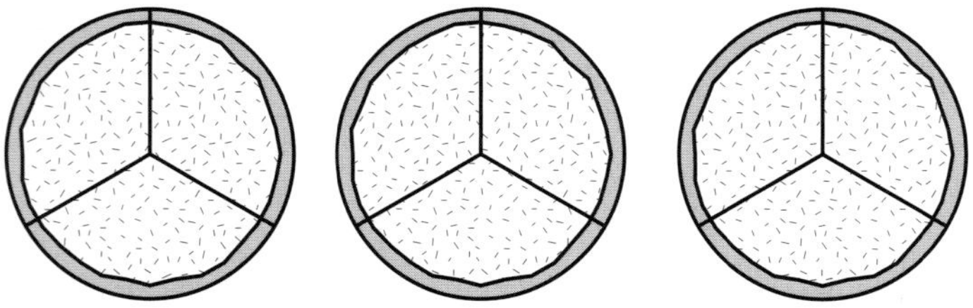

Mixed number =

Improper fraction =

# Fractions and decimals

| Place in the correct columns | Units | Tenths | Hundredths |
|---|---|---|---|
| **1.** 8.34 | | | |
| **2.** 7.21 | | | |
| **3.** 9.24 | | | |
| **4.** $6\frac{3}{10}$ | | | |
| **5.** $5\frac{7}{10}$ | | | |
| **6.** $9\frac{15}{100}$ | | | |
| **7.** $7\frac{12}{100}$ | | | |
| **8.** $4\frac{3}{100}$ (Be careful!) | | | |
| **9.** $3\frac{2}{100}$ (Be careful!) | | | |
| **10.** $7\frac{19}{100}$ | | | |
| **11.** $6\frac{47}{100}$ | | | |
| **12.** $9\frac{56}{100}$ | | | |

# Percentages and ratios

*Make sure you can explain HOW you solved these problems.*

1) At the gym club there are 2 boys for every 1 girl.
   10 girls are members of the club.
   How many members are boys?

2) Amy and Tom are sharing out some sweets.
   For every sweet Amy has, Tom has 2.
   Tom ends up with 20 sweets. How many does Amy end up with?

3) Chicken must be cooked for 50 minutes for every kg.
   How long should a 2 kg chicken be cooked for?

4) The recipe for fresh orange squash is 3 parts of orange juice for every 5 parts of water.
   a) How many glasses of water should be added to 3 glasses of orange juice?
   b) Jen has 3 litres of orange juice.
      How much orange squash can she make?
   c) James wants to make 16 litres of orange squash.
      How much orange juice will he need?

5) Mark and John share out counters.
   Mark gets 5 counters for every 2 counters that John gets.
   a) Mark gets 15 counters. How many should John get?
   b) When John gets 2 counters, how many should Mark get?
   c) When John gets 6 counters, how many should Mark get?

6) Write down three questions about this pattern of shapes.
   The questions must involve ratios.
   Try them on a friend.

# Percentages and ratios

1) Complete these sentences about the square below.

a) ________________ parts in 100 are grey.

b) ________________ parts in 10 are grey.

c) ________________ per cent of the square is grey.

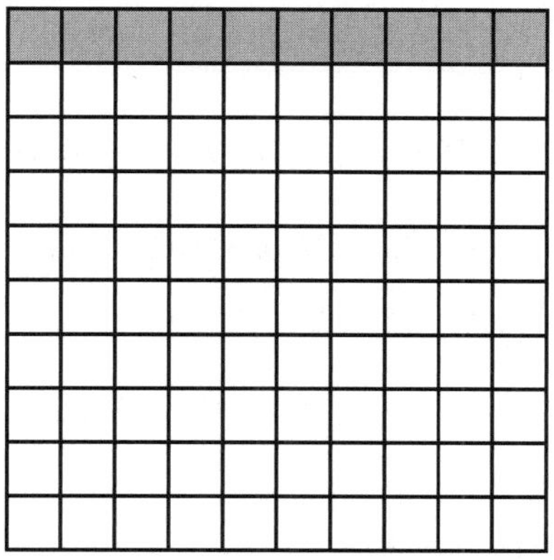

d) Shade in some more squares so that 15 parts in 100 are grey.

e) Shade in some more squares so that 20 per cent is grey.

2) Shade in half this square.

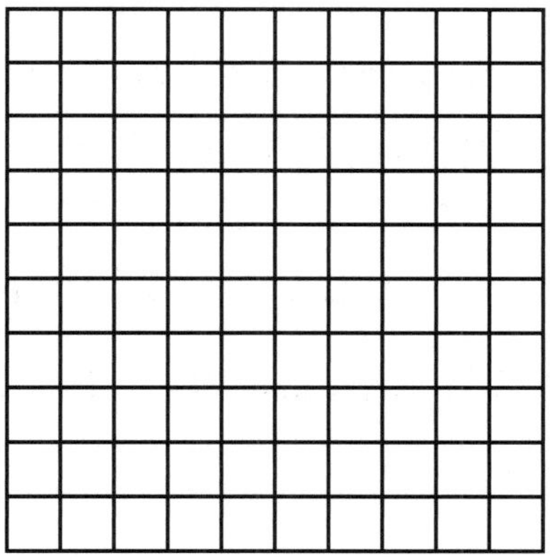

a) What per cent of the square is shaded? ________________

b) What per cent is not shaded? ________________

c) Shade in some more squares so that 60 per cent is shaded.

# Handling data

**Chart A**

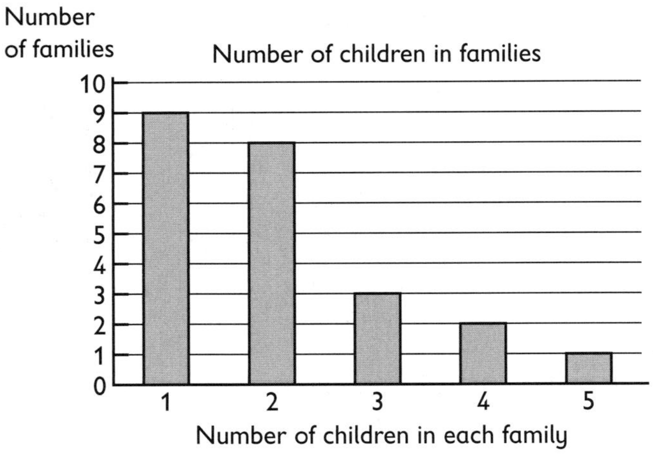


**Chart B**

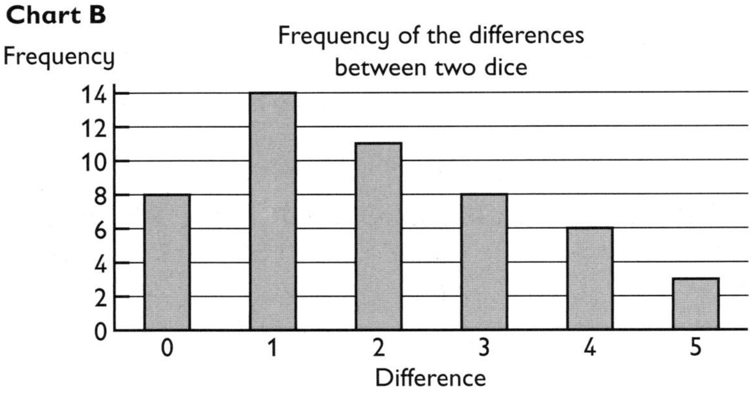


**Chart C**

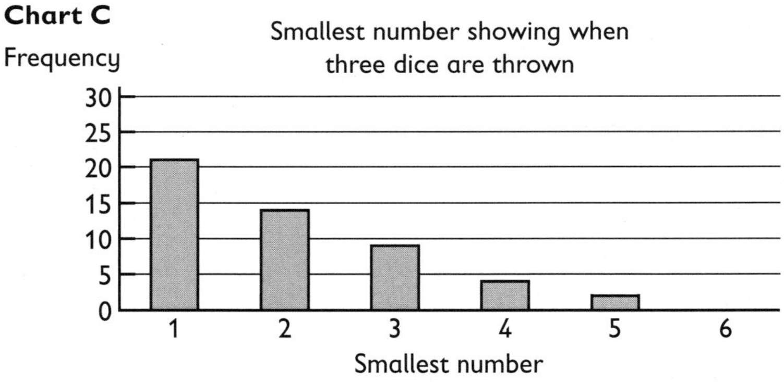


**Chart D**

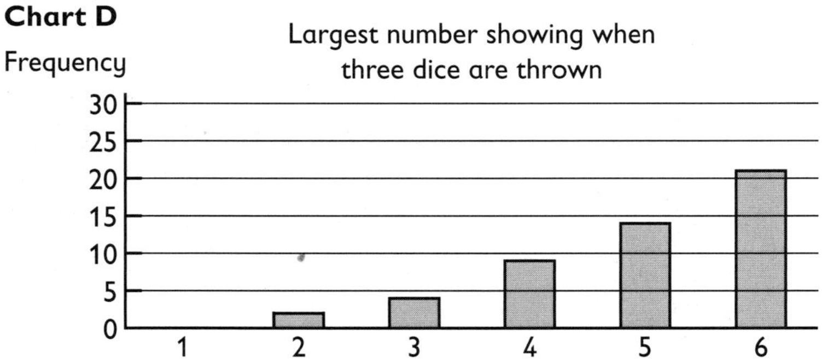

# Handling data

## Part 1

Here are two bar line graphs showing the frequency of total match scores for premier and first division games played on one Saturday.

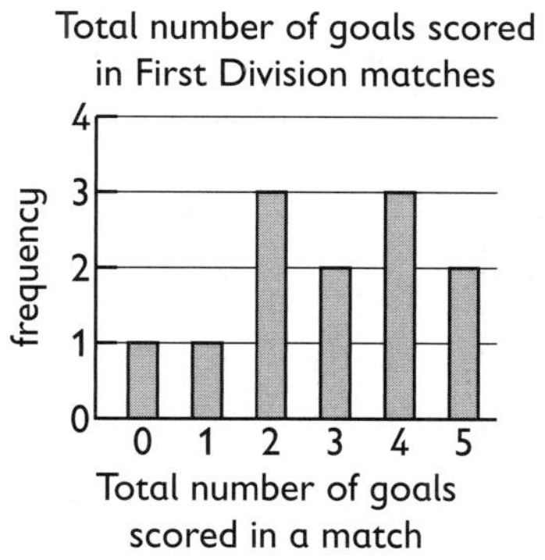


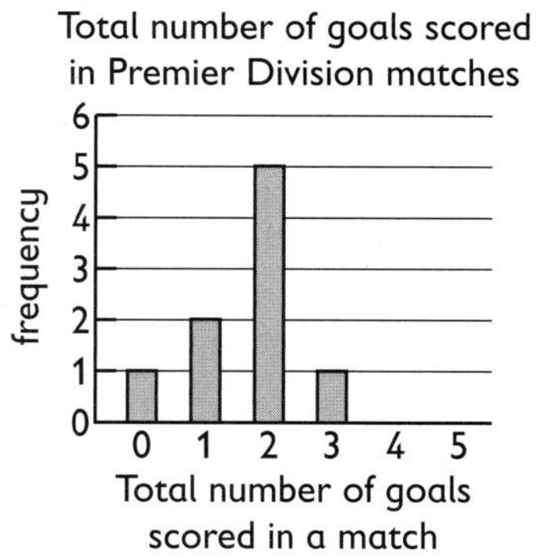


1) In the **first division** matches, in how many matches were:
   a) no goals scored?
   b) 1 goal scored?
2) In the first division, what was the maximum number of goals scored in a match? In how many matches did this happen?
3) How many first division matches were played?
4) In the **premier division** what was the maximum number of goals scored in a match? In how many matches did this happen?
5) In the premier division, which total score was the most frequent?

Looking at the two bar line charts, what differences are there between premier and first division football matches?

***Challenge:*** Draw some similar bar line charts for yourself. You will find the match scores in an old Sunday or Monday newspaper's sports pages.

## Part 2

This bar line chart shows how many times each number was thrown when a dice was rolled 100 times. Look at the bar line graph and answer the questions.

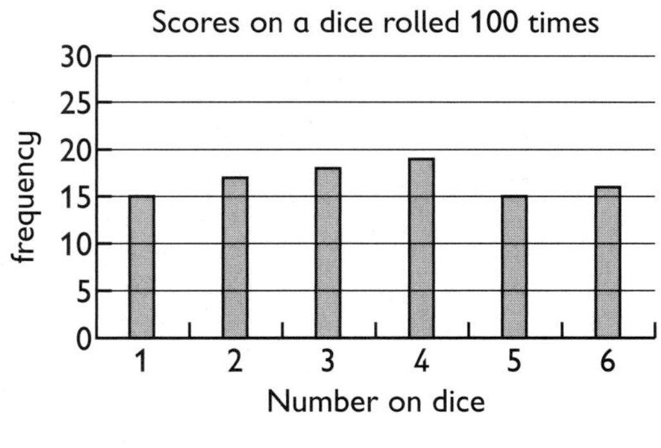


1) Which number was rolled most often?
2) How many times was a '1' rolled?
3) How many times was a '6' rolled?
4) If you did the experiment yourself would you expect to get exactly the same bar line chart?
5) Looking at the chart, which number is most likely to come up? How do you know?
6) James joins the tops of the bars, as shown below. Why do you think this is silly? (Hint: a score of $1\frac{1}{2}$?)

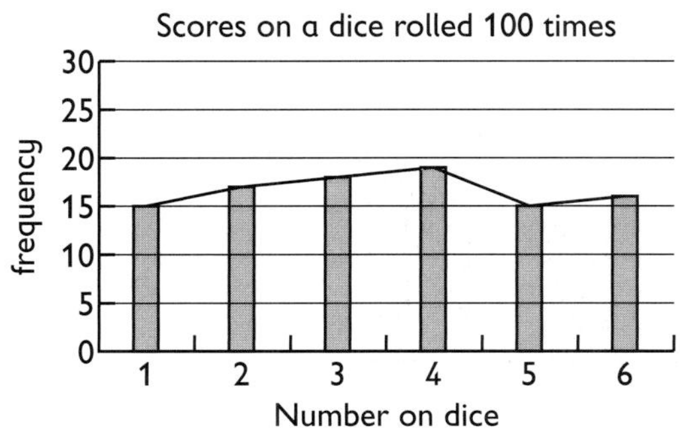


***Challenge:*** Repeat the experiment with two dice to find the frequency of the result of adding the two scores. You'll need to work together.

# Shapes

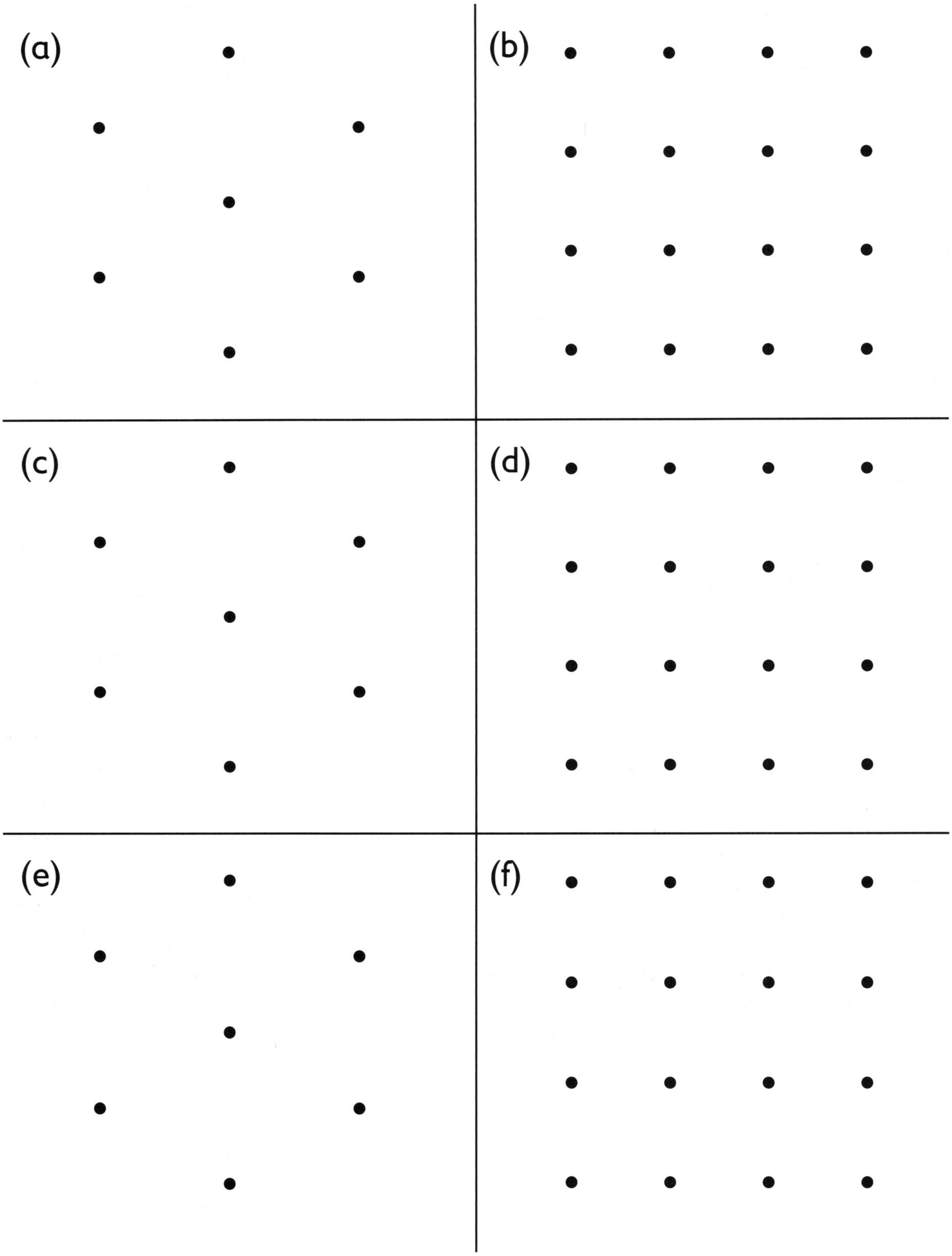

# Shapes

## Part 1

1) Here is a square you can make using dots as vertices. There are eight differently sized squares that can be drawn on a 5 dot by 5 dot grid. How many can you find? What about a 6 dot by 6 dot grid?

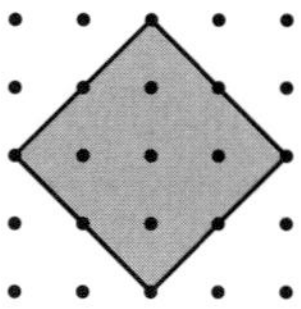

2) How many different polygons can you draw using dots as vertices on a 4 dot by 4 dot grid? Here are two.

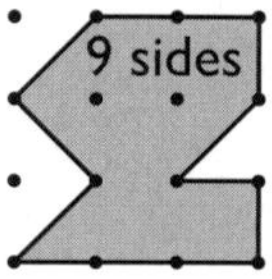


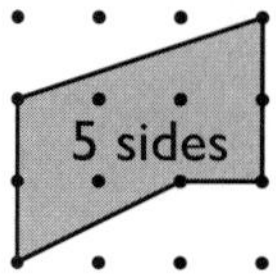


3) You will need some squared paper and scissors for this.
Draw a square like this: cut out a piece like this:

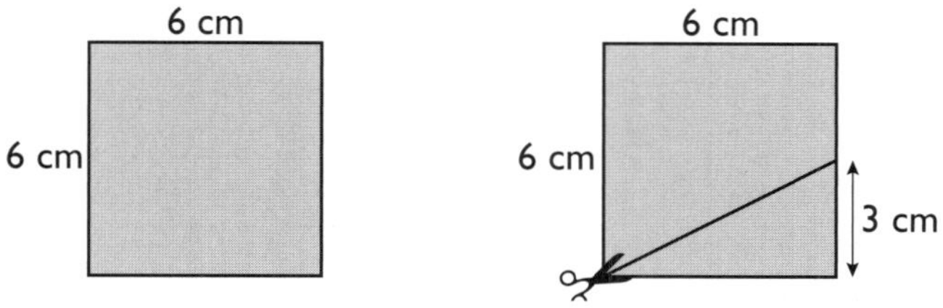


Sketch some of the different polygons you can make, like this one.

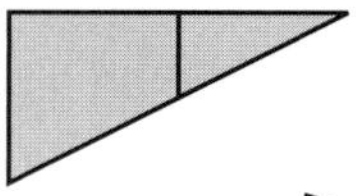

4) Draw a square.
Make a tracing of your square.
Name the different polygons you can make by moving the tracing.

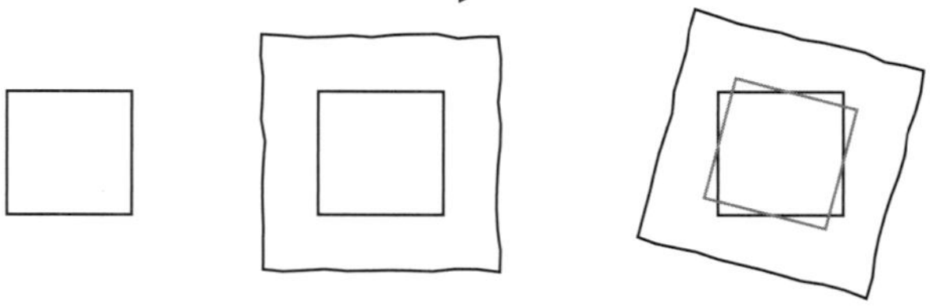

## Part 2

1) Make this tangram on squared paper or card and label the pieces as in the diagram.
We call the pieces of a tangram tans.
   a) How many different congruent pieces are there?
   b) What different shapes can you make with two C tans, one of which can be turned over?
   c) Write down the names of the tans labelled A, B, C and D.
   d) Can you make an equilateral triangle with two A tans and two B tans?
   e) Can you make a larger equilateral triangle with two A tans, two C tans and the D tan?
   f) What other shapes can you make using some or all of the tans?

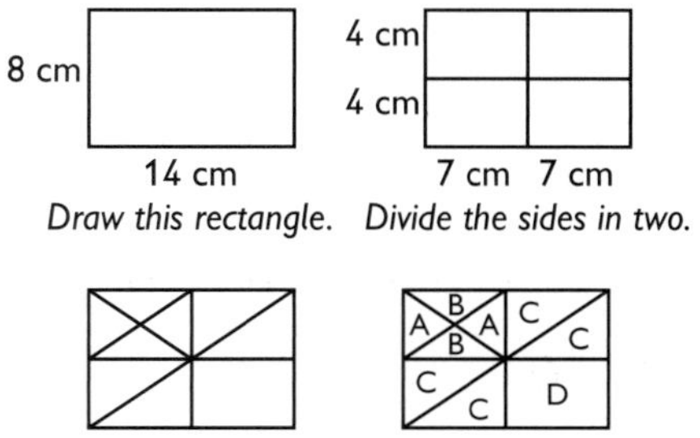


*Draw this rectangle.* *Divide the sides in two.*

*Draw these diagonals.* *Label the tans.*

2) Make a copy of this tangram and cut it out.

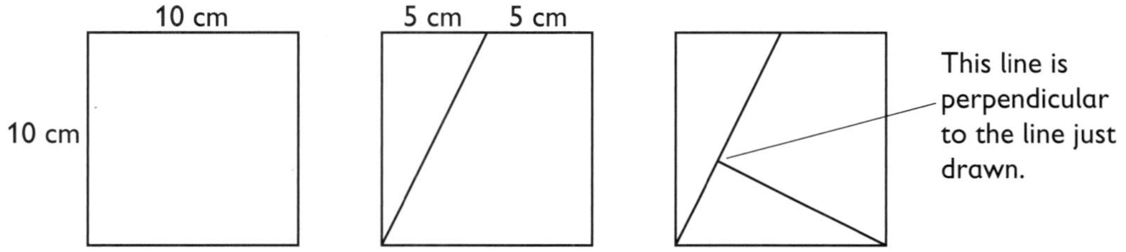


   a) Can you make a triangle out of 2 tans?
   b) Can you make a triangle out of 3 tans?
   c) What other shapes can you make from some or all of the tans?

# Measuring length

1) Circle in red as many boxes <u>in a line</u> as you can which give a total length of 10 centimetres. Some have already been done for you.

a)

| | | | | | | | | | | |
|---|---|---|---|---|---|---|---|---|---|---|
| 4 cm | 1 cm | 3 cm | 2 cm | 4 cm | 8 cm | 7 cm | 1 cm | 4 cm | 5 cm | 9 cm |
| 5 cm | 1 cm | 3 cm | 7 cm | 4 cm | 3 cm | 2 cm | 1 cm | 8 cm | 1 cm | 1 cm |
| 1 cm | 5 cm | 6 cm | 2 cm | 2 cm | 8 cm | 2 cm | 4 cm | 6 cm | 9 cm | 4 cm |
| 8 cm | 4 cm | 3 cm | 1 cm | 2 cm | 7 cm | 8 cm | 1 cm | 1 cm | 6 cm | 3 cm |

b)

| | | | | | | | | | | |
|---|---|---|---|---|---|---|---|---|---|---|
| 3 cm | 2 cm | 2 cm | 3 cm | 60 mm | 50 mm | 5 mm | 50 mm | 50 mm | 5 cm | 70 mm |
| 10 mm | 20 mm | 1 cm | 60 mm | 1 cm | 3 cm | 5 cm | 40 mm | 10 mm | 20 mm | 3 cm |
| 6 cm | 80 mm | 3 cm | 10 mm | 2 cm | 4 cm | 45 cm | 1 cm | 4 cm | 6 cm | 40 mm |
| 5 mm | 1 cm | 30 mm | 9 cm | 20 mm | 3 mm | 90 mm | 9 mm | 6 mm | 80 mm | 6 cm |

2) On this grid circle as many boxes <u>in a line</u> as you can which give a total length of 1 metre.

| | | | | | | | | | | |
|---|---|---|---|---|---|---|---|---|---|---|
| 10 cm | 5 cm | 2 cm | 75 cm | 50 mm | 70 cm | 10 mm | 20 cm | 30 mm | 30 m | 4 mm |
| 90 km | 90 m | 90 km | 10 mm | 50 m | 50 km | 10 cm | 60 cm | 30 cm | 10 cm | 40 mm |
| 50 cm | 10 cm | 50 mm | 45 cm | 5 m | 95 cm | 50 mm | 40 m | 40 km | 10 mm | 50 cm |
| 50 mm | 90 km | 50 mm | 5 cm | 45 cm | 5 cm | 5 km | 60 mm | 10 cm | 90 cm | 50 mm |
| 45 cm | 10 mm | 90 cm | 5 m | 5 cm | 95 mm | 5 m | 10 km | 50 cm | 10 km | 50 mm |
| 55 km | 45 m | 5 cm | 90 mm | 10 cm | 15 mm | 85 mm | 90 cm | 50 mm | 90 mm | 20 cm |
| 10 cm | 100 m | 5 mm | 5 cm | 20 cm | 50 mm | 15 cm | 40 cm | 5 cm | 9 km | 20 cm |
| 90 cm | 10 mm | 90 mm | 90 cm | 20 cm | 80 cm | 40 mm | 60 mm | 90 cm | 89 m | 60 km |

3) On this grid circle as many boxes <u>in a line</u> as you can which give a total length of 1 kilometre.

| | | | | | | | | | |
|---|---|---|---|---|---|---|---|---|---|
| $\frac{1}{2}$ km | 500 m | 500 cm | 500 mm | 400 cm | 600 m | 200 m | 300 m | 500m | 100 m |
| 250 m | 500 mm | 400 m | 500 cm | 500 m | 200 m | 100 m | 700 m | $\frac{1}{2}$ km | 100 cm |
| 250 m | 5 m | 100 mm | 900 m | 100 m | 200 m | 100 cm | 700 mm | $\frac{1}{2}$ km | 900 cm |
| 200 cm | 25 m | 900 mm | 50 m | $\frac{1}{2}$ km | 500 cm | 600 m | 300 cm | 500 cm | 300 m |
| $\frac{3}{4}$ km | 70 m | 100 m | 50 m | 5 mm | 100 cm | 400 cm | 700 cm | 500 m | 500 m |
| 250 m | 900 m | 400 cm | $\frac{1}{2}$ km | 95 mm | 500 cm | 600 m | 300 m | 100 m | 400 mm |
| 750 cm | 100 mm | 600 cm | 500 mm | $\frac{3}{4}$ km | $\frac{1}{4}$ km | $\frac{1}{2}$ km | 600 mm | 400 m | 600 mm |
| 250 mm | 900 m | $\frac{1}{2}$ km | 500 cm | 250 mm | 250 cm | 500 m | 500 cm | 500 mm | 400 cm |

# Measuring length

1) Fill in the correct units of length.
   a) A tall man is about 190__ tall.
   b) The ceiling in most houses is about 3__ from the ground.
   c) This worksheet is about 30___ wide.
   d) The perimeter of a school playground is about 400___.
   e) The world record for the high jump is just over 2___.
   f) An average exercise book is about 5___ thick.
   g) The distance between Manchester and Liverpool is about 30___ or 45___.
   h) An average door is about 3___ thick.

2) Make up two sentences like the ones above.

______________________________________________

______________________________________________

3) Jot down some objects you would measure in each of these units.

| Kilometres (km) | Metres (m) | Centimetres (cm) | Millimetres (mm) |
|---|---|---|---|
| | | | |
| | | | |
| | | | |
| | | | |

# Measuring

Write the times on these clocks in the 12 and 24 hr clock time.

morning

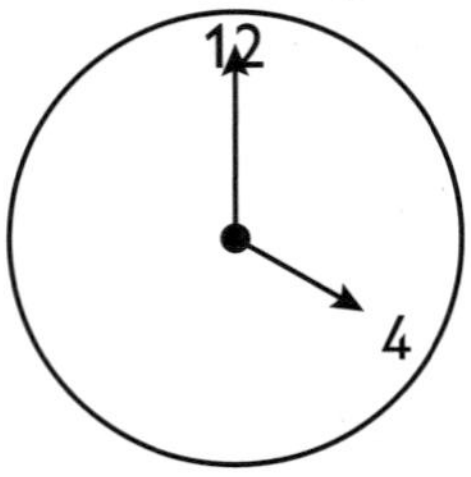


4.00 am

04:00

afternoon

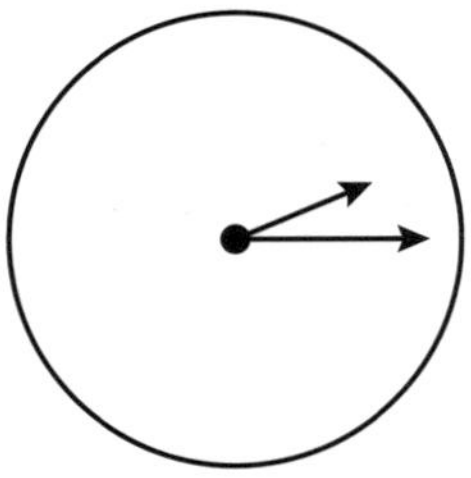

evening

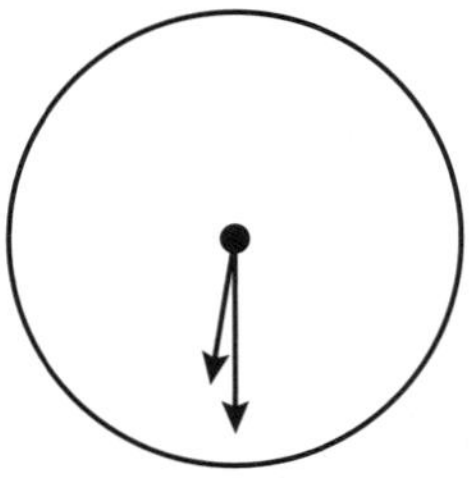

afternoon

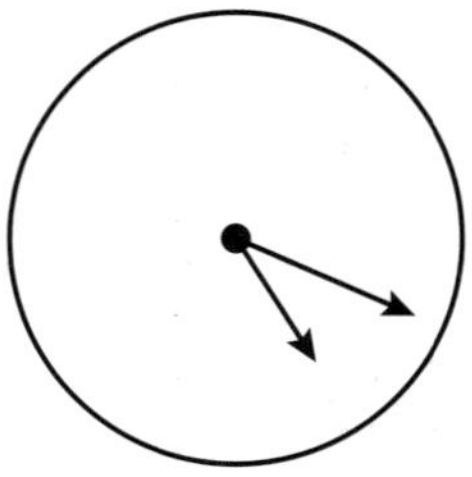

evening

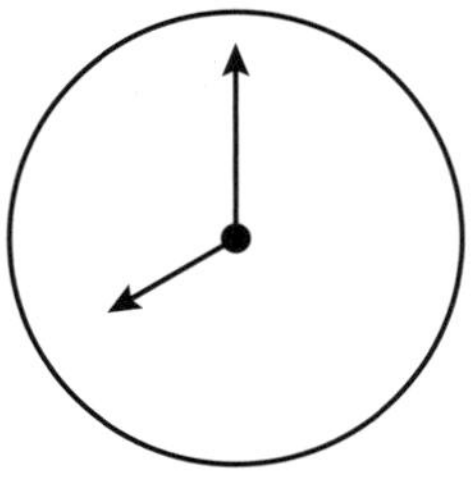

morning

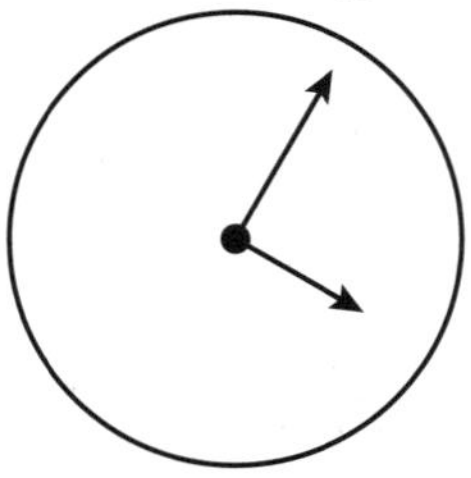

morning

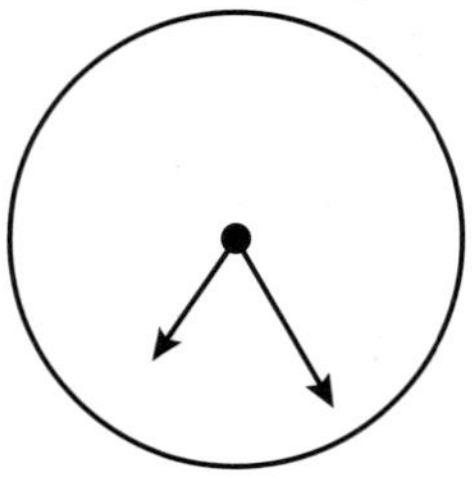

afternoon

evening

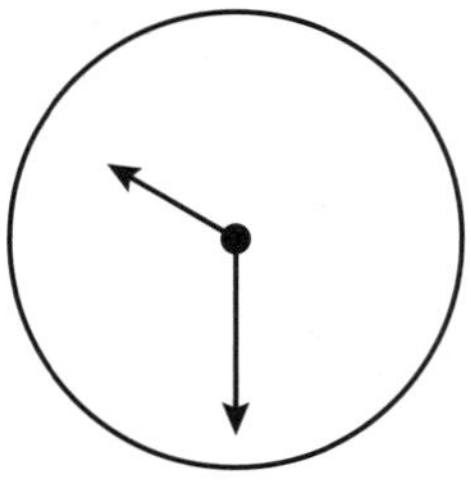

# Measuring

| | SUNRISE | SUNSET |
|---|---|---|
| JAN 1st | 08 : 50 | 16 : 32 |
| FEB 1st | 08 : 10 | 17 : 05 |
| MARCH 1st | 07 : 30 | 17 : 30 |
| APRIL 1st | 06 : 40 | 18 : 10 |
| MAY 1st | 06 : 00 | 18 : 45 |
| JUNE 1st | 05 : 10 | 19 : 50 |
| JULY 1st | 05 : 20 | 19 : 03 |
| AUGUST 1st | 06 : 00 | 18 : 40 |
| SEPT 1st | 06 : 40 | 18 : 00 |
| OCT 1st | 07 : 10 | 17 : 20 |
| NOV 1st | 07 : 50 | 16 : 30 |
| DEC 1st | 08 : 20 | 16 : 00 |

# Addition and subtraction

Attempt these calculations in the way shown.

$$\begin{aligned}874 - 356 &= 800 + 70 + 4\\ &- \underline{300 + 50 + 6}\\ &= 800 + 60 + 14\\ &\quad \underline{300 + 50 + 6}\\ &\quad \underline{500 + 10 + 8} = 518\end{aligned}$$

1. $$\begin{aligned}675 - 149 &= 600 + 70 + 5\\ &- \underline{100 + 40 + 9}\\ &= 600 + 60 + 15\end{aligned}$$

   ____________

   ____________

2. 727 − 219 =
3. 654 − 325 =
4. 571 − 263 =
5. 432 − 125 =
6. $$\begin{aligned}237 - 148 &= 200 + 30 + 7\\ &- \underline{100 + 40 + 8}\\ &= 100 + 120 + 17\\ &\quad \underline{100 + 40 + 8}\\ &\quad \underline{80 + 9} = 89\end{aligned}$$
7. 327 − 256 =
8. 428 − 359 =
9. 627 − 538 =
10. 831 − 649 =
11. 727 − 538 =
12. 624 − 439 =

# Addition and subtraction

USE CALCULATORS

## Section A

Make as many subtraction and addition problems using these digits.

1) $7, 3, 10 = 7 + 3 = 10, 3 + 7 = 10, 10 - 7 = 3, 10 - 3 = 7$
2) $8, 5, 13 =$ ____________________
3) $12, 15, 27 =$ ____________________
4) $35, 27, 62 =$ ____________________
5) $55, 12, 67 =$ ____________________
6) $112, 95, 207 =$ ____________________

## Section B

What calculations can be used to check these answers?

1) $727 - 512 = 215 \rightarrow 727 - 215 = 512$
$512 + 215 = 727$
$727 - 512 = 215$

Are these right or wrong? Show your working.

2) $625 - 112 = 513$ ____________________
3) $872 + 111 = 974$ ____________________
4) $327 + 265 = 592$ ____________________
5) $972 - 111 + 867$ ____________________
6) $875 + 122 = 957$ ____________________
7) $462 + 533 = 976$ ____________________
8) $372 + 213 = 585$ ____________________

**Copymaster 19**

# Number sequences

Use colour

| | | | | | | | | | |
|---|---|---|---|---|---|---|---|---|---|
| • | × | • | × | | | | | | |
| × | × | • | × | | | | | | |
| • | • | • | × | | | | | | |
| × | × | × | × | | | | | | |
| | | | | | | | | | |
| | | | | | | | | | |
| | | | | | | | | | |
| | | | | | | | | | |
| | | | | | | | | | |
| | | | | | | | | | |

Complete the pattern

$1 = 1$

$4 = 1 + 3$

$9 = 1 + 3 + 5$

$16 = 1 + 3 + 5 + 7$

$25 =$

$36 =$

$49 =$

$64 =$

$81 =$

$100 =$

# Number sequences

12 →

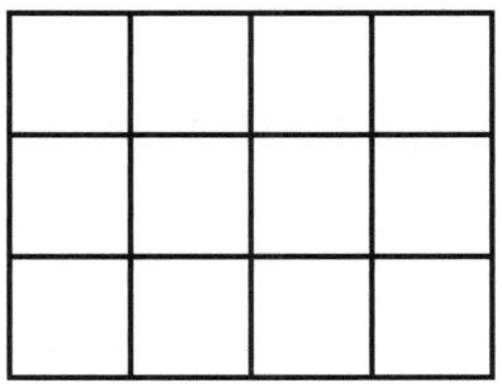

4 by 3 factors = 4 and 3

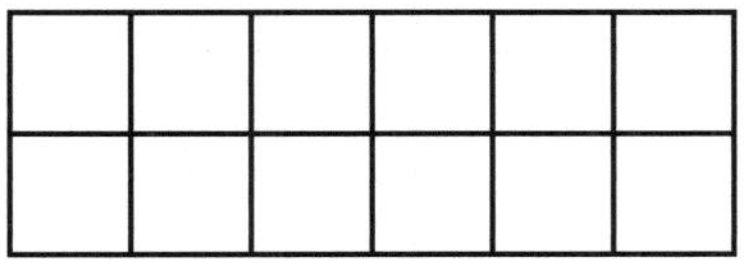

6 by 2 factors = 6 and 2

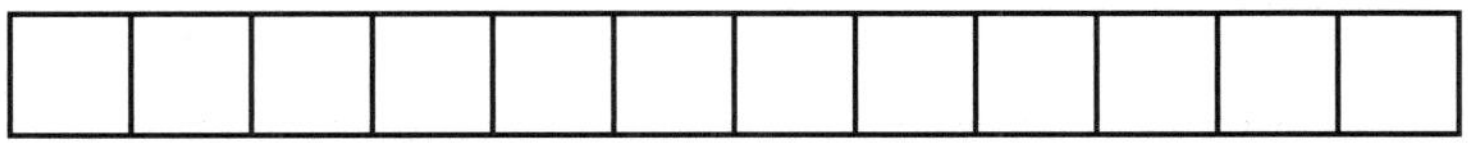

12 by 1
factors = 12 and 1

Factors of 12 are 4, 3, 6, 2, 12 And 1

15 →

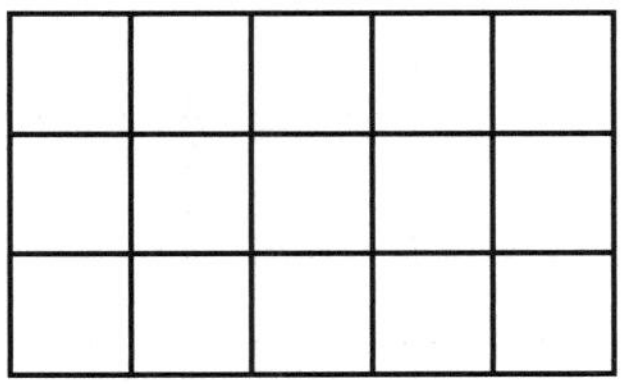

5 by 3 factors = 5 and 3

Any more rectangles for 15?

Do the same for:

21

32

36

Remember there might be more than one rectangle for each number.

## Copymaster 21

# Comparing and ordering numbers

| | | | | | | | | |
|---|---|---|---|---|---|---|---|---|
| 1 000 000 | 2 000 000 | 3 000 000 | 4 000 000 | 5 000 000 | 6 000 000 | 7 000 000 | 8 000 000 | 9 000 000 |
| 100 000 | 200 000 | 300 000 | 400 000 | 500 000 | 600 000 | 700 000 | 800 000 | 900 000 |
| 10 000 | 20 000 | 30 000 | 40 000 | 50 000 | 60 000 | 70 000 | 80 000 | 90 000 |
| 1 000 | 2 000 | 3 000 | 4 000 | 5 000 | 6 000 | 7 000 | 8 000 | 9 000 |
| 100 | 200 | 300 | 400 | 500 | 600 | 700 | 800 | 900 |
| 10 | 20 | 30 | 40 | 50 | 60 | 70 | 80 | 90 |
| 1 | 2 | 3 | 4 | 5 | 6 | 7 | 8 | 9 |

# Comparing and ordering numbers

Database of some small countries

| Country | Population | Capital city | Population of the capital city | Length of coastline in km |
|---|---|---|---|---|
| Andorra | 72,766 | Andorra la Vella | 16,151 | 0 |
| Bahrain | 590,042 | Manama | 140,402 | 161 |
| Barbados | 257,030 | Bridgetown | 9,466 | 97 |
| Belize | 219,296 | Belmopan | 44,087 | 386 |
| Benin | 5,709,529 | Porto-Novo | 179,138 | 121 |
| Botswana | 1,477,630 | Gaborone | 133,468 | 0 |
| Cyprus | 744,609 | Nicosia | 47,036 | 648 |
| Finland | 5,105,230 | Helsinki | 512,176 | 1,126 |
| Iceland | 270,292 | Reykjavik | 101,418 | 4,988 |
| Jamaica | 2,595,275 | Kingston | 103,962 | 1,022 |
| Mali | 9,653,261 | Bamako | 658,275 | 0 |
| Monaco | 31,719 | Monaco-Ville | 27,063 | 4 |

# Multiplication and division

## Section A

1) $19 \times 8 = 152$, so $21 \times 8 = 152 + \_\_\_\_ \times 8 = \_\_\_\_$

2) $20 \times 17 = 340$, so $21 \times 17 = 340 + \_\_\_\_ = \_\_\_\_$

3) $20 \times 17 = 340$, so $19 \times 17 = 340 - \_\_\_\_ = \_\_\_\_$

4) $10 \times 13 = 130$ and $2 \times 13 = 26$
so $12 \times 13 = \_\_\_\_ + \_\_\_\_ = \_\_\_\_$

## Section B

5) $(6 + 4) \div 2 = \_\_\_\_$

6) $(3 + 7) \times 4 = \_\_\_\_$

7) $(4 + \_\_\_\_) \times 3 = 21$

8) $(20 + \_\_\_\_) \div 4 = 6$

9) $30 \div (2 + \_\_\_\_) = 5$

10) $(1 + 2 + 3 + 4 + \_\_\_\_) \div 4 = 9$

## Section C

11) $14 \times 32 = 448$, so $448 \div 14 = \_\_\_\_$

12) $4 \times 87 = 348$, so $40 \times 87 = \_\_\_\_$

13) $963 \div 9 = 107$, so $107 \times 9 = \_\_\_\_$

14) $30 \times 30 = 900$, so $30 \times 28 = \_\_\_\_$

15) $16 \times 17 = 272$, so $17 \times 17 = \_\_\_\_$

# Multiplication and division

*Write down 2 division and 2 multiplication facts using these numbers:*

1) 7, 8, 56 ______ ______

2) 9, 8, 72 ______ ______

3) 6, 4, 24 ______ ______

4) 84, 12, 7 ______ ______

5) 36, 9, 4 ______ ______

6) 54, 6, 9 ______ ______

CALCULATE THESE

1) $\frac{6 \times 8}{8} =$ ______

2) $\frac{9 \times 7}{7} =$ ______

3) $\frac{8 \times 12}{3} =$ ______

4) $\frac{7 \times 11}{7} =$ ______

5) $\frac{10 \times 120}{2} =$ ______

6) $\frac{9 \times 12}{4} =$ ______

7) $\frac{11 \times 11}{121} =$ ______

8) $\frac{12 \times 12}{144} =$ ______

9) $\frac{7 \times 102}{7} =$ ______

FINALLY

$3(7 \times 2) \div 2 =$ ______

$5(9 \times 3) \div 3 =$ ______

$7(8 \times 7) \div 2 =$ ______

$9(8 \times 9) \div 2 =$ ______

# Problem solving

*Show your working so that someone else can understand what you have done – you need to write down every step.*

## Part 1

1) A plane has 152 seats. There are 87 people on board.
   How many empty seats are there?
2) There are 48 stickers on a sheet.
   a) How many groups of six can be taken from it?
   b) How many stickers will be left over?
3) There are 4 coaches for a school trip. Each coach can hold 52 pupils.
   How many pupils can all the coaches hold?
4) In a school there are 107 pupils in Year 5 and 132 in Year 6.
   How many are there altogether in Years 5 and 6?
5) The distance from London to Nottingham is 131 miles.
   It is then another 38 miles to Lincoln.
   How far is it from London to Lincoln if you go through Nottingham?
6) Amy is reading a book with 132 pages. So far she has read 85 pages.
   How many more pages has she left to read?
7) Share 14 biscuits between 4 people.
   a) How many biscuits does each person get?
   b) How many biscuits are left over?
8) What is the total cost of two 26p stamps and three 10p stamps?
9) A group of 3 people share a win of £81 on the lottery. How much does each person get?
10) On a school trip each ticket costs £6. How much will a class of 32 pay altogether?

## Part 2

1) Des has less than 20 books. When he counts them in fives, he has four books left over. When he counts them in fours, he has three left over. How many books does Des have?
2) Make three lists using only the numbers in 1 to 7 once, so that the sum of one list is three times the other. There are five different ways of doing this. How many can you find?

# Problem solving

## Part 1

*Show your working so that someone else can understand what you have done.*

| Name | Age |
|---|---|
| Kelly | 10 |
| Lisa | 6 |
| Amy | 4 |
| Martin | 9 |
| Ram | 5 |
| Anita | 7 |

1) Use this list to answer these questions.
   Who is:
   a) a year younger than Kelly? b) twice as old as Ram?
   c) 6 years older than Amy? d) 10 in four years' time?
   e) 11 in 7 years' time? f) half as old as Martin will be in a year's time?
2) A passenger plane has 40 rows of seats.
   There are 6 seats in each row.
   How many passengers can the plane carry?
3) Gianni is 9 years old. His father is 37. How much older is his father?
4) Make two lists using only the numbers 1 to 6 once, so that the sum of the numbers in one list is twice the sum of the other list. There are four different ways of doing this. How many can you find?
5) Leone went to a pet shop and bought 7 fish for £18. She only bought Angel fish and Neon fish. How many Angel fish did she buy if Angel fish cost £3 and Neon fish cost £2?
6) How could you make up a) 13p b) 19p c) 25p d) 12p using these stamps?

## Part 2

*Here are some calculations and short cuts. Do them and explain why or how they work. Sometimes an example can do most of the explaining for you. Work together in your group and help each other.*

1) a) $23 + 17$ b) $24 \times 2$ c) $86 \div 2$
2) a) $32 - 15$ b) $47 + 59$ c) $75 - 20$
3) a) $700 - 280$ b) $417 + 163$ c) $63 \div 2$
4) a) $3000 - 2831$ b) $654 + 286$
5) a) $15 \times 11$ b) $40 \times 30$
6) a) $49 \times 30$ b) $141 \times 5$
7) a) $8.2 \times 3$ b) $16 \times 8$
8) $\frac{1}{6}$ of 24
9) To divide a number by 4: divide it by two, then divide your answer by 2.
10) To multiply a number by 5: divide it by 2 and multiply the answer by 10.
11) To multiply a number by 9: multiply it by 10 and take the original number away from the answer.
12) Mark has to calculate $58 - 46$. He adds 4 to each number. This gives $62 - 50$, which is 12 … the answer to the original problem! What about $130 - 86$?
13) To multiply a number by 25: divide the number by 4 and multiply the answer by 100.
14) To multiply a number by 15: add half the number to itself and multiply the answer by 10.

# Fractions and decimals

*Arrange these values in order, smallest first.*

1) 2.7 cm, 8.6 cm, 3.4 cm, 5.7 cm, 5.4 cm

______________________________

2) 12.9 kg, 15.7 kg, 9.9 kg, 4.6 kg, 3.2 kg

______________________________

3) 12.72, 6.81, 19.31, 12.73, 12.72

______________________________

4) 8.67, 9.21, 3.63, 5.21, 6.93

______________________________

5) $8\frac{2}{3}$, $9\frac{1}{3}$, 6, $5\frac{2}{3}$, $5\frac{1}{3}$, 8

______________________________

6) $\frac{2}{4}$, $\frac{2}{2}$, $\frac{1}{8}$, $\frac{5}{8}$, $\frac{3}{4}$, $\frac{1}{4}$

______________________________

7) 3.6 m, 5.4 m, 2.7 m, 1.9 m, 10.3 m

______________________________

8) 9.25 km, 3.71 km, 2.67 km, 1.54 km

______________________________

9) 8.6 cm, 7.4 cm, 6.3 cm, 5.4 cm, 2.7 cm

______________________________

10) 12.01, 8.04, 3.62, 5.24, 8.31

______________________________

# Fractions and decimals

*Fill in this chart*

| MIXED NUMBER | DECIMAL | ROUNDED TO NEAREST WHOLE ONE |
|---|---|---|
| $2\frac{3}{10}$ | 2.3 | 2 |
| $3\frac{4}{10}$ | 3.4 | |
| $5\frac{2}{5}$ | | |
| $9\frac{1}{5}$ | | |
| $10\frac{2}{5}$ | | |
| $6\frac{7}{10}$ | | |
| | 8.8 | |
| | 9.2 | |
| | 7.6 | |
| | 15.4 | |
| $8\frac{2}{5}$ | | |
| $9\frac{1}{2}$ | | |
| $8\frac{7}{10}$ | | |
| $9\frac{2}{5}$ | | |
| $15\frac{6}{10}$ | | |
| $13\frac{1}{2}$ | | |
| $27\frac{3}{10}$ | | |
| $32\frac{4}{10}$ | | |
| $101\frac{6}{10}$ | | |
| $233\frac{4}{5}$ | | |
| $562\frac{6}{10}$ | | |

# Copymaster 29

# Shapes, lines and angles

1) Which of these skeleton cubes is the same as the one in this box? →

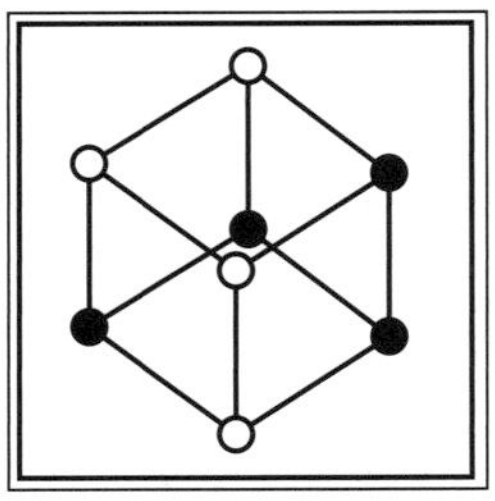

(a)

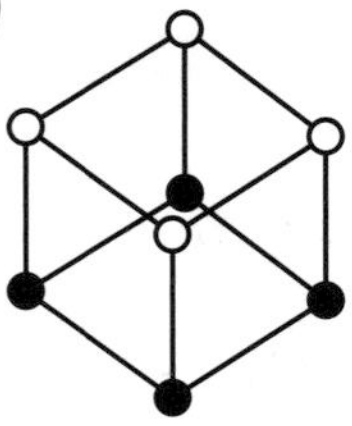

(b)

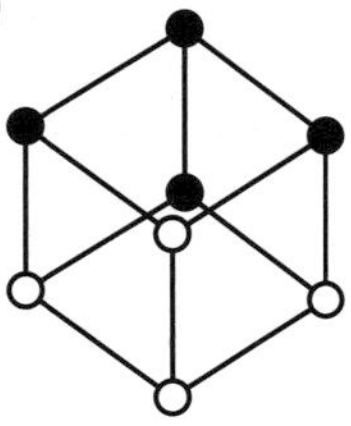

(c)

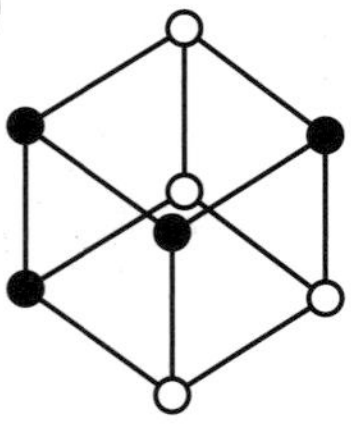

(d)

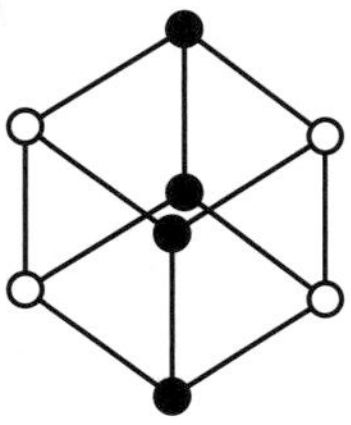

(e)

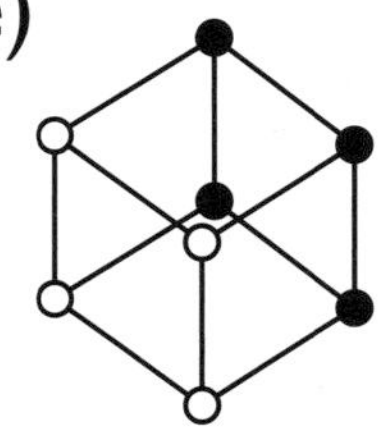

(f)

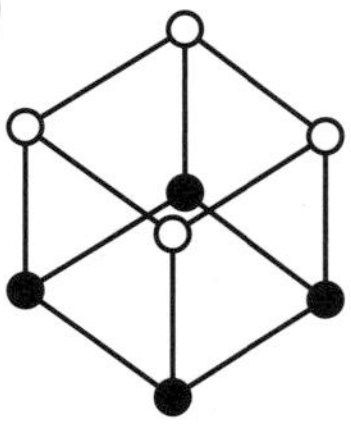

IF YOU GET STUCK OR WANT TO CHECK YOUR ANSWERS, MAKE THE MODEL OUT OF STRAWS AND PLASTICINE.

2) Make up and test on some friends a similar puzzle. Use these blank skeleton cubes.

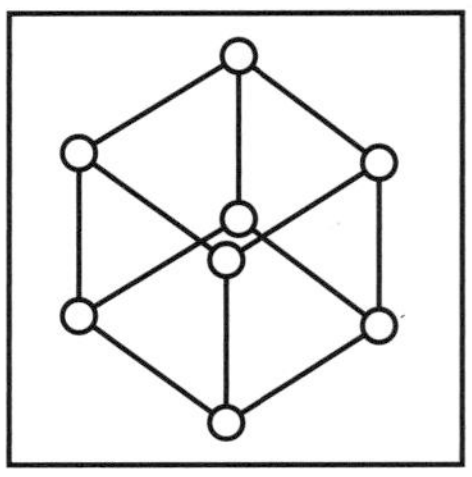

(a)

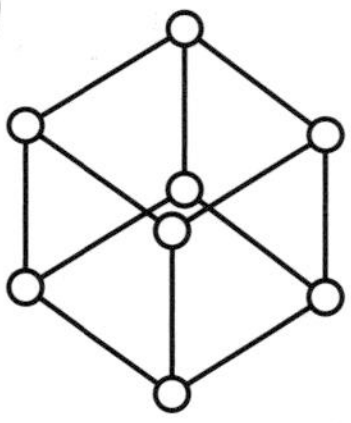

(b)

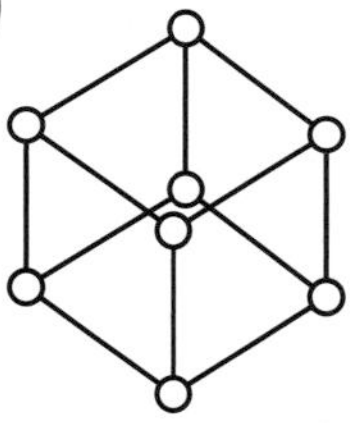

(c)

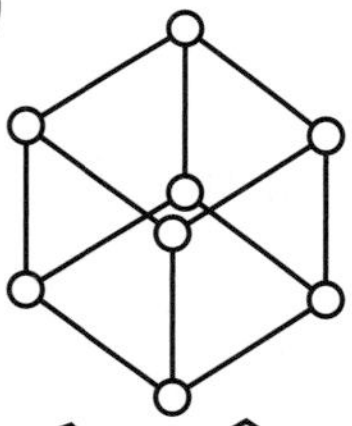

(d)

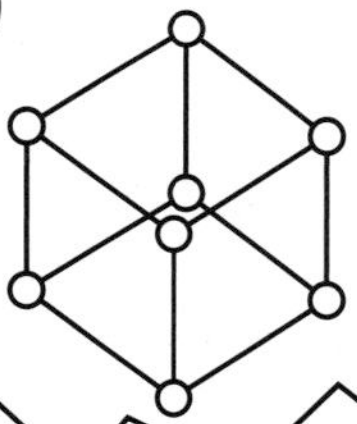

(e)

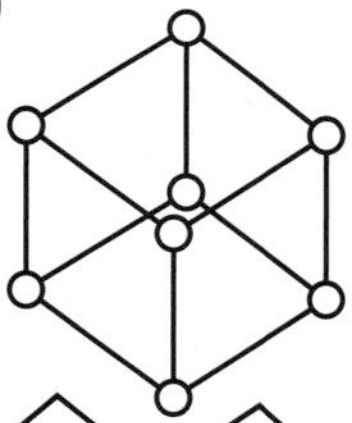

*Challenge:* how many different ways can just two pieces of plasticine be stuck on the vertices of a skeleton cube? These count as one way.

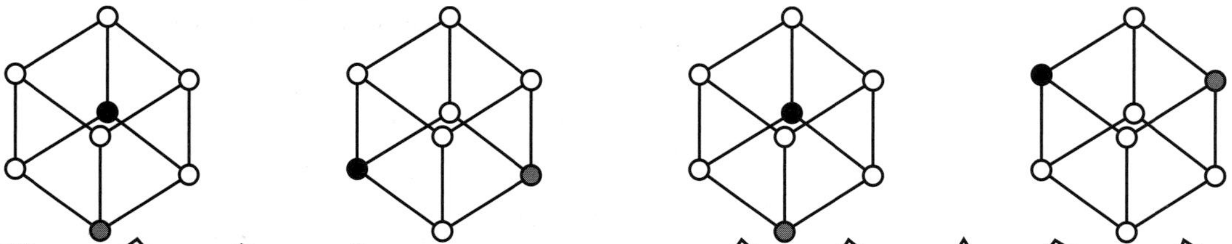

# Shapes, lines and angles

This net will fold up to make this open cube

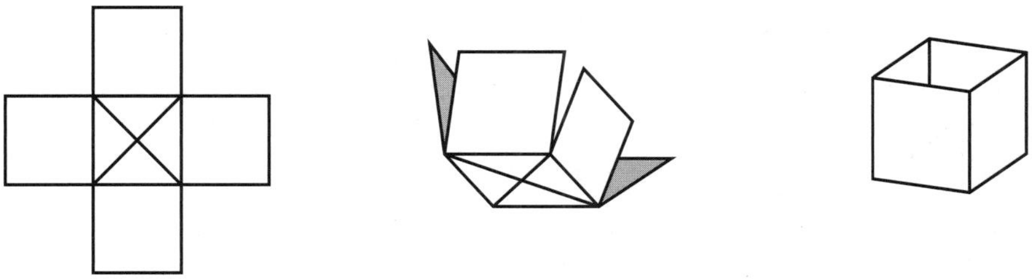

1) Which of these nets will make an open cube, with base 'X'?

(a)

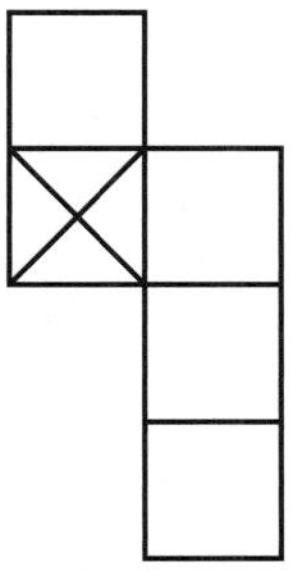

(b)

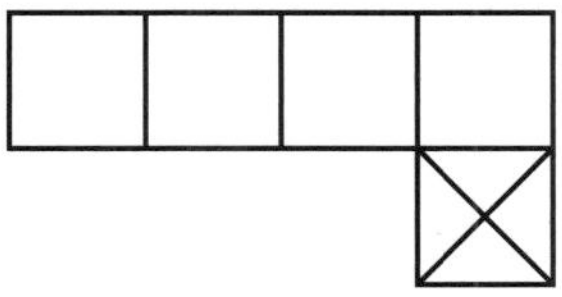

(c)

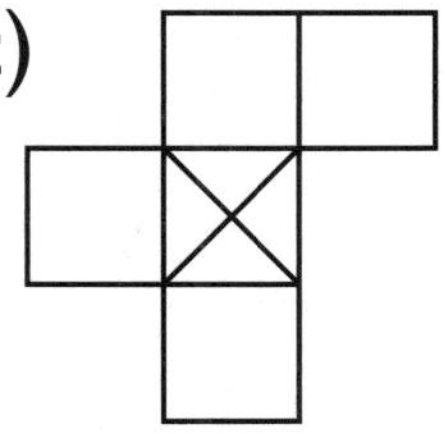

(d)

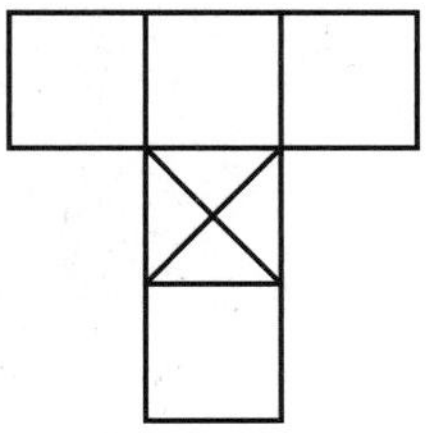

(e)

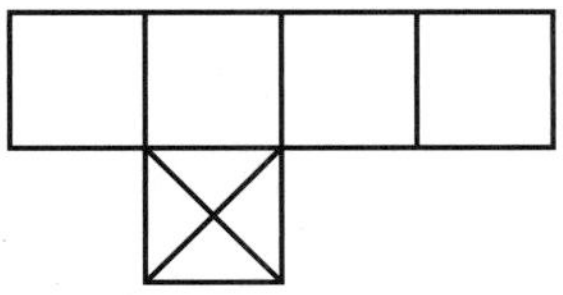

(f)

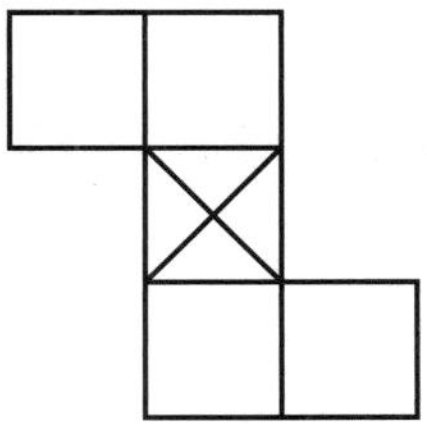

(g)

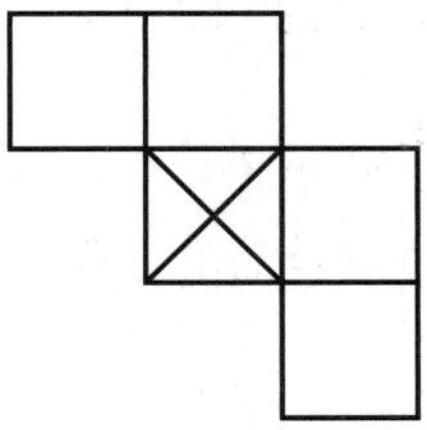

2) Which of these drawings are nets of cuboids?
Answer first just by looking.
Then check any you are unsure about by trying to make them.

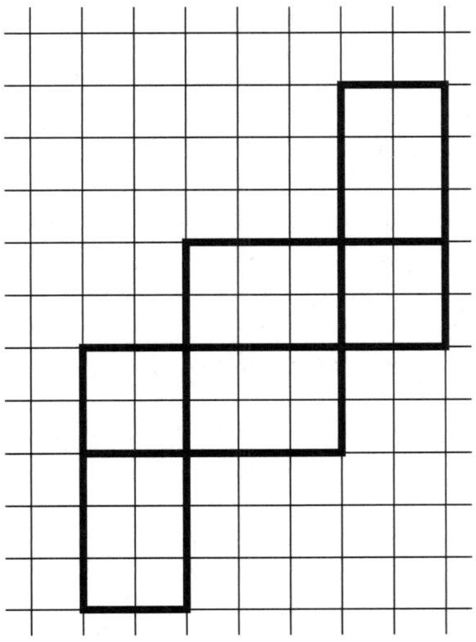

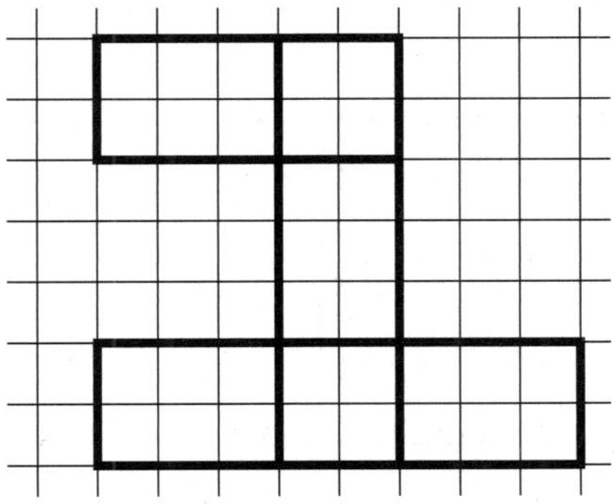

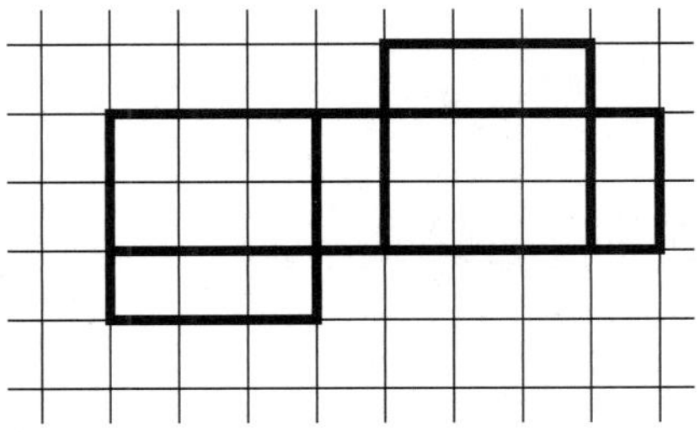

# Copymaster 31

# Area

1) What area does each of these plasters cover?

This small square has an area of 1 square centimetre.

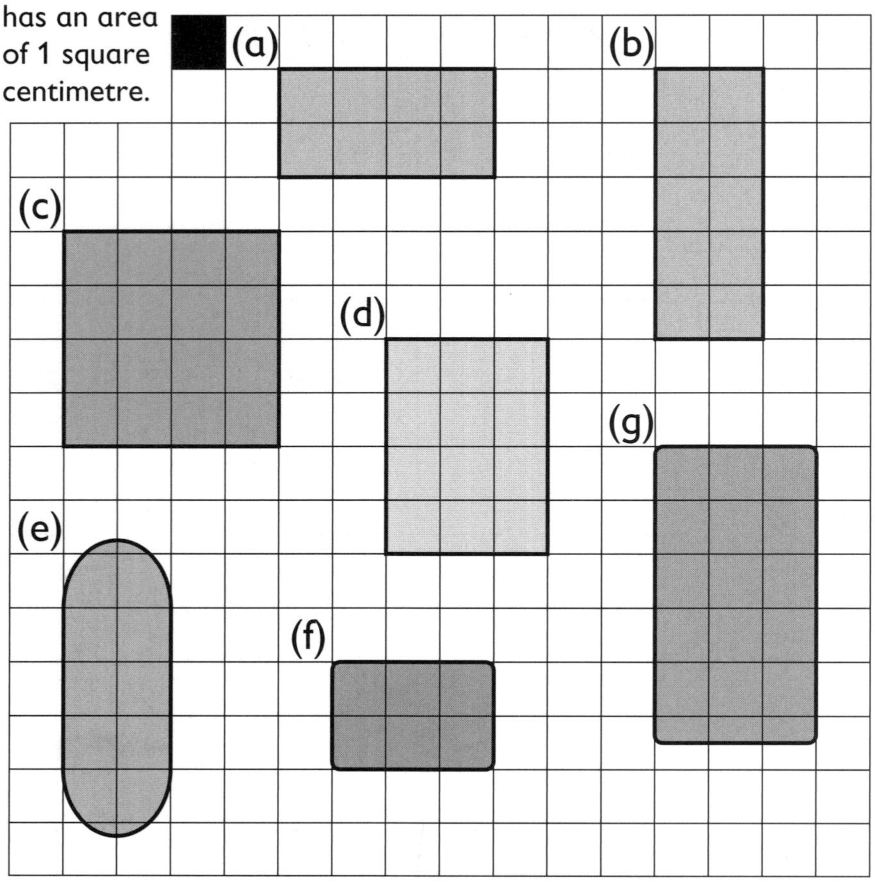


Not to scale

a) ____________

b) ____________

c) ____________

d) ____________

e) ____________

f) ____________

g) ____________

2) On this grid, made from centimetre squares, draw some shapes which have an area of 12 $cm^2$.

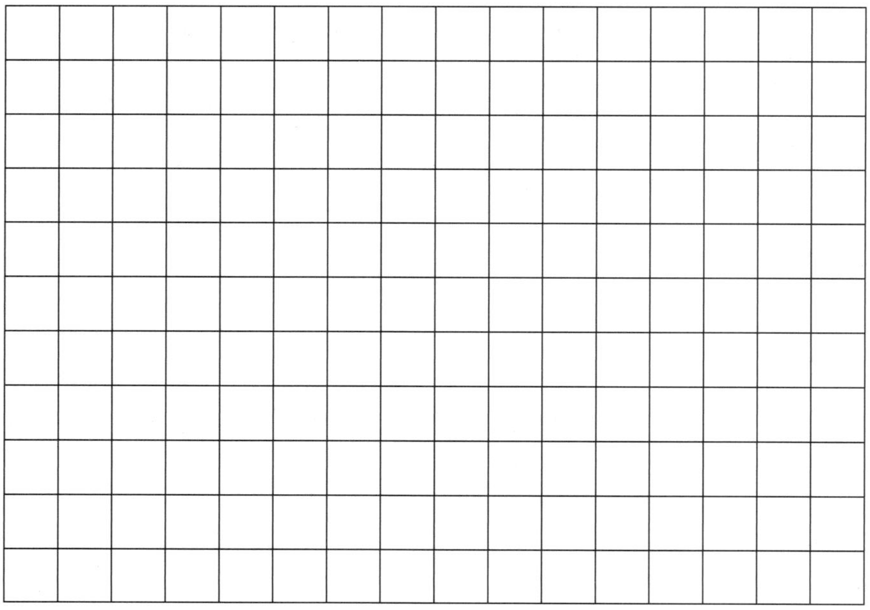

Not to scale

# Area

1) Which units would it be sensible to use for these?
The first one has already been done.
a) Area of a page in a book: $cm^2$ or square centimetres.
b) Area of a postage stamp: ______________________
c) Area of a table top: ______________________
d) Area of a football pitch: ______________________
e) Area of a full-stop: ______________________
f) Area of your class room: ______________________

2) Try to jot down in the table some things whose areas would be measured in:

| $mm^2$ | $cm^2$ | $m^2$ |
|---|---|---|
| | | |

3) For each of these choose the best answer:
a) The area of this sheet of paper: $6\ cm^2$ $60\ cm^2$ $600\ cm^2$ $6000\ cm^2$
b) The area of a bedroom floor: $1\ m^2$ $10\ m^2$ $100\ m^2$ $1000\ m^2$
c) The area of one side of a door: $6\ m^2$ $60\ m^2$ $600\ m^2$ $6000\ m^2$
d) Circle the approximate area of each of these rectangles:

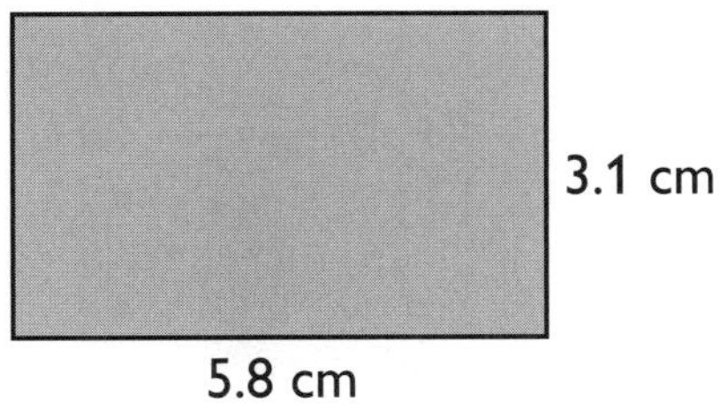


$15\ cm^2$ $18\ cm^2$ $21\ cm^2$ $24\ cm^2$

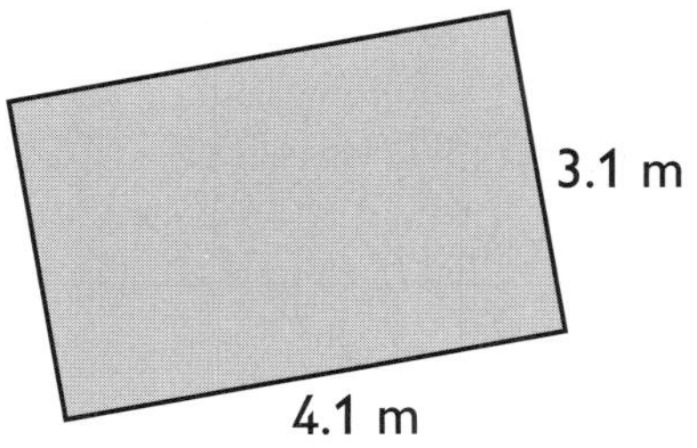


$1.2\ m^2$ $1.6\ m^2$ $12\ m^2$ $16\ m^2$

**Copymaster 33**

# Measuring mass

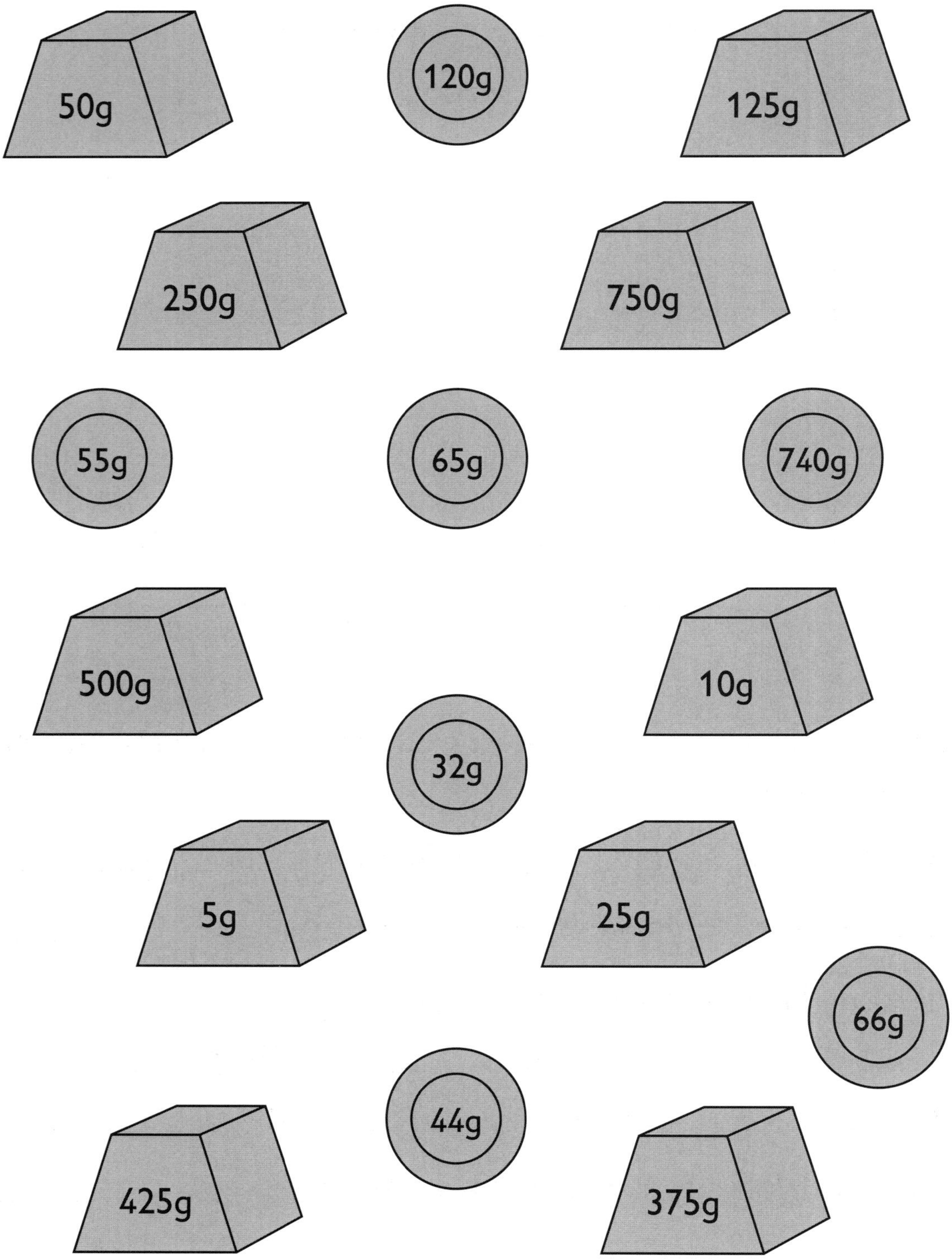


Can you write these weights in order, smallest first?

# Measuring mass

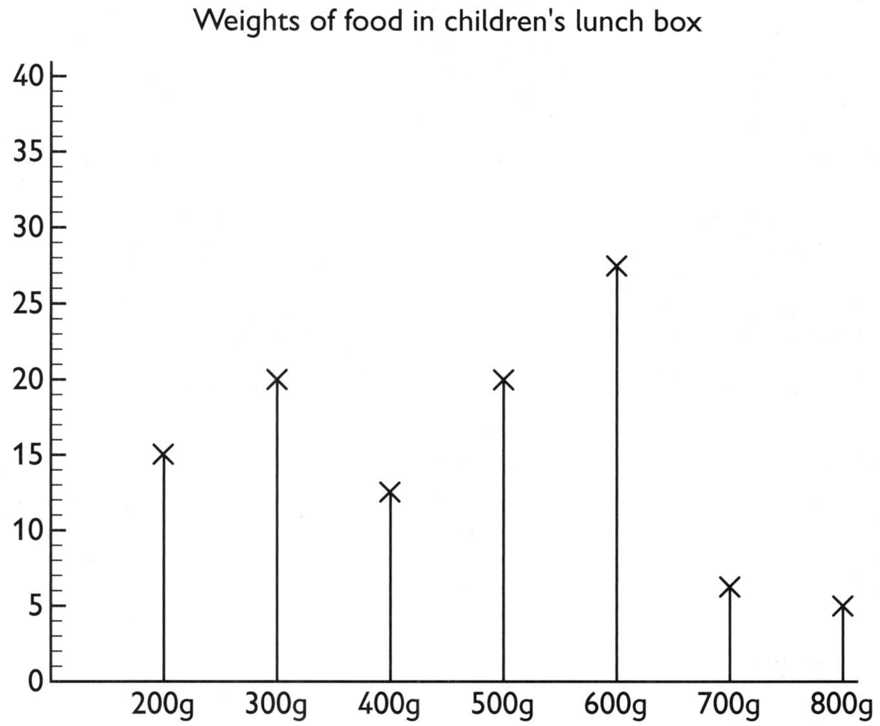


This is a bar line chart showing the weights of food in children's lunch boxes to the nearest 100 g.

1) What is the most common weight of food? ____________________

2) What is the least common weight of food? ____________________

3) How many children had food that weighed:

400 g → ________ 500 g → ________ 600 g → ________

200 g → ________ 600 g → ________ 800 g → ________ ?

4) How many children took part in the research? ____________________

## Copymaster 35

# Addition and subtraction

Complete these mathematical sentences:

1) 260 + 30 = __________
2) 260 − 30 = __________
3) 124 − 30 = __________
4) 320 + 220 = __________
5) 37 + 39 = 37 + 40 − 1 = __________
6) 29 + 83 = 30 + 83 − __ = __________
7) 126 + 68 = 126 + 70 = __________
8) 353 − 48 = 353 − 50 + 2 = __________
9) 423 + 38 = 423 + __ − 2 = __________
10) 260 + 29 = __________

Jot down the answers to these:

11) 35 + 59 = __________
12) 66 − 29 = __________
13) 312 + 48 = __________
14) 824 − 68 = __________
15) 727 − 89 = __________
16) 126 + 77 = __________
17) 298 + 157 = __________
18) 720 + 398 = __________
19) 498 + 377 = __________
20) 457 − 297 = __________

Solve these – think before you calculate!

21) 399 − 201 + 67 = __________
22) 510 − 170 = __________
23) 920 − 450 = __________
24) 800 − 320 = __________
25) 1405 + 798 = __________
26) 178 + 67 − 59 = __________
27) 57 + 39 + 79 = __________
28) 57 − 33 + 179 = __________
29) 398 + 299 + 57 = __________
30) 548 − 120 + 11 = __________

# Addition and subtraction

## Section A

Complete these number sentences:

1) $5.3 + 6.4 = (5 + 6) + (0.3 + 0.4) = (\_\_\_) + (\_\_\_) = \_\_\_\_$
2) $6.9 + 3.7 = (6 + 3) + (0.9 + 0.7) = (\_\_\_) + (\_\_\_) = \_\_\_\_$
3) $1.6 + 6.7 = (1 + 7) + (\_\_\_ + \_\_\_) = (\_\_\_) + (\_\_\_) = \_\_\_\_$
4) $3.65 + 1.21 = (3 + 1) + (0.6 + 0.2) + (0.05 + 0.01)$
$= 4 + (\_\_\_) + (\_\_\_) = \_\_\_\_$
5) $32.8 + 11.5 = (30 + 10) + (2 + 1) + (0.8 + 0.5)$
$= 40 + 3 + (\_\_\_) = \_\_\_\_$
6) $6.8 - 2.1 = \_\_\_\_$
7) $17.8 - 10.2 = \_\_\_\_$

## Section B

Complete these written calculations:

8)
```
  4.3
 +1.8
 ----
  _._
```

9)
```
  6.6
 +1.7
 ----
  _._
```

10)
```
  3.8
 +4.7
 ----
  _._
```

11) 4.3 − 2.7
```
  4. 3
  2. 7
 -----
  __.__
```

12) 8.49 − 1.73
```
  8.49
  1.73
 -----
  __.__
```

13) 8.44 − 1.76
```
  8.44
  1.76
 -----
  __.__
```

## Section C

Calculate:

14) $17 + 39$
15) $1.7 + 3.9$
16) $0.17 + 0.39$
17) $8.42 - 3.61$
18) $3.61 + 4.81$
19) $56.1 - 12.7$
20) $72.5 - 4.6$
21) $4.6 + 67.9$

# Money problems

1) Carmen has a collection of 10 CDs. 4 cost £2.50. 6 cost £3.50. How much did they cost altogether?

_______________

_______________

2) Paul went to 6 football matches. 3 cost him £12.50 each. 3 cost him £15 each. How much did going to the football matches cost Paul?

_______________

_______________

3) Joanna collected money for charity in three tins. 2 of the tins contained £4.75 each. The other tin contained £5.60. How much did Joanna collect altogether for charity?

_______________

_______________

4) 4 shops counted their takings at the end of the day. 2 of the shops had made £27.50 each. The other 2 shops collected £60.40 between them. How much did all four shops have?

_______________

_______________

5) Philip had to make 3 bus journeys. One journey cost £3.25, the other two £3.60 and £4.10. How much did the journeys cost altogether?

_______________

_______________

# Money problems

Work out the cost of the following orders.

1) 6 CDs at £5.50 each. ________________

2) 8 BOOKS at £6.75 each. ________________

3) 9 PENS at £0.75 each. ________________

4) 10 VIDEOS at £9.99 each. ________________

5) 12 SANDWICHES at £1.75 each. ________________

TOTAL [ ]

*Then*

1) Return 1 CD to the shop ________________

2) Return 2 BOOKS. ________________

3) Return 3 PENS. ________________

4) Return 2 VIDEOS. ________________

5) Return 6 SANDWICHES. ________________

How much will the bill be in total now? [ ]

Add these totals

| 1) | 2) | 3) |
|---|---|---|
| £ | £ | £ |
| 4.75 | 1.68 | 5.22 |
| 3.22 | 2.13 | 6.13 |
| +6.14 | +5.14 | +4.19 |
| ____ | ____ | ____ |

# Properties of numbers

Before you calculate these number sentences, decide if the answer is going to be odd or even.

| | *ODD or EVEN?* | *ANSWER* |
|---|---|---|
| 1) $3 + 9 + 13 =$ | | |
| 2) $23 + 11 + 33 =$ | | |
| 3) $17 + 18 + 14 =$ | | |
| 4) $20 + 32 + 15 + 17 =$ | | |
| 5) $(32 + 3) - 17 =$ | | |
| 6) $(41 + 7) - 12 =$ | | |
| 7) $(53 + 8) - 11 =$ | | |
| 8) $27 + 15 + 29 =$ | | |
| 9) $33 + 17 + 16 + 4 =$ | | |
| 10) $29 + 11 + 15 =$ | | |
| 11) $50 + 20 + 40 + 30 =$ | | |
| 12) $35 + 17 + 12 + 11 =$ | | |

# Properties of numbers

Write out the multiples of the following lists from these starting numbers.

Multiples of

| | | |
|---|---|---|
| 6 | 18 → | 96 |
| 7 | 21 → | 119 |
| 8 | 64 → | 160 |
| 9 | 72 → | 153 |

Draw a circle to show which of these numbers are:

Divisible by 5.

55 42 74 25 22 30 33 67

Divisible by 4.

98 52 48 60 36 32 54 20

Divisible by 10.

37 120 40 101 30 32 130

## Copymaster 41

# Multiplication and division

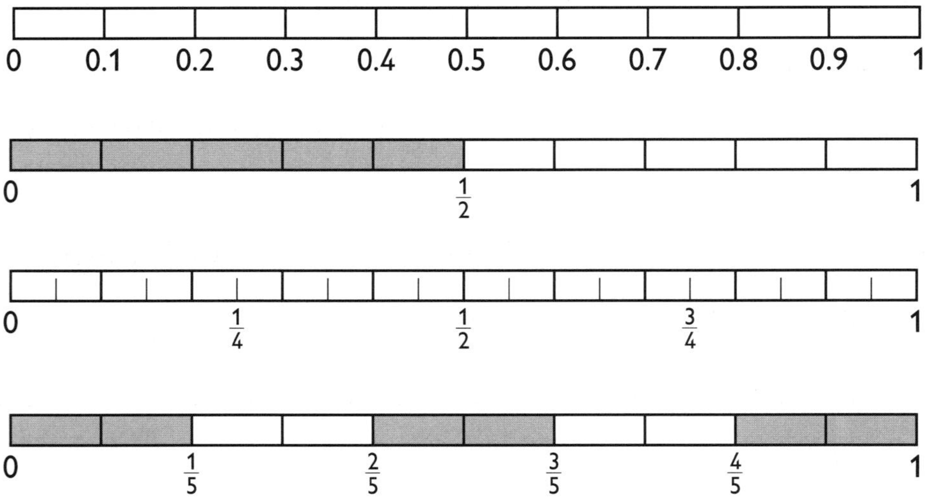


### Section A

1) $17 \div 2 = \ldots \frac{\ldots}{\ldots} = \ldots . \ldots$

2) $22 \div 5 = \ldots \frac{\ldots}{\ldots} = \ldots . \ldots$

3) $19 \div 4 = \ldots \frac{\ldots}{\ldots} = \ldots . \ldots$

4) $122 \div 5 = \ldots \frac{\ldots}{\ldots} = \ldots . \ldots$

5) $67 \div 4 = \ldots \frac{\ldots}{\ldots} = \ldots . \ldots$

6) $97 \div 2 = \ldots \frac{\ldots}{\ldots} = \ldots . \ldots$

### Section B

Calculate these. Give your answers with **fractions** not remainders.

7) $161 \div 4$ ______________

8) $487 \div 5$ ______________

9) $437 \div 5$ ______________

10) $881 \div 4$ ______________

### Section C

Calculate these. Give your answers with **decimals** not remainders.

11) $246 \div 4$ ______________

12) $516 \div 5$ ______________

13) $661 \div 2$ ______________

14) $367 \div 5$ ______________

# Multiplication and division

1) Amy has saved £48. How many CDs costing £9 can she buy?

   ______________

2) Eggs are stored in boxes of 12 eggs. How many boxes will be filled by 70 eggs? ______________

3) Cola is sold in 6 can packs. Tom needs to buy 20 cans for a party. How many packs will he need to buy? ______________

4) Buses hold 54 passengers. How many buses will be needed for 250 people? ______________

5) Carpet tiles are sold in boxes of 10 tiles.
   Mena calculates she needs 22 tiles. How many boxes of tiles does she need? ______________

6) Nails are sold in boxes of 50.
   How many full boxes can be filled with 845 nails? ______________

7) A lift will carry a maximum of 8 people.
   How many journeys will it have to make to carry 26 people to the top floor? ______________

8) James needs to post 62 letters, but he has no envelopes.
   Envelopes are sold in packs of 20.
   How many packs does he need to buy? ______________

9) A class has 32 pupils in it. Each table seats 6 pupils.
   How many tables are needed to seat the whole class?

   ______________

10) Marbles are sold in bags of 12.
    How many full bags will be needed for 90 marbles? ______________

11) There are 70 pupils in a year group. Each pupil needs a pencil.
    The pencils come in boxes of 12 pencils.
    How many boxes of pencils are needed for every pupil in a year group? ______________

# Money problems

## Section A

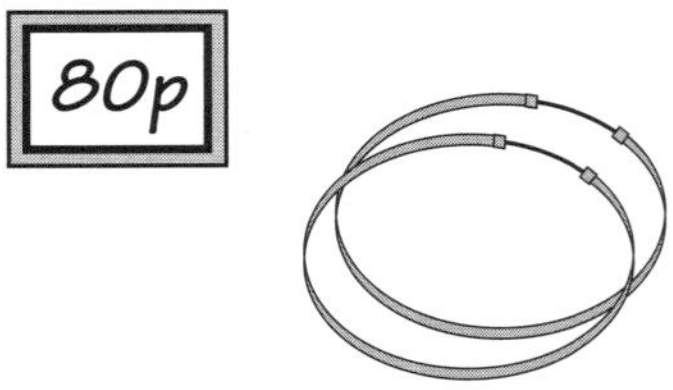


1) These earrings are reduced by 50%.
   How much do they cost now? __________

2) Janet works for a big store.
   She gets 25% off anything she buys in the store.
   A coat costs £40 in the store. How much could Janet save? __________

3) Before this sale a belt cost £5.

   **All prices cut by 50%**

   a) How much cheaper would it be in the sale? ______________
   b) How much cheaper would a bag costing £2.80 be? ______________

4) Complete these number sentences, using the numbers from this list:

   10 15 20 25 30 40 50 60 75

   _____% of _______ = _______
   _____% of _______ = _______
   _____% of _______ = _______

5) This is on the side of a new bottle of shampoo.

   **25% more!**

   The old bottle used to contain 200 ml of shampoo.
   How much more shampoo is in the new bottle? ______________

6) You have two 27p stamps and two 33p stamps. If you send a parcel using one or more of your stamps, what might it cost? ______________

## Section B

1) Kath wants to make some extra money by making gift tags from old cards, glitter and gold thread. She gets the old cards for nothing. Glitter costs £2.40 and gold thread costs £1.60. The glitter and gold thread is enough for 100 tags.

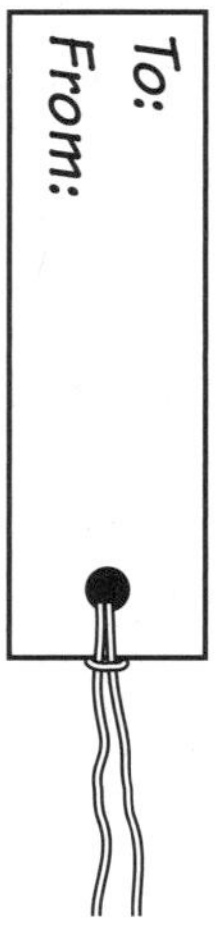


   a) How much goes each tag cost to make? ____________
   b) Kath sells the tags for 6p each.
      How much profit does Kath make on 100 tags? __________
   c) What profit would Kath make if she increased her price by 50% per tag? ______________

## Part 1

Chewing gum 38p

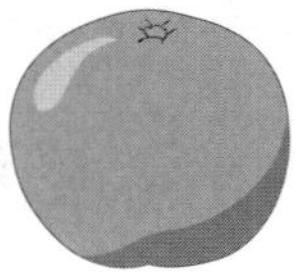
Orange 25p

Crisps 48p

Apple 19p

1) How many oranges can you get for 50p? ______________
2) Petra buys a chewing gum. She pays with a £1 coin.
   How much change should she get? ______________
3) How many apples could you buy for £1? ______________
4) Will £1 be enough to buy an orange, a packet of crisps and an apple?
   If it is, how much change should you get? ______________
5) Will £1 be enough to buy all four things on sale? ______________
6) How much would it cost to buy a class of 32 pupils an apple each? ______________
7) Imagine you had £1 to spend. What would you buy? How much would you have left over? ______________

## Part 2

Join each problem to the correct calculation and work out the answer.

| |
|---|
| A Euro is worth 63p. How much are 5 Euros worth? |
| Amy has £63 in the bank. She pays in £5. How much has she in the bank now? |
| Anil saves the same amount each week. After 5 weeks he has saved £6.30. How much does he save a week? |
| James has £6.30 birthday money. He saves £5 and spends the rest. How much does he spend? |
| In Year 6 there are 63 pupils. Each pays 50p for a school trip. How much is this in total? |
| Five people share £63. How much should they each receive? |

| |
|---|
| £63 + £5 = |
| £6.30 − £5 = |
| £0.63 × 5 = |
| 63 × £0.50 = |
| £63 ÷ 5 = |
| £6.30 ÷ 5 = |

# Fractions, decimals, percentages

Calculate these amounts. The first one has been done for you.

$\frac{2}{3}$ of 12 = 12 ÷ 3 = 4 × 2 = 8

$\frac{3}{7}$ of 56 = ____________________

$\frac{4}{9}$ of 72 = ____________________

$\frac{8}{12}$ of 108 = ____________________

$\frac{3}{9}$ of 36 = ____________________

$\frac{7}{8}$ of 96 = ____________________

$\frac{3}{10}$ of 200 = ____________________

$\frac{5}{11}$ of 110 = ____________________

$\frac{9}{18}$ of 36 = ____________________

$\frac{10}{15}$ of 165 = ____________________

# Fractions, decimals, percentages

Complete this table.

| | | | | |
|---|---|---|---|---|
| 0.2 | = | $\frac{2}{10}$ | = | 20% |
| 0.4 | = | | = | |
| | = | $\frac{3}{10}$ | = | |
| 0.7 | = | | = | |
| | = | | = | 80% |
| 0.9 | = | | = | |
| 0.5 | = | | = | |

Fill in the missing answers.

37% = $\frac{37}{100}$ = 0.37

26% = ☐ ☐

18% = ☐ ☐

27% = ☐ ☐

14% = ☐ ☐

# Ratio & proportion

Fill in these tables.

1) *Ratio* – 1 box for every 4 sweets (1 : 4)

| BOXES | **SWEETS** |
|---|---|
| 3 | |
| 8 | |
| 7 | |
| 9 | |

2) *Ratio* – 2 apples for every 6 children (2 : 6)

| **APPLES** | **CHILDREN** |
|---|---|
| 2 | |
| 4 | |
| 8 | |
| 12 | |

3) *Ratio* – 4 frogs for every 6 ponds (4 : 6)

| **FROGS** | **PONDS** |
|---|---|
| 4 | |
| 8 | |
| 16 | |
| 20 | |

4) *Ratio* – 6 eggs for every 3 boxes (6 : 3)

| **EGGS** | **BOXES** |
|---|---|
| 12 | |
| 18 | |
| 24 | |
| 30 | |

# Ratio & proportion

## THEME 4

*STATEMENT – Paul has one book for every two that Graham has.*

- So Paul has $\frac{1}{2}$ as many books as Graham.
- Graham has twice as many books as Paul.
- Paul has $\frac{1}{3}$ of the total number of books and Paul has $\frac{2}{3}$.

1) If Graham has 20 books how many has Paul got?

________________________________________

2) If Paul has 15 books how many has Graham got?

________________________________________

3) If Graham has 60 books how many has Paul got?

________________________________________

*STATEMENT – Alice has one sticker for every 3 that Faye has.*

4) If Alice has 3 stickers how many has Faye got?

________________________________________

5) If Alice has 9 stickers how many has Faye got?

________________________________________

6) If Faye has 36 stickers how many has Alice got?

________________________________________

Copymaster 49

# Handling data

1) 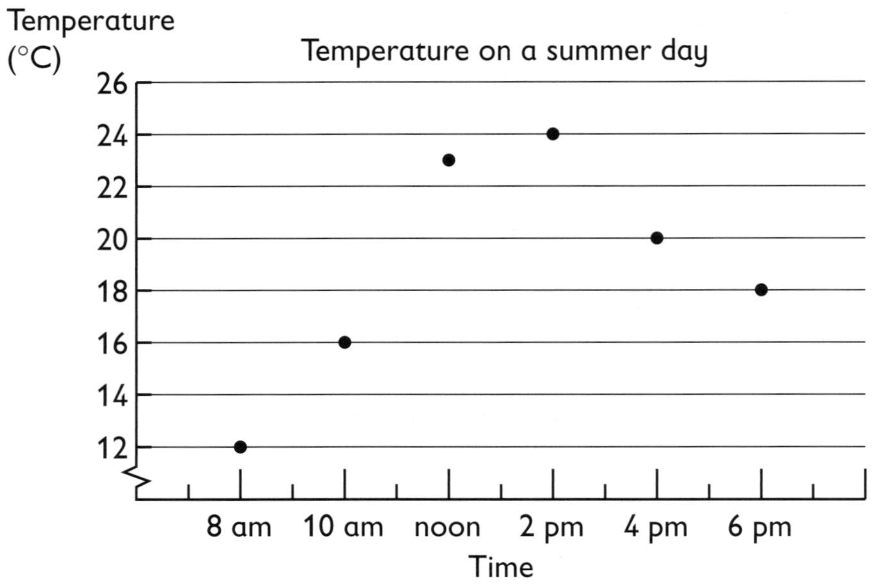


2) 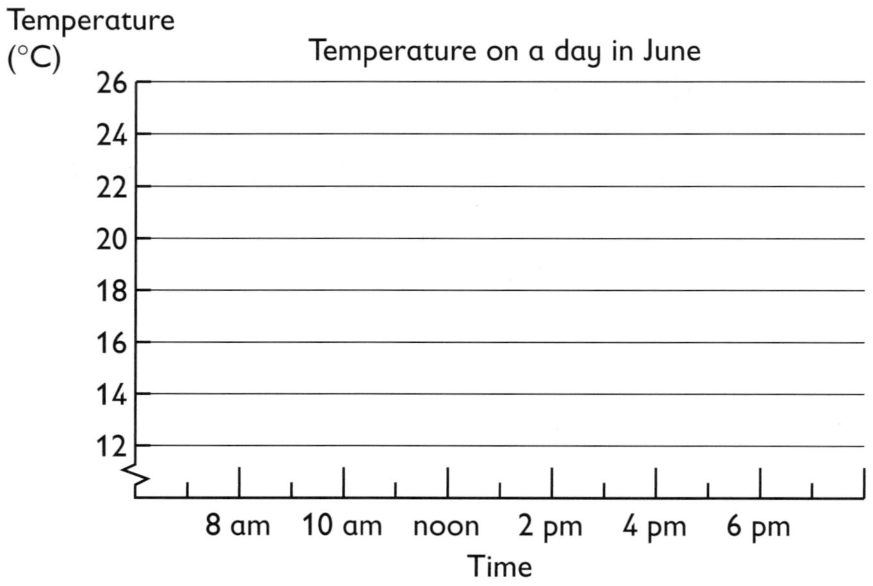


| Time | 8 am | 10 am | noon | 2 pm | 4 pm | 6 pm |
|---|---|---|---|---|---|---|
| Temperature °C | 12 | 14 | 23 | 21 | 20 | 18 |

# Handling data

1) This graph shows the noise level in a school hall over 1 day.

Noise level in a school hall over one day

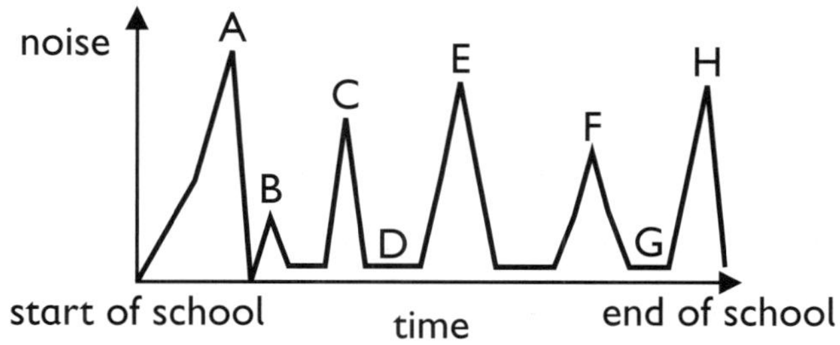


2) This graph shows the amount of water in a bath.

Taking a bath

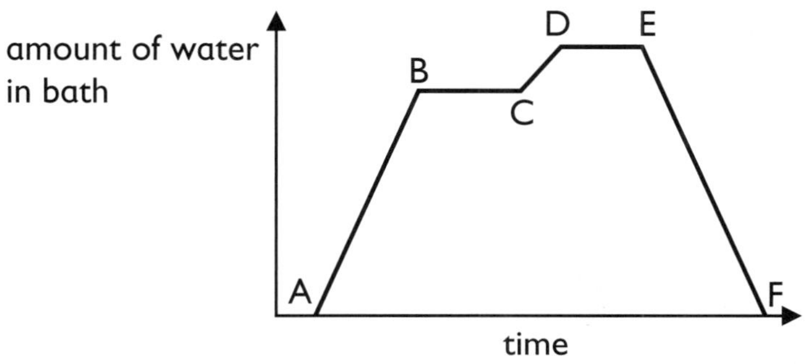


3) This graph shows the level of water in a rain barrel during the month of April.

Level of water in rain barrel during April

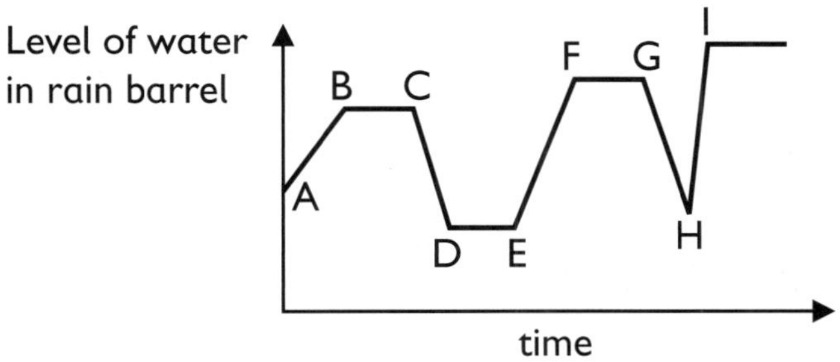


4) This graph shows the amount of water in a tank which is being filled from a water tap.

A tank filled with water
from water tap

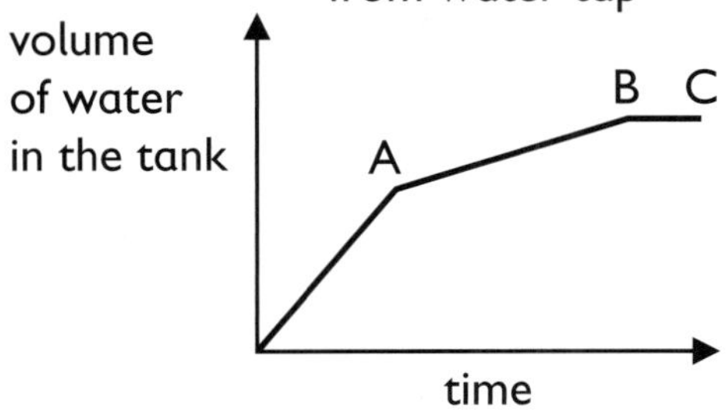

# Reflections and symmetry

You will need a mirror and some squared paper.

1) Draw a cross on the squared paper.
Investigate how the distance from the cross to the mirror changes the distance between the cross and its reflection or **mirror image**.
Try to spot a rule.

2) Look at this shape.
The arrows go round clockwise.
Look at an image of the shape in a mirror. Which way do the arrows in the image of the shape go?

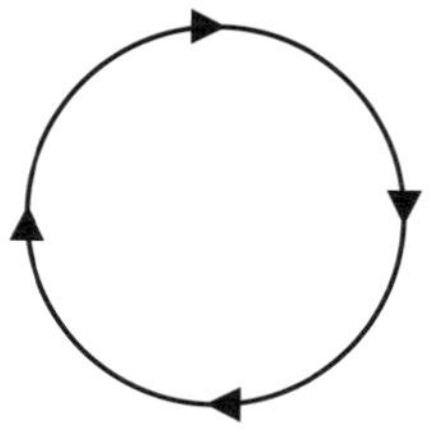

3) Look at the image in a mirror when you put a mirror along the dotted lines in these shapes.
Jot down the name of the polygon made from the shape and its image.

a) 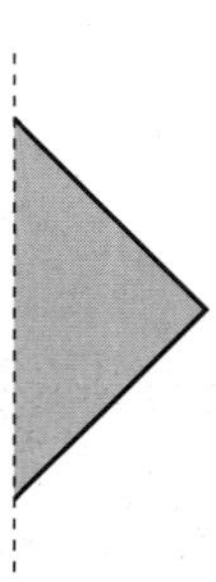 ______________

b)  ______________

c) 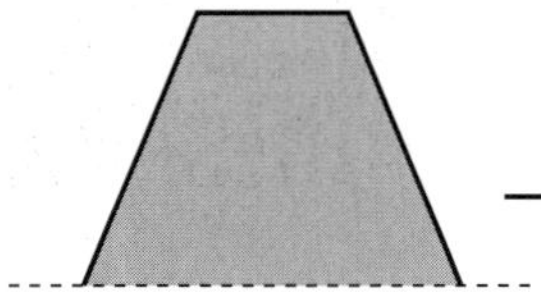 ______________

d) 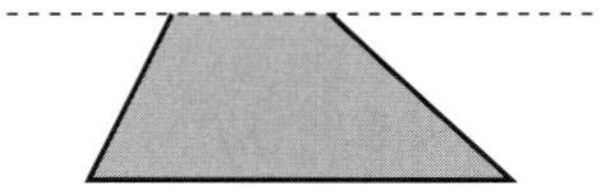 ______________

4) Place your mirror so that you can see:

2 circles

3 circles

4 circles

5 circles

and so on up to 16 circles.

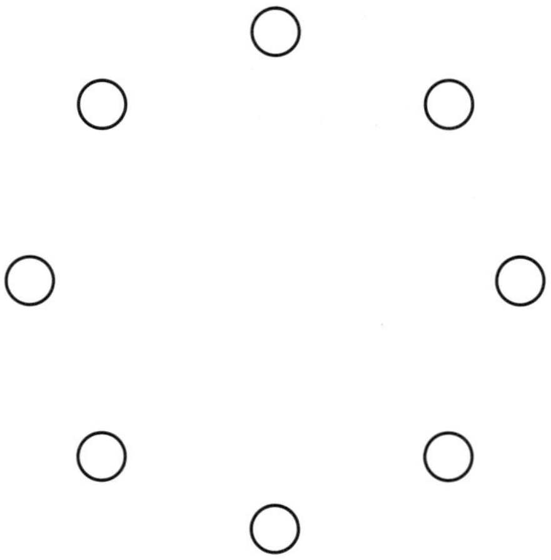

# Reflections and symmetry

1) Here are some shapes.
Tick (✓) those which have reflection symmetry.
Cross (✗) those which don't have reflection symmetry.

a) 

b) 

c) 

d) 

e) 

f) 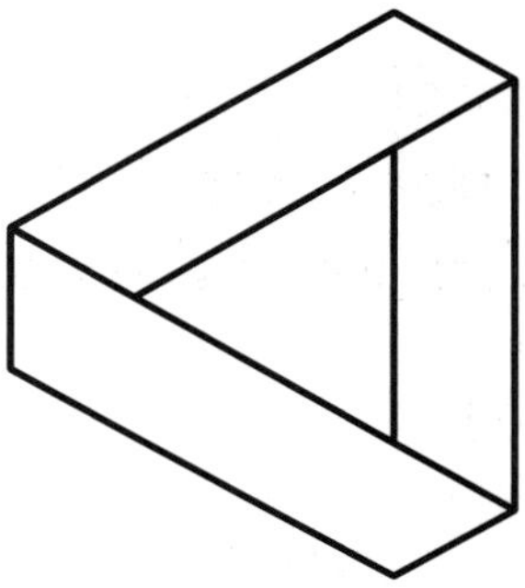

g) 

h) 

i) 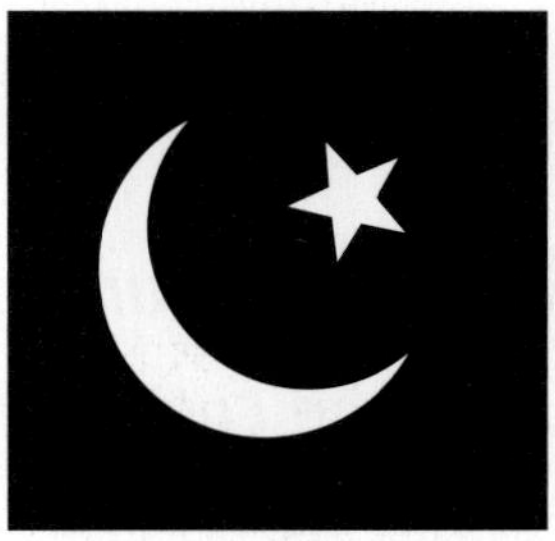

j) 

k) 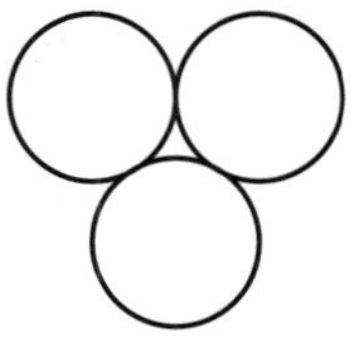

# Plan a holiday!

| *Destinations* | *Currency* | *Distance from London* |
|---|---|---|
| ARGENTINA | 4 *PESOS* for every pound | 12 000 km |
| AUSTRALIA | $2\frac{1}{2}$ *DOLLARS* for every pound | 17 000 km |
| FRANCE | $1\frac{1}{2}$ *EUROS* for every pound | 85 km |
| KUWAIT | $\frac{1}{2}$ *DINAR* for every pound | 5000 km |
| SINGAPORE | $2\frac{1}{2}$ *DOLLARS* for every pound | 12 000 km |
| SOUTH AFRICA | 15 *RAND* for every pound | 11 000 km |

| | *Cost from London* | *Speed 750 km an hour* |
|---|---|---|
| Argentina | £300 | |
| Australia | £600 | |
| France | £50 | |
| Kuwait | £200 | |
| Singapore | £250 | |
| South Africa | £275 | |

*Work out your journey time to each destination.*
*Calculate the cost of your journey in pounds and the local currency equivalent.*
*You should use a calculator.*

| **Destination** | **Journey time** | **Cost of travel (£)** | **Cost in local currency** |
|---|---|---|---|
| Argentina | | | |
| Australia | | | |
| France | | | |
| Kuwait | | | |
| Singapore | | | |
| South Africa | | | |

# Journey planning

## THEME 7

| *Destinations* | *Currency* | *Distance from London* |
|---|---|---|
| ARGENTINA | 4 *PESOS* for every pound | 12 000 km |
| AUSTRALIA | $2\frac{1}{2}$ *DOLLARS* for every pound | 17 000 km |
| FRANCE | $1\frac{1}{2}$ *EUROS* for every pound | 85 km |
| KUWAIT | $\frac{1}{2}$ *DINAR* for every pound | 1000 km |
| SOUTH AFRICA | 15 *RAND* for every pound | 11 000 km |
| SINGAPORE | $2\frac{1}{2}$ *DOLLARS* for every pound | 12 000 km |

| | *Cost from London* | *Speed 750 km an hour* |
|---|---|---|
| Argentina | £300 | |
| Australia | £600 | |
| France | £50 | |
| Kuwait | £200 | |
| South Africa | £250 | |
| Singapore | £275 | |

---

*Estimate and then calculate the difference in journey times (use a world map) between:*

1. London and Argentina and London and Australia
2. London and France and London and Kuwait
3. London and South Africa and London and Singapore
4. London and Argentina and London and France
5. London and South Africa and London and Australia
6. London and France and London and Singapore.

*Estimate and then calculate the difference in the cost of travel between the above destinations:*

a) in pounds     b) in local currency

# Capacity

| |
|---|
| 1 pint = 568 ml<br>8 pints make 1 gallon. |

pint bottle = 568 ml

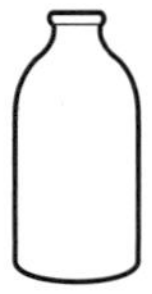

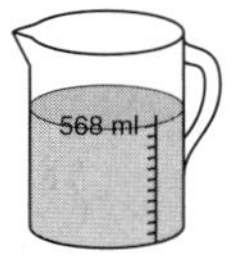


8 pint bottles = 1 gallon

1136 ml = ____ pints

2272 ml = ____ pints

3976 ml = ____ pints

5112 ml = ____ gallons ____ pints

6816 ml = ____ gallons ____ pints

7384 ml = ____ gallons ____ pints

3 gallons 4 pints = _______ ml

5 gallons 3 pints = _______ ml

6 gallons 4 pints = _______ ml

25 pints = ____ gallons ____ pints

36 pints = __·__ gallons

52 pints = __·__ gallons

84 pints = __·__ gallons

# Capacity

James drank 200 ml of cola. John drank 350 ml of lemonade and Paul drank 300 ml of water.

How much drink is that altogether _____?

Hannah drank 300 ml of water. Kerry drank 500 ml of water and Katie 400 ml of water.

How much water is that in litres and millilitres? ___ l ___ ml

4 bottles contained the following amounts of liquid:

Bottle 1 300 ml Bottle 2 650 ml Bottle 3 3800 ml Bottle 4 900 ml

What is the total amount in litres and millilitres? ___ l ___ ml

Convert these amounts into millilitres.

3 litres _____ $2\frac{1}{2}$ litres _____ $2\frac{3}{4}$ litres _____

$5\frac{1}{2}$ litres _____ $1\frac{1}{4}$ litres _____ $1\frac{1}{2}$ litres _____

# Copymaster 57

## Section A

Complete these calculations.

1) 27 + 36 + 13 = (20 + 30 + 10) + (7 + 6 + 3) = (60 + 16) = ____________
2) 54 + 61 + 34 + 28 = (50 + 60 + 30 + 20) + (… + … + … + …) = ____________
3) 80 + 40 + 70 = ____________
4) 3 + 9 + 5 + 7 = ____________
5) 570 + 250 = ____________
6) 620 − 380 = ____________
7) 500 + 638 = ____________
8) 1263 − 400 = ____________
9) 5.7 + 2.5 = 5.7 + 2 + ___ = ____________
10) 6.2 − 3.8 = 6.2 − 3 − 0.8 = ____________

## Section B

Complete these number sentences.

1) [________] − 7984 = 19
2) 8003 − [________] = 19
3) 800 + [________] + 400 = 1500
4) 27 + 36 + [________] = 76
5) 0.24 + [________] = 0.36
6) 6.8 − [________] = 4.2
7) 0.95 − [________] = 0.78
8) 0.56 + [________] = 0.70
9) 2.4 + 8.7 = [________]
10) 6.3 − 4.8 = [________]

## Section C

1) Write six subtractions that have 0.15 as an answer.

________________________________________

________________________________________

2) Try to find a easy way to calculate:
1 + 2 + 3 + 4 + 5 + 6 + 7 + 8 + 9 + 10 + 11 + 12 + 13 + 14 + 15

________________________________________

________________________________________

3) Andy wrote this: 26 + 28 + 30 + 32 + 34 = 5 × 30 = 150
Try to figure out his method and use it to find:
74 + 76 + 78 + 80 + 82 + 84 + 86

________________________________________

________________________________________

# Addition and subtraction

In pairs solve these problems: Don't forget to jot down all your working out.

1) What change do you get from £20 for £12.65? ________________
2) Petrol costs 83p per litre. What should you pay to fill a 5 litre can? __________
3) The deposit on a £800 computer is 10%. How much is the deposit? __________
4) Four people share equally the cost of a £72 meal.
How much does each person pay? ________________
5) I think of a number, then divide it by 15.
The answer is 15. What is the number? ________________
6) A quick way to multiply a number by 21 is to double the number, multiply this by 10, and add the number. Use this method to calculate $43 \times 21$.
________________
7) $15 \times 191$ is 2865. Use this to calculate $16 \times 191$. ________________
8) Double a number is 4 less than 30. What is the number? ________________
9) What is the change from £1 for two kiwi fruit at 28p each? ________________
10) Ali is 1.45 cm tall. He is 6 cm shorter than Emile. How tall is Emile? __________
11) Buns are 10 for £1. What do 4 buns cost? ________________
12) A bus had 44 passengers on it. Twelve got off and 8 got on. How many were on the bus then? ________________
13) I think of two numbers. Added together they make 60. One of the numbers is 10 more than the other. What is the smaller number? ________________
14) There are 32 pupils in Inram's class. A quarter of the class are away with flu: of these, half are girls. How many girls are away with flu? ________________
15) Mark buys three 27p stamps and two 25p stamps. How much change should he get from £5? ________________
16) 25g is about one ounce. There are 16 ounces in a pound. About how many grams is a quarter of a pound? ________________
17) Amber's granddad started secondary school in 1957 when he was 11 years old. In what year was he 21 years old? ________________
18) A bag contains an equal number of 10p coins and 20p coins.
There is a total of £3 in the bag. How many coins are there of each kind?
______________________
19) Put the numbers 2, 3, 7, 8, 14 and 18 into two lists which have the same sum.
20) I divide a number by five, double the answer and get 8. What was my number?
______________________

# Properties of numbers

True or False.

1) $28 + 16 + 24 = 70$ ________

2) $33 + 3 + 3 = 60$ ________

3) $40 + 4 + 12 = 33$ ________

4) $14 + 13 + 9 = 36$ ________

5) $27 - 6 - 4 = 17$ ________

6) $33 - 5 - 7 = 25$ ________

7) $63 - 2 - 3 = 58$ ________

8) $37 - 3 - 2 = 35$ ________

9) $67 - 53 - 1 = 13$ ________

10) $32 + 13 + 3 = 50$ ________

11) $51 + 11 + 4 = 64$ ________

12) $34 + 9 + 42 = 85$ ________

13) $70 + 8 + 21 = 99$ ________

# Properties of numbers

1) I am a multiple of 7 between 40 and 50 ________

2) I am a multiple of 9 between 50 and 60 ________

3) I am a 2-digit number between 63 and 65 ________

4) I am a 3-digit number between 110 and 122 which is a multiple of 11 ________

5) I am a 3-digit number between 140 and 150 which is a multiple of 12 ________

6) I am a 4-digit number between 1121 and 1133 which is a multiple of 10 ________

7) I am a 4-digit number between 1232 and 1237 which is a multiple of 9 ________

8) I am a 5-digit number between 11 231 and 11 236 which is a multiple of 5 ________

# Homework Copymaster 1

This week we have been doing multiplication and division.

Explain and show your working.

## Section A

1) I think of a number, add 2, then multiply by 5. The answer is 25.
   What was my number? ____________________

2) There are 136 books on the top shelf, and 59 on the bottom shelf. A total of 40 books are removed. How many are left? ____________________

3) In a class of 32 children, one quarter are ill and a half are away on a school trip.
   How many children are left in the class? ____________________

4) John has 6 shelves of comics in his room. Three of the shelves have 20 comics each. Two have 15 each and one has 21 comics on it.
   How many comics does John have? ____________________

5) Kate has a pack of 32 biscuits.
   She eats a quarter of them on Monday, and half of what's left on Tuesday.
   How many has she left on Wednesday? ____________________

## Section B

1) Amy has 24 stickers and Ben has 16 stickers. Carole has twice as many as Amy and Ben combined. How many does Carole have? ____________________

2) Jan pays £20 for two pairs of jeans and a top.
   The top costs £6. What is the cost of one pair of jeans? ____________________

3) An adult giraffe is 3 times the height of a newborn giraffe.
   The adult giraffe is 6 m tall. How tall is the newborn giraffe? ____________________

4) Jack and Paul together have 150 stickers.
   Jack has twice as many as Paul.
   How many do they each have? ____________________

5) In a computer game a sword and dagger are worth 300 copper pieces altogether. The sword is worth 200 copper pieces more than the dagger. How much is the dagger worth? ____________________

This week we have been solving mathematical problems.

1) Tom collects football stickers in a book.
The book has 32 pages. There is a space for 4 stickers on each page.

a) How many stickers can the book hold? ________________
b) He buys 8 stickers a week. ________________
If none of them are the same, how long will it take to fill the book?
________________
c) How long will it take Tom to half fill his sticker book? ________________

2) A shop sells torches and batteries. It has 21 torches and 25 batteries.
Each torch needs two batteries.

a) How many batteries are needed for all the torches? ________________
b) How many more batteries will be needed for all the torches? ________________

3) Here are the number of pupils in each year in a school.

| *Year* | *Number of pupils* |
|---|---|
| R | 24 |
| 1 | 38 |
| 2 | 45 |
| 3 | 40 |
| 4 | 43 |
| 5 | 45 |
| 6 | 42 |

a) How many pupils are there in Year 1 and Year 2 altogether? ________________
b) Each pupil in Year 3 needs two pencils.
How many pencils are needed for the whole year? ________________
c) Year 5 and Year 6 have lunch at the same time. All of them have lunch.
In the dining hall each table seats six pupils.
How many tables are needed to seat Year 5 and Year 6? ________________
d) Half the pupils in the school live on the local housing estate.
How many pupils is this? ________________

# Homework Copymaster 3

This week we have been looking at fractions and decimals.

Place these amounts on the number lines.

1) 0 — 0.5 — 1 — 1.5 — 2

a) 0.2 b) 0.7 c) 1.3 d) 1.7 e) 1.9

2) 0 — 5 — 10

a) 1.5 b) 2.5 c) 5.3 d) 7.5 e) 8.5

3) 0 — 5 — 10

a) $4\frac{1}{2}$ b) $3\frac{1}{2}$ c) $5\frac{1}{4}$ d) $7\frac{1}{2}$ e) $8\frac{1}{2}$

4) 0 — $\frac{1}{2}$ $\left(\frac{5}{10}\right)$ — 1 — $1\frac{1}{2}$ $\left(1\frac{5}{10}\right)$ — 2

a) $\frac{5}{10}$ b) $\frac{7}{10}$ c) $1\frac{1}{10}$ d) $1\frac{8}{10}$ e) $\frac{9}{10}$

5) 0 — $\frac{50}{100}$ — 1

a) $\frac{10}{100}$ b) $\frac{30}{100}$ c) $\frac{60}{100}$ d) $\frac{90}{100}$ e) $\frac{40}{100}$

# Homework Copymaster 4

This week we have learnt how to calculate percentages and ratios.

## Section A

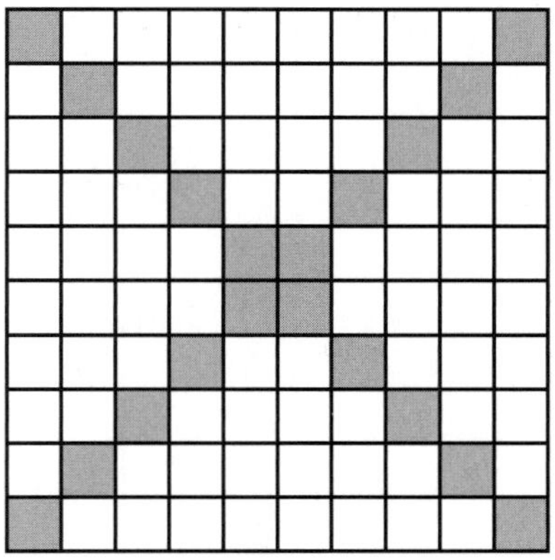

1) a) What percentage of the big square is shaded?

   ______________________________

   b) What percentage is unshaded?

   ______________________________

   c) How many more squares need to be shaded so that 25% of the big square is shaded?

   ______________________________

2) What percentage of each of these shapes is shaded?

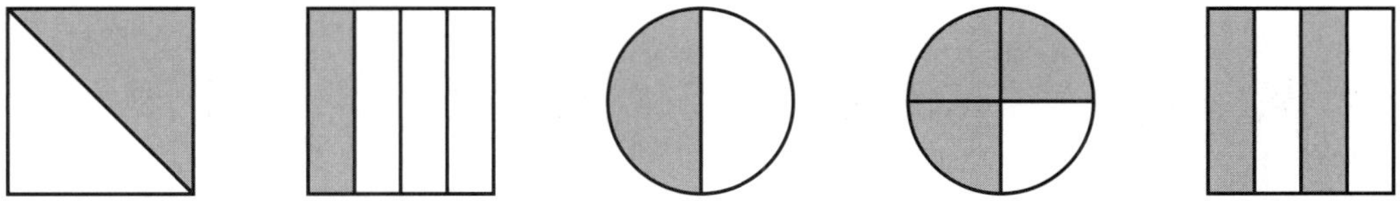

(a) (b) (c) (d) (e)

_______ _______ _______ _______ _______

3) Shade 25% of each of these shapes.

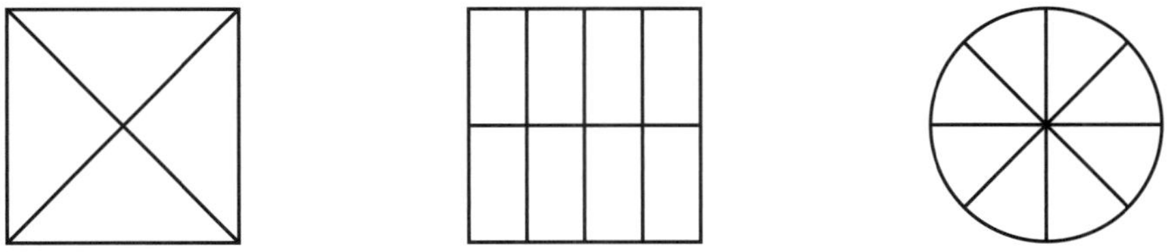

(a) (b) (c)

## Section B

1) To make mortar for making a brick wall you need a mixture of sand and cement. The mixture is 1 part of cement for 3 parts of sand.

   a) How much sand should be added to 2 shovelfuls of cement? ____________

   b) How much cement should be added to 9 shovelfuls of sand? ____________

   c) In 4 shovelfuls of mortar how much is cement? ____________

   d) What percentage of mortar is cement? ____________

   e) What percentage of mortar is sand? ____________

# Homework Copymaster 5

This week we have learnt how to handle data.

Chart showing some people's choice of number from 1 to 9

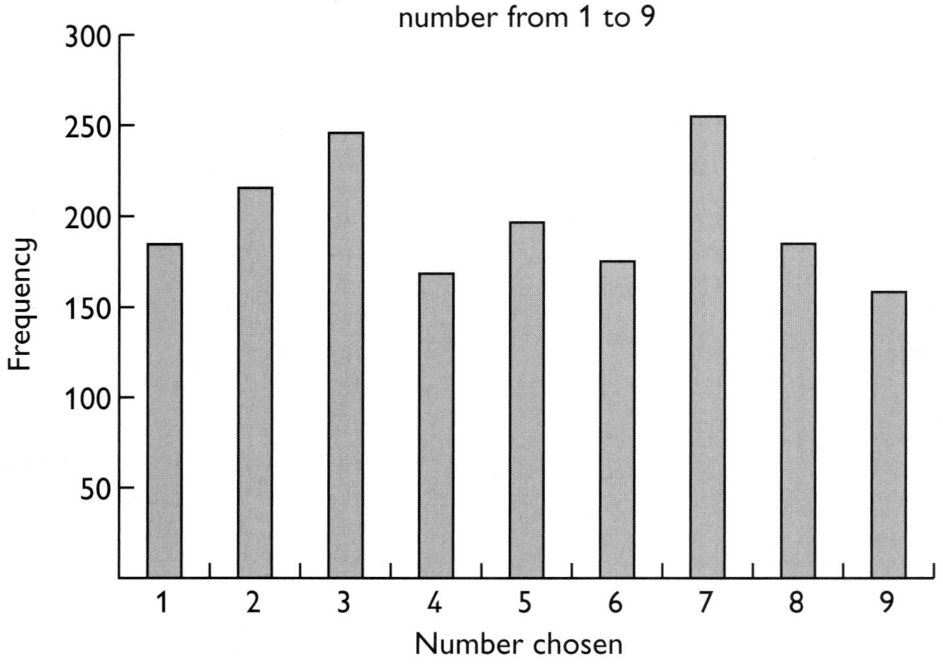


**1** About how many people chose:

a) 5 ____________ b) 9 ____________ c) 1? ____________

**2** Which number was chosen the most? ____________

This number is called the mode.

**3** About how many people were asked to choose a number? ____________

This week we have looked at shapes and their properties.

Link the shape or property with its description by drawing a line.

POLYGON

HEXAGON

My name is for all four sided shapes

I have four sides, all equal in length. My four angles are right angles

I am a triangle with all three sides equal

ISOSCELES TRIANGLE

OBLONG

EQUILATERAL TRIANGLE

I have six sides

My name is for all four sided shapes

SEMI-CIRCLE

QUADRILATERAL

CONGRUENT

I am made from eight straight lines

I am a triangle with just two sides equal

SQUARE

BISECT

I am half a circle

SCALENE

My name means 'exactly the same as but in a different position'

I am a rectangle but not with all four sides equal in length

PARALLEL

I am a triangle with no two sides equal in length

I am another word for 'divide into two parts'

VERTEX

I'm a pair of straight lines which are always the same distance apart

OCTAGON

PENTAGON

I am the proper name for the corner of a shape

I am a closed shape whose sides are all straight lines.

HEPTAGON

# Homework Copymaster 7

This week we have been estimating and measuring length.

*Estimate, fill in the table. Check, fill in the table. Calculate the difference.*
*At the end calculate the total difference.*

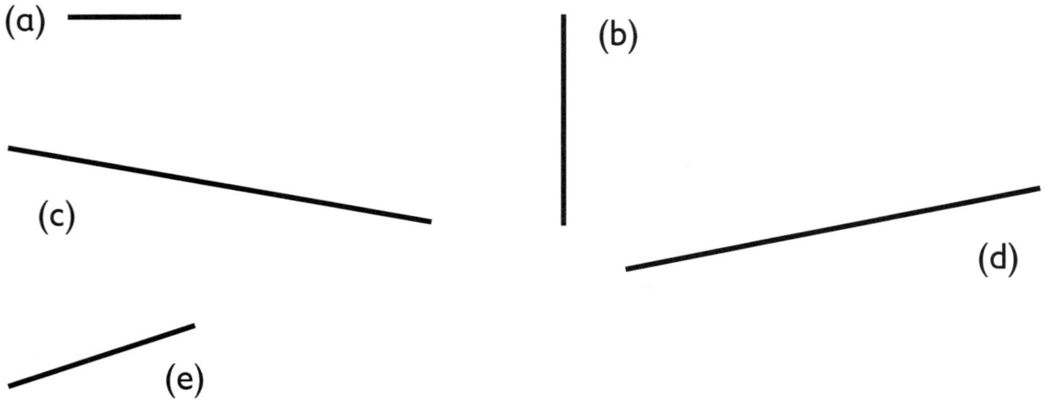


| Line | Estimated Length (millimetres/mm) | Measured Length (millimetres/mm) | Difference (millimetres/mm) |
|---|---|---|---|
| a | | | |
| b | | | |
| c | | | |
| d | | | |
| e | | | |

Estimate the perimeters of these shapes. Don't forget to use sensible units!

a)

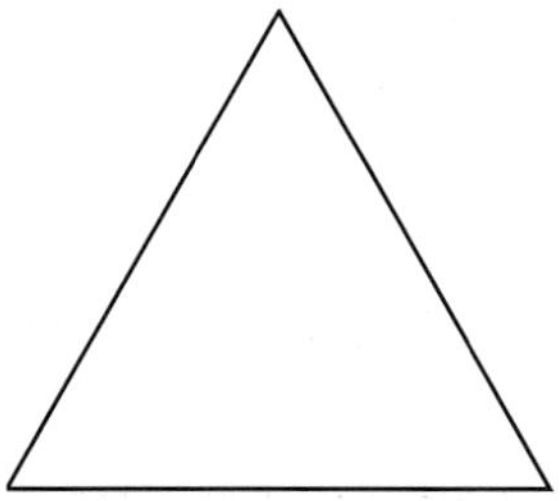

____________________

____________________

b)

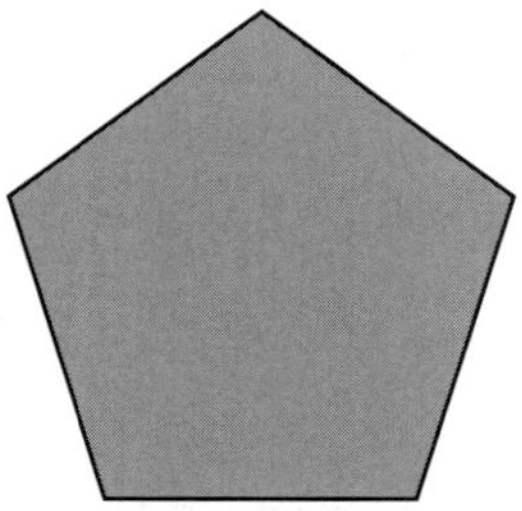

____________________

____________________

c)

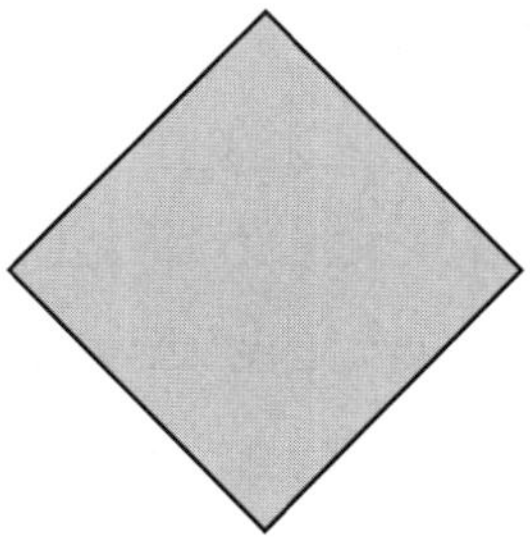

____________________

____________________

This week we have been looking at measurement including time.

## Time problems

1 A maths lesson starts at 09:25 and finishes 50 minutes later.
At what time does it end?

______________________________

2 A coach journey takes 90 minutes.
If the journey ends at 13:15, at what time did it start?

______________________________

3 Carmen leaves home at 07:45 and arrives at school at 08:20.
How long does her journey take?

______________________________

4 A film starts at 14:35 and ends at 17:05.
Will a 3-hour videotape be long enough to record it?

______________________________

5 School starts at 08:50 and ends at 15:20. How long is the school day?

______________________________

6 Richard gets up at 06:45. He spends 30 minutes getting ready and 1 hour and 15 minutes driving to work. At what time does he arrive at work?

______________________________

7 A train finishes its $3\frac{1}{2}$ hour journey at 2:05 pm. At what time did the journey start?

______________________________

8 A film lasts $2\frac{1}{2}$ hours. It starts at 11:40 a.m. At what time does it finish?

______________________________

# Homework Copymaster 9

This week we have been looking at addition and subtraction.

Complete these addition problems as the example shows:

$$\begin{aligned}322 + 431 &= 300 + 20 + 2 + 400 + 30 + 1\\ &= 700 + 50 + 3\\ &= 753\end{aligned}$$

$$\begin{aligned}232 + 641 &= 200 + 30 + 2 + 600 + 40 + 1\\ &= 800 + 70 + 3\\ &= \_\_\_\_\_\_\_\_\_\_\_\_\_\_\_\_\_\_\_\_\end{aligned}$$

147 + 327 = ____________________

364 + 436 = ____________________

527 + 271 = ____________________

647 + 238 = ____________________

Also:

$$\begin{aligned}438 - 53 &= 400 + 30 + 8 - 500 - 3\\ &= 300 + 130 + 8 - 50 - 3\\ &= 300 + 80 + 5 = 385\end{aligned}$$

$$\begin{aligned}364 + 77 &= 300 + 60 + 4 - 70 - 7\\ &= 200 + 160 + 4 - 70 - 7\\ &= 200 + 150 + 14 - 70 - 7\\ &= \_\_\_\_\_\_\_\_\_\_\_\_\_\_\_\_\_\_\_\_\end{aligned}$$

271 − 89 = ____________________

234 − 57 = ____________________

546 − 79 = ____________________

627 − 49 = ____________________

# Homework Copymaster 10

This week we have been learning about number sequences.

- Answer these:

**1** $4^2$ ______ **2** $3^2$ ______ **3** $8^2$ ______ **4** $9^2$ ______

**5** $7^2$ ______ **6** $12^2$ ______ **7** $11^2$ ______ **8** $15^2$ ______

$^2$ = squared (or times by itself)

- What are the factors of these numbers?

25 ____________________

36 ____________________

42 ____________________

3 ____________________

7 ____________________

19 ____________________

- Draw rectangles to show the factors of 30, 40 and 20

e.g.

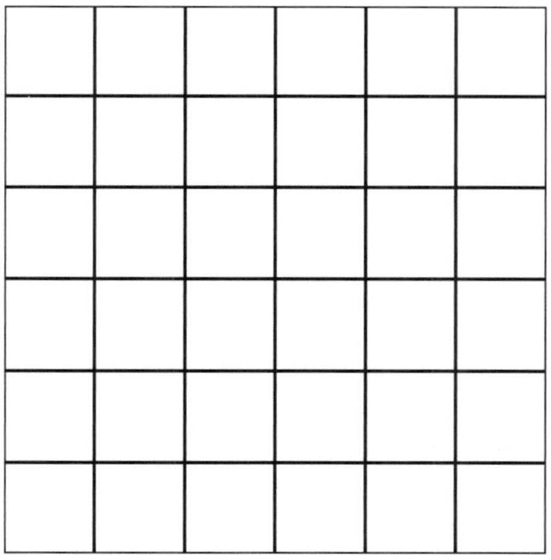

6 by 5 = 30

Factors = 6 and 5

- Are there more factors/rectangles to show for 30? ______________

- $2^2 + 3^2 = 13$ (*not* $5^2$) $4^2 + 3^2 =$ ______ $5^2 + 6^2 =$ ______

$8^2 - 7^2 =$ ______ $7^2 - 3^2 =$ ______ $4^2 - 2^2 =$ ______

# Homework Copymaster 11

This week we have been comparing and ordering numbers.

Complete these number sentences with either <, or =, or >

Less than  Greater than

**1** 5 + 4 + 7 □ 3 + 5 + 8

**2** 4 + 3 □ 3 + 1

**3** 5 + 4 □ 8 + 7

**4** 6 + 7 + 3 □ 7 + 9 + 4

**5** 8 + 3 + 2 □ 7 + 10 + 5

**6** 9 + 4 + 3 + 6 □ 5 + 7 + 12 + 10

**7** 6 + 5 + 3 + 7 + 10 □ 9 + 4 + 3 + 12

**8** 9 + 6 + 4 + 10 □ 5 + 4 + 6 + 11

Complete these number sequences

**1** 2, 4, 8, ___, ___.

**2** 27, 24, 20, ___, ___.

**3** 38, 41, 37, 41, ___, ___,

**4** 22, 33, ___, ___, 66

**5** 10, −20, −50, ___, ___.

This week we have been working on multiplication and division.

FILL IN THESE GRIDS.

| × | 4 | |
|---|---|---|
| 3 | | 24 |
| 2 | | 16 |

| × | | 8 |
|---|---|---|
| | 21 | 24 |
| 4 | 28 | 32 |

| × | 5 | 3 |
|---|---|---|
| 6 | | |
| 2 | | |

| ÷ | 32 | 64 |
|---|---|---|
| 4 | | |
| 8 | | |

| ÷ | 63 | 72 |
|---|---|---|
| 3 | | |
| 9 | | |

| ÷ | | |
|---|---|---|
| 9 | 9 | 15 |
| 3 | 27 | |

# Homework Copymaster 13

This week we have been solving mathematical problems.

*Show your working so that someone else can understand what you have done – you need to write down every step.*

**1** If I double a number, then subtract 5, the answer is 7. What is the number?

**2** Jane is older than Kim, Kim is older than Sean, Sean is younger than Jane and Rachael is older than Jane. List these people from oldest to youngest.

**3** Dina and Paul together have 270 stickers. Dina has twice as many stickers as Paul. How many stickers does each of them have?

**4** James has twice as many marbles as John. John has twice as many marbles as Peter. Peter has 10 marbles. How many marbles do they have altogether?

**5** Leone went to a pet shop and bought 20 fish for £45. She only bought Angel fish and Neon fish. How many Angel fish did she buy if Angel fish cost £3 and Neon fish cost £2?

**6** The product of three whole numbers is 42. Their sum is 12. What are the three numbers?

**7** A group of children have a total of 18 counters. Some have 5 counters.
a) What could be the total number of these counters?
b) The rest have 2 counters each.
What could be the total number of these counters?
c) How many children are there in the group?

**8** Rachael opened a book. The page numbers added up to 243. What pages did she open to?

**9** I'm thinking of a whole number less than 20.
When I divide it by 2 it gives a remainder of 1. What could it be?
When I divide it by 7 it gives a remainder of 1. What could it be? What number am I thinking of?

This week we have been working on fractions and decimals.

To find $\frac{3}{10}$ of 50 → divide 50 by the denominator and times the numerator

$= 50 \div 10 \times 3$

$= 15$

Do the same for

$\frac{3}{4}$ of 60 → ______________________

$\frac{2}{3}$ of 60 → ______________________

$\frac{4}{5}$ of 60 → ______________________

$\frac{3}{6}$ of 60 → ______________________

$\frac{9}{10}$ of 60 → ______________________

$\frac{5}{7}$ of 60 → ______________________

$\frac{6}{8}$ of 60 → ______________________

$\frac{3}{12}$ of 60 → ______________________

$\frac{9}{11}$ of 60 → ______________________

# Homework Copymaster 15

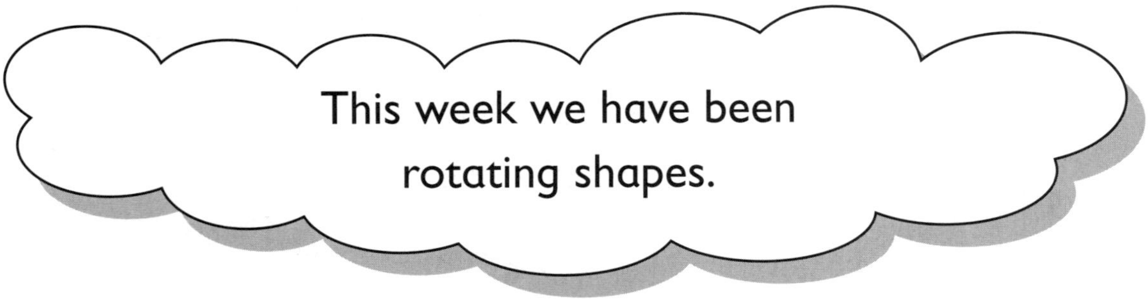


On squared paper copy one of these shapes.

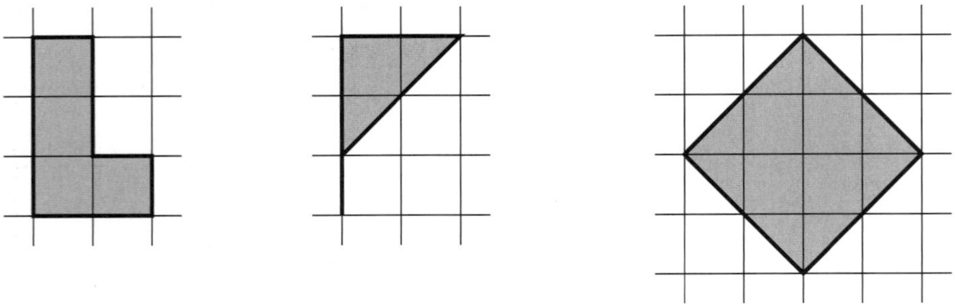

a) Make a pattern by rotating it by rotations of 90° each time.
Like this:

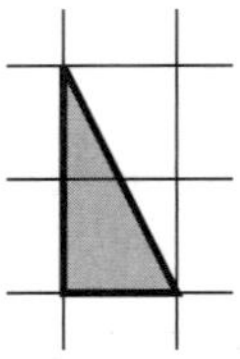

Will make this pattern:

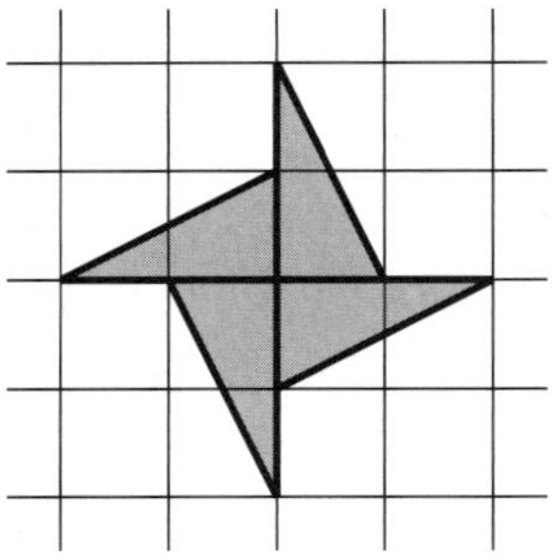

b) Make a pattern by rotating one of these shapes by 45°.

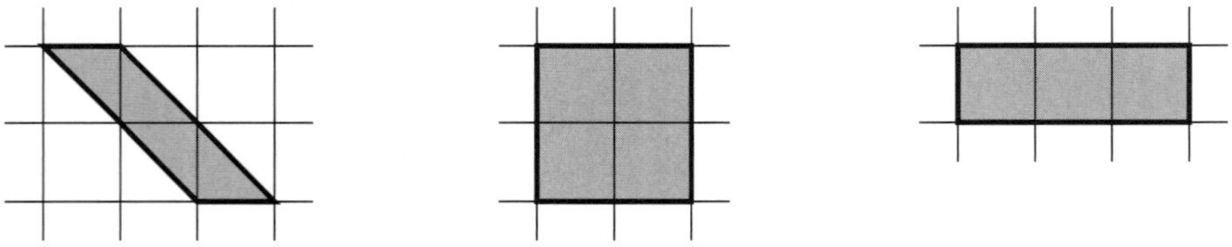

c) Boxes are moved across the floor by rotating them end over like this:

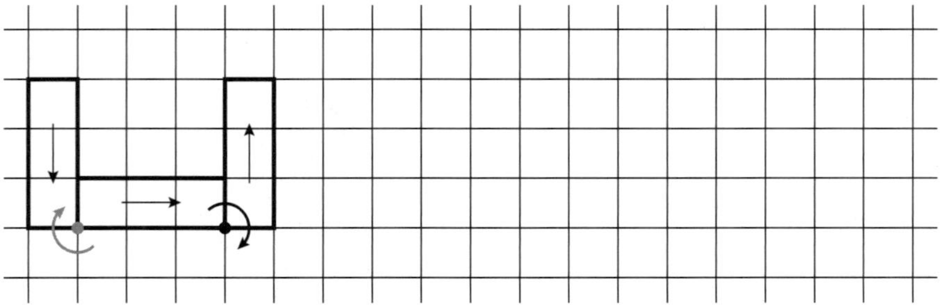

Carry on the drawing for another three rotations.

This week we have been looking at area.

**1** All these rectangles are drawn on centimetre squares.
Count the number of squares in one row. Count the number of rows.
Then, without counting, jot down the area of each rectangle.

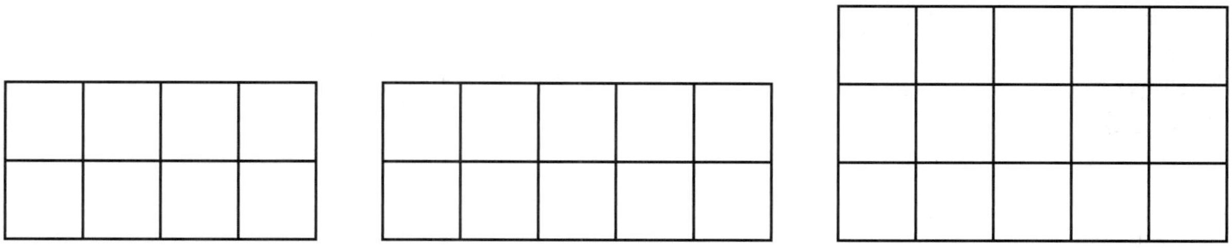

a) ________ b) ________ c) ________

**2** Put your transparent grid on each rectangle below.
Count the number of squares in one row. Count the number of rows.
Then, without counting, jot down the area of each rectangle.

a) ________ b) ________ c) ________

**3** Find the areas of these rectangles. Do not use your transparent grid.

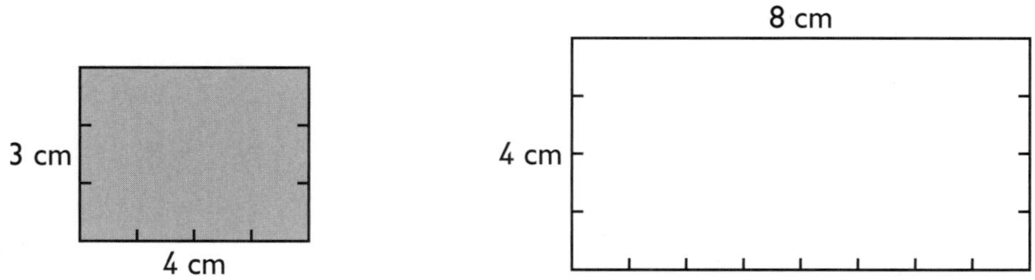


a) ________ b) ________

**4** By measuring their sides with a ruler find the areas of these rectangles.

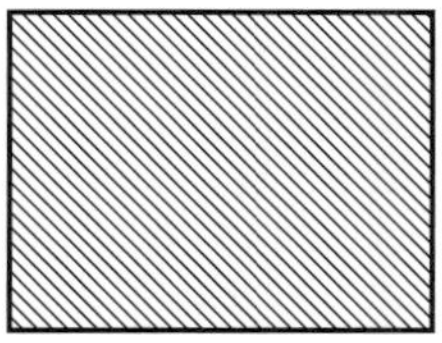

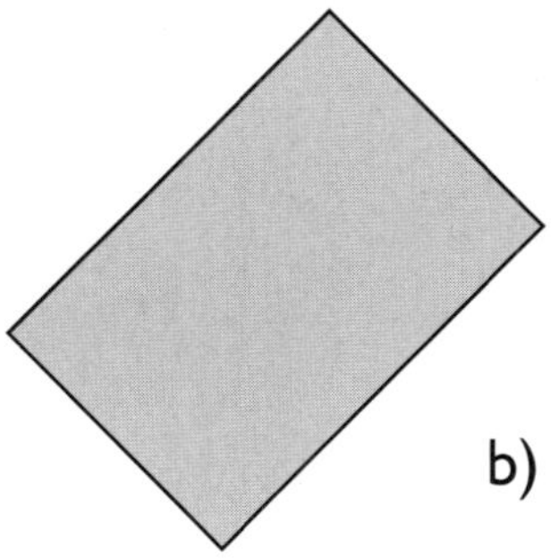

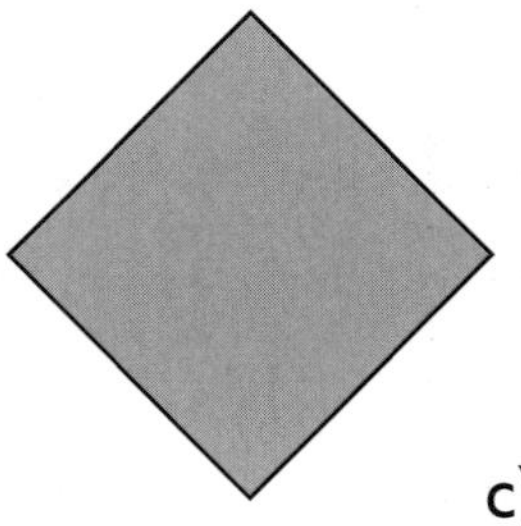

a) ________ b) ________ c) ________

# Homework Copymaster 17

This week we have been looking at measuring mass.

Look through your food cupboard and list items that weigh between the following limits.

50 g → 200 g

201 g → 300 g

301 g → 400 g

401 g → 500 g

501 g → 1 kg

This week we have been adding and subtracting decimal numbers.

### Section A

Complete these number sentences:

**1** 5.3 + 6.4 = (5 + 6) + (0.3 + 0.4) = (___) + (___) = ___

**2** 6.9 + 3.7 = (6 + 3) + (0.9 + 0.7) = (___) + (___) = ___

**3** 8.41 + 3.57 = (8 + 3) + (0.4 + 0.5) + (0.01 + 0.07) = 11 + 0.9 + (___) = ___

### Section B

Complete these written calculations:

**4**
```
  4 . 3 8
 +1 . 8 7
 --------
  _ . _ 5
 --------
  _   1
```

**5**
```
  6 . 0 7
 +1 . 1 9
 --------
  _ . _ _
 --------
      _
```

**6**
```
  7 3 . 8
      4 . 5
 ----------
  _ _ . _
 ----------
      _
```

**7**
```
  7.54 = 7 + 0.5 + 0.04
 -2.16 = 2 + 0.1 + 0.06
         --------------
       = 7 + ___ + 0.14
         2 + 0.1 + 0.06
         --------------
         _ + ___ + ___ = 5.38
```

**8**
```
 7.54 − 1.81
      6 . 15
      7 .  5 4
      1 .  8 1
 -------------
     __ . __ _
```

Calculate

**9** 1.2 + 2.3 + 1.2 ____________

**10** 4.5 − 2.3 ____________

**11** 3.9 + 2.9 ____________

**12** 4.4 − 1.8 ____________

**13** 8.82 − 1.17 ____________

**14** 7.65 + 1.17 ____________

**15** 9.42 − 6.68 ____________

**16** 6.68 + 2.74 ____________

**17** 2.40 + 6.85 + 6.33 ____________

**18** 12.9 + 7.3 ____________

### Section C

Calculate:

**19** 1.53 + 2.3 ____________

**20** 6.1 + 2 + 5.1 ____________

**21** 6.81 − 2.5 ____________

**22** 8.8 − 1.25 ____________

**23** 24.9 + 6.25 ____________

**24** 24.3 − 1.25 ____________

# Homework Copymaster 19

This week we have been looking at money problems.

Give your child any supermarket bills which they can check for correct addition.

They should then pretend to return certain items and take the price off the final amount.

Total this bill:

£
2.75 – Oranges
0.13 – Gum
5.12 – Chicken
6.15 – Bubble bath
3.22 – Soup
5.11 – Fish
6.19 – Washing powder

£ ____

Return the oranges, gum and chicken.

How much will the bill be then? ______________________

Then buy 2 more items at £2.75 and £3.24.

Add these amounts to the new bill. ______________________

This week we have been looking at the properties of numbers.

Complete this table.

**MULTIPLE OF**

| | |
|---|---|
| 24 | 4, 6, 12, 2, 1, 8, 3 |
| 16 | |
| 35 | |
| 50 | |
| 29 | |
| 54 | |
| 60 | |

What numbers could go on this Venn diagram?

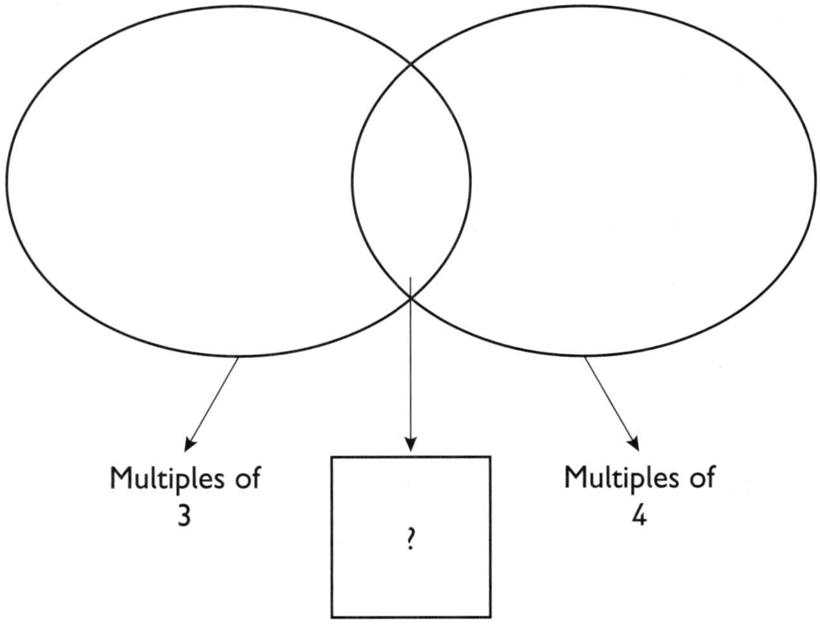

# Homework Copymaster 21

This week we have been looking at multiplication and division.

**Section A**

**1** Use just the fact $101 \times 11 = 1111$ to find

a) $1111 \div 11 =$ ______________ b) $11 \times 101 =$ ______________

**2** $301 \times 11 = 3311$, so $301 \times 22 =$ ______________

**3** $10 \times 43 = 430$ and $3 \times 43 = 129$, so $13 \times 43 =$ ______________

**4** $200 \div 10 = 20$, so $400 \div 20 =$ ______________

**5** $600 \div 10 = 60$, so $600 \div 5 =$ ______________

**Section B**

**6** $308 \div 7 = 44$, so $308 \div 14 =$ ______________

**7** $33 \times 22 = 726$, so $726 \div 11 =$ ______________

**8** $10 \times 17 = 170$, so $2 \times 5 \times 17 =$ ______________

**9** $123 \times 22 = 2706$, so $124 \times 22 =$ ______________

**10** $4 \times 15 \times 8 = 480$, so $15 \times 4 \times 4 =$ ______________

**Section C**

**11** $50 = 100 \div 2$ Use this to find a simple rule to multiply a number by 50.
Use your rule to calculate:

a) $36 \times 50$ ______________ b) $44 \times 50$ ______________

**12** Give some examples of this short-cut in use.
*To find the sixth of a number, find a third of the number and halve it.*

______________________________________________

______________________________________________

This week we have been solving money problems.

| Bill's Burgers | |
|---|---|
| Burger | £1.58 |
| Veggieburger | £1.45 |
| Cheeseburger | £2.05 |
| French fries | £1.10 |
| Side salad | 85p |
| Cola | 80p |
| Milk shake | £1.10 |

**1** Complete these bills for Bill.

How much change from £5?

______________________

1 burger............
1 French fries......
Total = ........

**2** Will £5 be enough?

______________________

1 burger............
1 cheeseburger......
2 French fries......
Total = ........

**3** Will £10 be enough? If not, how much more is needed?

______________________

2 veggieburgers......
3 cheeseburgers......
4 milk shakes........
1 cola...............
Total = .........

**4** Three friends share this bill equally. How much should they each pay?

______________________

2 burgers............
2 French fries.......
1 side salad.........
2 colas..............
Total = .........

# Homework Copymaster 23

This week we have been looking at fractions, decimals and percentages.

- Find 10% of these amounts.

£2.70 ______ £1.60 ______ £1.35 ______ £1.94 ______ £1.72 ______

200 g ______ 150 g ______ 62 g ______ 95 g ______ 173 g ______

- Find 20% of these amounts.

600 m ______ 250 m ______ 160 m ______ 280 m ______ 200 m ______

260 km ______ 320 km ______ 540 km ______ 130 km ______

- Take 50% off these amounts. What are you left with?

£2.70 ______ £3.80 ______ £5.60 ______ £8.90 ______

- Take 25% off these amounts. What are you left with?

£2.80 ______ £1.60 ______ £2.40 ______ £1.00 ______ £5.60 ______

This week we have been looking at ratio and proportion.

**FRUIT BASKET RATIOS**

Look at the ratio statements below. Write in the numbers. The first one has been done for you. After you have completed the ratios, draw the correct number of fruit next to the second basket to keep the ratio the same.

1)

2 for every 1

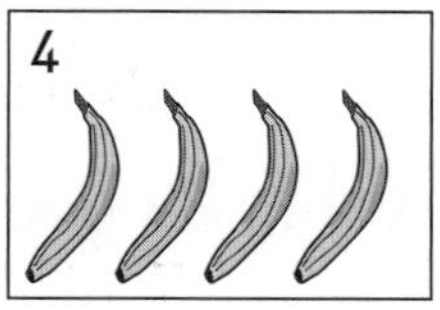


2)

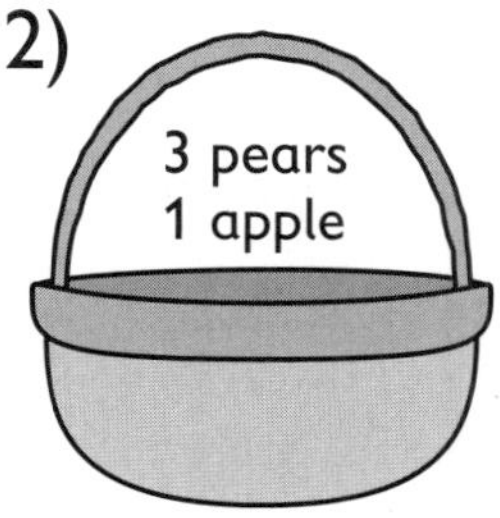


... for every ...

3)

... for every ...

4)

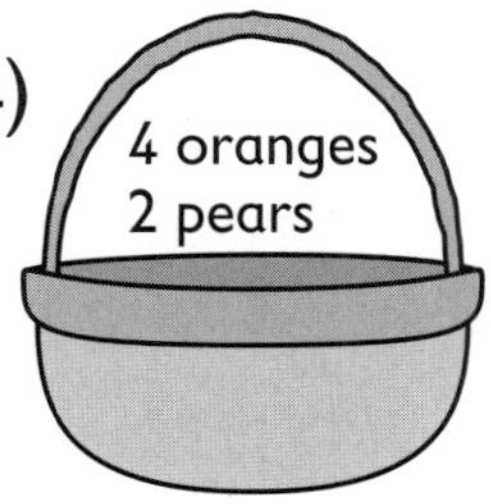


... for every ...

5)

... for every ...

# Homework Copymaster 25

This week we have been handling data.

You will need a calculator for these problems and investigations.

**1** Use your calculator to help you find the missing numbers:

a) $501 \times \_\_\_ = 10521$    b) $\_\_\_ \times 40 = 13080$

c) $15075 \div \_\_\_ = 1005$    d) $492 \div \_\_\_ = 12$

**2** What do you notice when you multiply any 3-digit number by 1001?

________________________________________

Experiment with some different 3-digit numbers.

**3** Investigate this pattern of calculations. What do you notice?

$37 \times 3 = \_\_\_\_\_\_\_\_$

$37 \times 6 = \_\_\_\_\_\_\_\_$

$37 \times 9 = \_\_\_\_\_\_\_\_$

and so on …

**4** Find the smallest number which is in both the 13 times table and the 7 times table.

________________________________________

**5** Consecutive numbers follow on from each other:
3 and 4 are consecutive numbers, as are 67 and 68.
The product of two consecutive numbers is 1056.

What are the two numbers? ____________________

**6** What is the remainder to $1678 \div 117$? ____________________

**7** Find the missing number: $37 \times \_\_\_ \times 13 = 3367$

This week we have looked at lines of symmetry and reflections.

**1** Draw in the lines of symmetry in each of these.
Check your lines of symmetry using a mirror.

a)

b)

c)

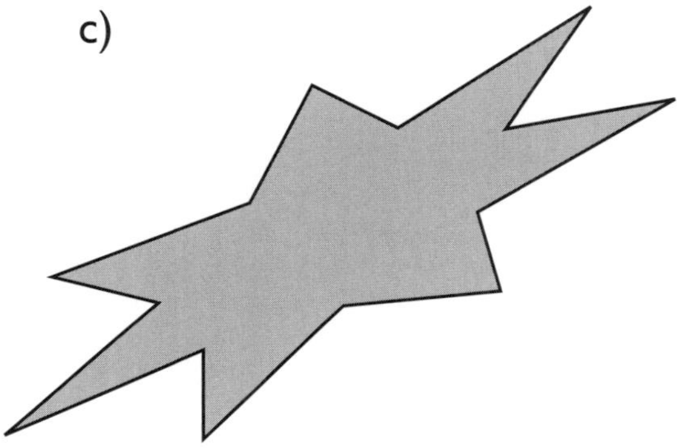

d)

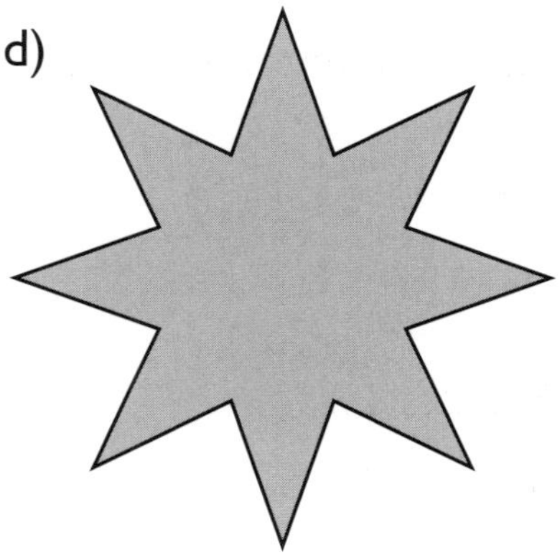

e)

f)

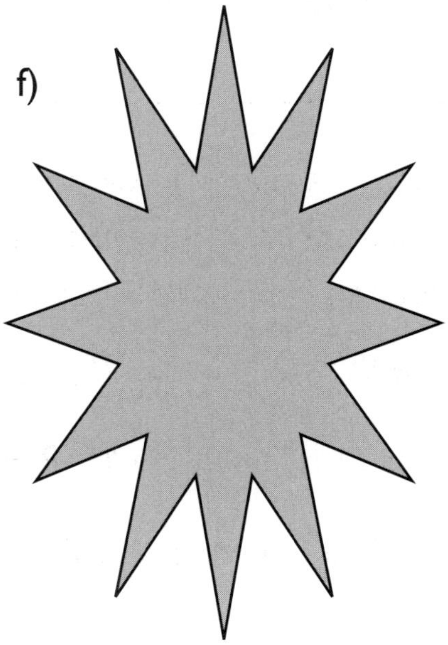

# Homework Copymaster 27

This week we have been solving time problems.

*Time yourself at doing the following*

1 Hopping on each leg 25 times each. __________

2 Standing up and sitting down 30 times. __________

3 Saying your alphabet through A to Z. __________

4 Saying your 5×, 6×, 10× tables one after the other. __________

5 Reading a page of your reading book. __________

6 Making your bed. __________

7 Sweeping the kitchen floor. __________

8 Counting from 1 to 100. __________

9 Stacking up 15 books. __________

10 Walking around your house. __________

What were you fastest at? ____________________

What were you slowest at? ____________________

This week we have been looking at capacity.

Look in your food cupboard and around the kitchen to find 10 containers which have their capacity in litres, millilitres or pints. Fill in the chart.

| | **Description** | **Capacity** (ml, l or pints) |
|---|---|---|
| 1. | ______________ | __________ |
| 2. | ______________ | __________ |
| 3. | ______________ | __________ |
| 4. | ______________ | __________ |
| 5. | ______________ | __________ |
| 6. | ______________ | __________ |
| 7. | ______________ | __________ |
| 8. | ______________ | __________ |
| 9. | ______________ | __________ |
| 10. | ______________ | __________ |

- Which holds the most? ______________________
- Which holds the least? ______________________
- Try and write some statements about how many of one container will fit into another. (You don't need to be completely accurate.)

______________________________________________

______________________________________________

# Homework Copymaster 29

This week we have been doing mental addition and subtraction.

1 Increase 180 by 47. ____________________

2 How many less than 405 is 98? ____________________

3 How many more than 925 is 1060? ____________________

4 500 less than 720. ____________________

5 What must be taken from 220 to leave 55? ____________________

6 16 add 30 add 27. ____________________

7 137 take away 35. ____________________

8 Jot down three pairs of numbers with a difference of 499. ____________________

9 Subtract 60 from 235. ____________________

10 What is the sum of 126 and 343? ____________________

11 What must I add to 720 to make 908? ____________________

12 Decrease 94 by 76. ____________________

13 How many altogether are 212 and 225? ____________________

14 7346 add 30. ____________________

15 What is the difference between 165 and 340? ____________________

16 678 subtract 105. ____________________

17 570 added to a number is 620. What is the number? ____________________

18 Take 70 from 363. ____________________

19 Add 500 to 7356. ____________________

20 What is the total of 174 and 315? ____________________

This week we have been looking at the properties of numbers.

## WHICH NUMBER AM I?

1 I am a 2-digit number between 10 and 20. I am a multiple of 3 and the sum of my digits is 3.

______________________________

______________________________

2 I am a 2-digit even number between 20 and 40. The sum of my digits is 6 and I am in the 6 times table.

______________________________

______________________________

3 I am the smallest number divisible by both 2 and 5.

______________________________

______________________________

4 I am a 2-digit odd number less than 100. I am a square number and the sum of my digits is 9.

______________________________

______________________________

5 I am a number divisible by 2, 4, 5 and 10. I am greater than 30 and less than 50.

______________________________

______________________________

6 I am a 2-digit number. The sum of my digits is 9. I am divisible by 5 and smaller than 50.

______________________________

______________________________

# Notes

# Notes